Out of Step

Out of Step

A
DANCER
REFLECTS

ALIDA BELAIR

MELBOURNE UNIVERSITY PRESS

First published 1993
Reprinted in paperback 1994
Printed in Malaysia by SRM Production Services Sdn. Bhd. for
Melbourne University Press, Carlton, Victoria 3053

This book is copyright. Apart from any fair dealing for the
purposes of private study, research, criticism or review, as
permitted under the Copyright Act, no part may be reproduced by
any process without written permission. Enquiries should be made
to the publisher.

© Alida Belair 1993

National Library of Australia Cataloguing-in-Publication entry

Belair, Alida, 1944–
  Out of step: a dancer reflects.

  Includes index.
  ISBN 0 522 84660 2.

  1. Belair, Alida, 1944– . 2. Ballerinas—Australia—Biography.
  3. Ballet dancers—Australia—Biography. I. Title.

792.8092

*For my Mother and Father
with love*

Contents

1	First Steps	*1*
2	Pure Theatre	*17*
3	The *Wunderkind*	*26*
4	Old Roles, New Rivals	*40*
5	Number 358	*50*
6	Out of My Depth	*59*
7	A Foreign Body	*74*
8	Russian Style	*82*
9	Ballerina in the Bush	*92*
10	A Student Again	*104*
11	Departure	*111*
12	Exploring London	*121*
13	The Road to Moscow	*132*
14	At the Bolshoi	*140*
15	On the Tightrope	*154*
16	The London Ballet	*170*
17	A Chance and No Chance	*185*
18	'The Name is Alida'	*202*
19	A Classical Cul-de-Sac	*216*
20	Bon Voyage	*236*
21	A State of Anonymity	*251*
22	An Errant Swan	*258*
	Index	*271*

Illustrations

Dancing at Gerrie's wedding	*2*
Performing in the back garden	*3*
Madame Borovansky	*4*
Monsieur and Madame Souquet	*6*
Alida and her mother in Toulouse, April 1945	*8*
Alida's parents on the beach at Blankenberg, 1946	*10*
Aged eight, in full regalia	*15*
Uncle Maurice with Alida, Blankenberg, 1946	*21*
The snow scene in *Nutcracker*, Sydney, 1956	*35*
Courtesy of *The Australian Women's Weekly*	
A tiny ballerina and her fans, Adelaide, 1957	*36*
Courtesy of the *Adelaide News*	
With Monsieur Borovansky, Sydney, 1956	*38*
Courtesy of the *Sydney Morning Herald*	
Meeting the Governor in Adelaide, 1957	*45*
Courtesy of the *Adelaide Advertiser*	
The travelling circus	*48*
MacRobertson Girls High School photograph, 1958	*51*
Harry and friends, 1952	*61*
In the throes of anorexia, 1957	*68*
Alida in *Persephone*	*75*
Christmas with the Kinmonts	*83*
During the Bolshoi Ballet Company's tour, 1959	*88*
With Paul Grinwis during the Arts Council tour, 1961	*94*
The touring company at Mount Isa, 1961	*101*

The beautiful Lely	*114*
Alida in London, 1962	*126*
Packing to go to Russia, 1962	*133*
The Bolshoi's *Walpurgisnacht*	*144*
The prized Bolshoi pass	*146*
In the Bolshoi tunic	*152*
The programme for *Sleeping Beauty*	*158*
Dell Brady and Alida, 1963	*162*
The London Ballet debut, 1963	*171*
In the dressing room	*177*
Making up for *Swan Lake*	*178*
Marie Rambert	*187*
In the Ballet Rambert's *Giselle*	*198*
Don Quixote, 1964	*208*
Rehearsing for *Coppélia*	*213*
In Spain, 1964	*219*
Vamping it up in *Cul de Sac*, 1964	*222*
Simon Sempill, 1967	*227*
In Joyce Graeme's *Giselle*	*233*
Mr and Mrs Glasbeek, 1966	*241*
At the National Ballet Company, Washington, DC, 1966	*244*
Stevan Grebel	*247*
The American Ballet Theatre, 1968	*260*
Mr Yagisawa and his grandson, Tokyo, 1968	*268*

1

First Steps

As soon as I walked into the grand ballroom I was seduced. I smelt the sense of occasion and threw myself into this new world with all the confidence of one who has found her natural habitat.

The year was 1950. Barely twelve months earlier my parents had come to Australia in a decrepit Italian tub, leaving behind their home in Antwerp and the Europe that had betrayed them. Now we were assembling for a celebration. My family had taken the trip from Melbourne to Sydney to attend my cousin Gerrie's wedding. At six years of age, as flowergirl-elect, I was not unaware of my important role in the festivities.

My costume was most becoming: yards and yards of soft pink tulle, pink satin bonnet and shoes, and a beautiful posy, which I held with concentrated ceremony. Mother had even managed to wax my fine, straight hair into Shirley Temple ringlets.

The music began, and I was off. My swirling, swishy skirts seemed to give me flight. I was in costume, the orchestra was playing, and I couldn't help noticing that all the other people had left the dance floor to form a ring around me. Now I was in my element. I lost myself to the music and the joy of movement. I whirled and jumped, coaxed and teased, until the early hours of the morning.

I am told that I was dubbed the belle of the ball. One of the onlookers suggested that my mother seek some formal training for her 'gifted' progeny by consulting the telephone book for a local ballet school. My mother obliged, and inadvertently created a monster.

2   Out of Step

Little Alida dances at Gerrie's wedding.

My parents chose a school of dance located in a church hall just a few blocks away from home. I was enrolled in the Saturday morning class, along with my cousin Big Alida, who was six years older than I. We began our ballet tuition in a hall packed with children of indeterminate age, size and talent. Encouraged by our doting mothers, we coerced the adult members of the family into paying for the privilege of watching us go through our routines in the garden.

We soon became stars of the academy. After only a few lessons we were permitted to totter around *sur les pointes* on heavy black leather 'toe' shoes. We struggled up on to our points with bent knees and uplifted heads, and hobbled around to the honky-tonk music until a blistered or bleeding toe forced us to retire. We displayed our wounds as indisputable evidence that we were suffering for our art.

When the time came for our first annual concert, we practised our roly-poly cartwheels, high kicks and splits like veteran troupers. Like performing animals, we were rewarded with sweets at the end of each session.

Performing in the back garden: Harry partners the two Alidas.

Auntie Maria and Uncle Nico were summoned from Sydney to see their nieces perform. I don't think they were prepared for such a variety show. In one routine I was a cutie-pie doll, dressed in a blue satin sequined costume. I kept going in a different direction from all the other little dollies, much to the amusement of the audience, but I overstepped the mark when I came back on stage to sing 'I've got a lovely bunch of coconuts'. While I could look coy and sweet, sing I could not.

The big number was a duo, with Big Alida as Bo-Peep and yours truly as that troublesome sheep. Big Alida looked as pretty as a nursery-rhyme picture, and I am certain that I was suitably quaint in my fleecy-tailed costume. Our parents were enthralled by our vaudeville routine, but Auntie Maria sat stunned, her face registering horror at this travesty of ballet. As tactfully as possible, she suggested that it was time to find a more serious school of ballet, one where our 'obvious' talents could be developed in the tradition of classical dance.

The telephone book was consulted again. This time the national origins of the teacher took precedence over the location of the school.

4   Out of Step

My mother looked no further than 'B' for Borovansky. Everyone knew that the best dance teachers came from Russia.

When my mother and I arrived at the school we were ushered into Madame Borovansky's office and introduced to the stone-like figure sitting behind the desk. There was no smile of welcome, no reassuring

Madame Borovansky

words, just a frozen, imperious gaze. Madame Xenia Borovansky was a White Russian, aristocratic in the extreme, and treated plebeians like us with undisguised disdain. Her tall, elegant physique was offset by a disconcertingly unattractive face with large, protruding eyes, which she used to frightening effect.

It was not going to be a congenial encounter. Blinded by maternal love, or made foolish by nervousness, my mother sang the praises of Big Alida and myself: 'They have danced principal roles and, yes, they are already on points. Their former teacher regards them as very advanced pupils'. Throughout this spiel Madame Borovansky remained sphinx-like. She let my mother run out of steam, then rolled her enormous eyes and said, 'We shall see how good they are. Bring them along on Saturday'. That was it. End of interview.

The following Saturday Big Alida and I turned up at the Elizabeth Street academy, neatly attired in our lime tunics with monogrammed pockets. We both felt confident enough to preen and posture as we waited for the class to commence. The double doors swung open and Madame made her entry, mink coat draped over her shoulders. With a cigarette dangling from the corner of her mouth, she said, 'Good morning, class. First position: *pliés*'.

'My God, what is that?' Big Alida whispered.

'*Battements en croix*, class.' We stood open-mouthed, frozen. The French commands just kept coming. We could neither understand the terminology nor copy the rest of the class, because we had never taken part in a structured ballet class before. Bewildered and humiliated, we broke down and wept. Madame did not say a word to us; she simply left us skulking at the back of the class for the rest of the lesson.

Eventually the torture ended. The doors opened, and Big Alida and I retreated into the dressing room. Xenia Borovansky stalked past my mother, who had been watching the class through a slit in the door, along with the other mums. 'Well, and what do you think of your little stars now?' she said.

We were enrolled at the Borovansky Ballet Academy.

As the daughter of Jewish refugees in hiding, I did not have a large audience when I made my entrance into the world. I was born on 9 January 1944, in a small hospital at Villeneuve-sur-Lot in the south of France. I had hardly made my presence felt when I was whisked off to lie low, as far as possible from the public eye. My conception, I am told, was not intended, though it was well rehearsed. 'What else were we supposed to do, lying on that straw in the stable for twenty-four hours a day?' my mother would ask. Forty years later, I still didn't quite know what to make of that question. I might have preferred a little more intent.

Two days after I was born a sympathetic doctor warned my mother that the Nazis were coming. She took a nerve-racking bus ride back to the relative safety of the stable at the Souquets' farm in Tournon. Though they were only poor subsistence farmers, Monsieur and Madame Souquet harboured seven Jewish fugitives: my parents, my nine-year-old brother Harry, another married couple, a dentist, and me.

Later I would gaze at old photographs of the Souquets and wonder why these real-life saviours bore no resemblance to the heroes that graced the silver screen. The camera captures Madame Souquet staring sternly from a heavily moustached face, wearing an ill-fitting dress. Her diminutive husband is the epitome of the French peasant.

I could see why my mother had whispered her doubts to Dad. Surely they had come to the wrong place for help? Life for Jews on the run in Vichy France was fraught with danger. Not all the 'safe houses' were safe, and many people who knocked on the wrong door were turned over to the local gendarmerie.

But the Souquets' farm turned out to be an uncomfortable abode of miracles. These two shabby, impoverished heroes were defiant in a

Monsieur and Madame Souquet on the steps of their farmhouse

world taken leave of its senses. At enormous risk to themselves and their two children, the Souquets took us in and cared for us as if we were members of their own family. Even Monsieur's meagre ration of tobacco was shared with my father. '*Monsieur Glasbeek, il y a du tabac*', Monsieur Souquet would call, and without the slightest hesitation he would cut it square down the middle.

I would not be writing this story if my parents had not been among the small minority of European Jewry who were pessimistic enough to believe that the unbelievable could happen. When my parents heard that the Germans had entered their district, they walked out of their home, turned off the chicken soup simmering for that evening's meal, packed a tiny bundle of the barest necessities and made their way to Antwerp Central Railway Station, destination unknown. Although they were convinced of the need to leave Belgium, they had no real idea where they should go. No one could have foreseen the dimensions of the tragedy to come, but Hitler had already made one thing clear by 1940: in this war the Jews could not expect to be classified as members of any European country's civilian population.

By the time I rolled out into an inhospitable world, my nine-year-old brother had already assumed most of the responsibilities of adulthood. Harry's childhood ended the day our parents closed the front door of their Boomgaadstraat house and left Antwerp for four years. I am told that my brother risked life and limb to visit his mother and baby sister in hospital, but when he arrived he turned up his nose and said, 'Don't tell me I walked all that way in mortal danger for that horrible wrinkly tomato'.

'I was blissfully unaware of our perilous situation. Years later my parents would laugh as they described how I suckled away happily, while everyone around me was consumed with anxiety and suffering from varying degrees of malnutrition. I managed to remain clamped to my mother's bountiful breasts for eighteen months. Whenever the Germans or Vichy gendarmes were seen approaching the farm, my mother would run out into the surrounding woodlands with me attached firmly to the breast, in case I should utter a sound and give everyone away. Her fears were groundless. Oblivious to all the fuss, I remained round, tomato-red and completely contented.

In August 1944 the Midi was liberated. At last our family was able to come out of hiding and return to Toulouse. In spite of their euphoria at having survived the war against the odds, my parents found it difficult to say goodbye to the Souquets, whom they had grown to love. When

8   Out of Step

Coming out of hiding: Alida's mother, with her well-worn fur coat, with Alida in Toulouse, April 1945

my parents offered to repay them financially, the Souquets were quite offended. They believed they had taken the only possible course of action for French patriots. Forty years later my brother learnt that the Souquets had never discussed the time when they had hidden Jewish people. None of the children born after 1945 knew about their parents' heroism.

Not until March the following year could we return to Belgium and begin the task of returning to some semblance of normal life and regaining a sense of identity. But first we had to endure a frightful train journey from France to Belgium in one of the despicable wagons that had transported Jews to the death camps.

When we returned there was a joyous reunion with my mother's brother, Uncle Maurice Gosler, his wife Rosa and their daughter, Big Alida—three Jews who had miraculously survived the Nazi killing machine. Most of our relatives were less fortunate. My parents learnt of the deaths of both sets of parents, six of my father's brothers and sisters, my mother's eldest brother and most of their extended family and friends. Antwerp seemed like a ghost town; Marken, the Jewish district of Amsterdam, was no longer.

The end of the war did not herald an automatic return to normality. The persecution had irrevocably changed my parents, and extinguished much of their old way of life. Even though the war had reinforced their agnosticism, it had also made them realize that they could not sever themselves from the destiny of the Jewish community.

It took nine months of legal wrangling to reclaim the family home from the Belgian family who had moved in while we were in hiding. Unmoved by our pathetic appearance, they refused to let us enter the house on our first day in Antwerp. As we had nowhere else to go, we were still Displaced Persons. We thought ourselves fortunate to be given refuge in a crowded Jewish hostel, where we slept on the floor alongside skeletal survivors of the concentration camps. The horrors of the holocaust were revealed as the survivors trickled in, still in their striped suits, with shaven heads, gaunt and ill; they were living corpses.

I was the apple of everybody's eye, and while I still suckled at my mother's breast I was almost completely in charge. Imagine my outrage when I was thrown into a cold, unfriendly isolation ward. At eighteen months I had contracted diphtheria from contact with other refugees. Right from the start I made it clear that I had no intention of staying in this dreadful place, but to my horror my parents disappeared. I found myself alone, surrounded by complete strangers. I was passed from hand to hand, pummelled and prodded, laid on my back, weighed, washed and bedded. All the while I screamed indignantly. It was some time before I forgave my parents and decided to love them again.

Materially we were soon back on our feet. My father was an excellent diamond-cutter, and his skills were very much in demand in post-war Antwerp. We spent two or three months of every year at the fashionable Belgian seaside resort of Blankenberg. My parents seem to have had a compulsion to immortalize our family in photographs, and many years later the Blankenberg photos were a particular source of pleasure to me. My parents' sheer happiness illuminates every picture: my mother, rounder than in pre-war photos, impeccable in the latest seaside fashions, and my strong, handsome father, a courageous young couple, ready to meet the future with confidence and optimism.

But my parents felt an all-consuming need to get as far away as possible from the killing grounds of Europe. They decided to migrate to Australia, partly because my mother's sister Maria already lived in Sydney with her husband and son, but mainly because Australia was far, far away. As there was no diamond-cutting industry in Sydney, it was decided that Melbourne should be our future home.

Looking to the future: Alida's parents on the beach at Blankenberg, 1946

The fortunes of the Glasbeek and Gosler families were by now entwined. Uncle Maurice's wartime experiences made the adjustment to normal life difficult. After two years in a Nazi concentration camp, he had been loaded on to the train bound for Auschwitz. But he managed to cheat death. In what must have been a one-in-a-million lapse of German efficiency, a guard had forgotten to bolt one of the wagon doors, and my uncle jumped from the moving train. Malnourished and suffering from beriberi, conspicuous because of his shaven head and prison garb, he managed to make his way on foot from the Polish border to the south of France, where he was reunited with his wife and daughter.

Although Uncle Maurice returned to his former work as a singer at the Antwerp opera, the Goslers found it hard to manage financially, so my father adopted them as his own. Our money and our home were shared equally, as were our vacations—the Goslers came to Blankenberg with us each year—and now our trip to Australia. This was no ostentatious gesture; for my father, it was just the natural thing to do.

'We thought we had received a windfall. Your Dad and I had never seen so much money. Two whole suitcases filled to the brim with bundles of lira. One ice-cream later in Naples and our load was considerably lighter. Poor Dad—I realized we weren't millionaires after all!' My mother would tell me this anecdote over and over again. When she spoke of the past she tended to highlight the rare, whimsical moments, preferring to shove disturbing memories into less accessible recesses of her mind.

Family snapshots show us boarding the *Toscano*, the ship that was to take us to Australia, looking very much the archetypal migrant family. We were weighed down with enormous suitcases and a huge assortment of unnecessary sundries.

The six weeks on board were miserable for most of the family. The menu consisted almost entirely of pasta, three meals a day. We had paid first-class fares for third-class accommodation, but we considered ourselves lucky to have obtained a passage at all, as there was unprecedented pressure on passenger ships leaving Europe. Temporary discomfort seemed a small price to pay for a second chance at life.

The voyage was no great trial for Harry, who found some chess-playing Italians on board. For my part, I managed to endear myself to the ship's captain, and the relationship had significant fringe benefits. After I had spent the day trotting around by his side, the captain would give me armfuls of fresh bread rolls, which were otherwise reserved for the first-class passengers. To the members of my family, down in the bowels of third class, the rolls were a welcome relief from the eternal pasta. By the time we reached Melbourne, Harry spoke a fair amount of Italian, I was delighted at my proven ability to win an audience, and the adults were ready to believe that the earth was flat and we would soon come to the edge.

To come to a new country with such a different culture is a momentous event for a five-year-old. I was looking forward to meeting my relations in Australia, having heard so much about their wealth, and about Auntie Maria's beauty. Indeed, I had a recurring dream in which my aunt and uncle were dressed in sumptuous robes and glittering crowns, and seated on two elevated golden thrones to receive their guests. I would approach them along an aisle carpeted in red velvet, and one of these two regal beings would take me up and set me on his or her lap, where I would be hugged and kissed, engulfed in a cloud of heavy perfume.

The *Toscano* docked at Port Melbourne, and my mother glimpsed my aunt and uncle on the pier below. Both sisters shrieked with delight. I watched my mother laugh joyfully, and then break down in tears. This strange behaviour made me rather apprehensive. My father lifted me on to the railing. I remember feeling confident that I would win Auntie and Uncle's approval, because everyone on board had already commented on the outfits that Big Alida and I were wearing. We were dressed in identical silk embroidered dresses from Russia. My fine hair was braided and pinned on top of my head, set off with the world's biggest chocolate-box bow.

But I was bitterly disappointed when I peered down from the railing and identified my aunt and uncle as two crownless, robeless individuals standing in the middle of the crowd. On board ship we had been aware that the Italian passengers regarded us as outsiders. Now, to my dismay, I noticed that we also looked different from the people waiting down below.

To make matters worse we had to wait on board for an interminable time, and Uncle Maurice decided to break into a series of songs. I am sure that he originally only wanted to serenade his sister and brother-in-law, but his beautiful voice captured the hearts of the waiting crowd below. Responding to their attention, he went from strength to strength. I think he would have gone on forever if we had not been called to customs.

My first day at school did little to dispel my sense of difference. Big Alida and I were despatched to the local state school in East Malvern, while Harry was enrolled in Melbourne High. I was considered lucky to be starting school at the preparatory level. I would be the only member of the family who would have the opportunity to learn to read and write English virtually as a first language. No doubt it wouldn't be long before I began to think in English as well.

But as far as I was concerned I might just as well have landed on Mars. There were shrieking children all over the place. I deduced that this place was not at all kosher. Those kids understood the lingo, they knew what was going on, and they still did not like it! And I looked different. Eager to make a good first impression, my mother had sent me off in my best hand-knitted dress, which barely covered my panties, new long white socks, black patent leather shoes, and that embarrassing Easter-egg bow on top of my European coiffure. All I wanted to do was melt into the background, but I had to resign myself to becoming the curiosity piece. The teachers and children touched me and stared at me as if my feelings had already left the room. They gesticulated frantically and mouthed words in an exaggerated fashion. I was a misfit, humiliated and abandoned. I sat and cried all day, imagining what would happen if my mother did not come back and I had to live out the rest of my life as if I were deaf and dumb. Even if my mother did decide to reappear, I decided, I would refuse to return to this madhouse.

When I told her this, my mother was sympathetic, but refused to yield to my demand. I was sent back to sit out another day of torment.

Thank God for the five-year-old's sponge-like brain! I soon began to feel as comfortable with English as my native Dutch, although it took me a long time to lose the stilted, plum-in-the-mouth precision of the foreigner edging her way into a new language. The headmaster was impressed by my efforts, and took every opportunity to display my new-found skills by asking me to read aloud. 'Listen carefully, class', he would say. 'The little Dutch girl has only been in the country for a few months, and she is already speaking better English than you.' My classmates were less than impressed.

At the Borovansky Ballet Academy the gods had mercy on us. Madame Borovansky was taken ill and forced to rest from teaching for a year. Her replacement, Corrie Lodders, was a plump, affable little lady. Though she could not have looked less like a ballerina, she was kind and patient, and before very long I became devoted to her.

I made rapid progress, and Miss Lodders advised my mother to replace my normal class with a private one, so that I could develop at my own pace. My mother needed little persuasion. For my part, although I worked alone and without musical accompaniment for the entire year, that one hour became the highlight of my existence.

At the end of the year a tearful Corrie Lodders broke the news that she had been dismissed because Madame Borovansky was returning to the Academy. The very thought made me shiver with fear. In her absence Madame's face had acquired even more sinister connotations, and her return was the most ghastly catastrophe I could imagine.

Miss Lodders was planning to open her own studio, and suggested I follow her. My mother, however, had become more ballet-wise. We had now seen several Borovansky productions, and realized that the Borovansky school was the finest in Australia. My mother's pragmatism sealed my fate.

Six glorious weeks of school holidays in the sun and on the beach did much to allay my fears of having to face the ogre again. Somehow or other I found myself in the Academy's dressing room, preparing to accept the worst with the bravest face I could manage. A brand new tutu boosted my confidence a little. This impractical uniform became the bane of my mother's existence. The more I became entrenched in the ballet ethos, the more fastidious I became. I insisted that Mother wash and starch my tutu so that the frills stood out horizontally, and my mother spent hours ironing those recalcitrant frills for her undeserving daughter.

After my apprehensions, the encounter with Madame was a pleasant anticlimax. I was not eaten alive, persecuted nor even screamed at. Madame Borovansky could not have been sweeter; in fact, she seemed thrilled with her new little pupil.

This time my mother was invited rather than summoned to the office. She was cordially received by Madame's secretary, who even drew up a chair for her to await the great lady's arrival. It was plain that Madame had forgotten the circumstances of our first meeting. When the secretary introduced my mother, Madame registered no sign of recognition. The cold eyes thawed just enough to project some sincerity when she described me as an exceptionally talented child who was destined to go far, providing I was given the correct tuition.

'You have a child prodigy, Mrs Glasbeek', Madame announced. 'Are you prepared to make the necessary sacrifices for her future?'

At home the news was received with mixed feelings. My mother was thrilled to be credited with another exceptional child—Harry having already gained recognition as a 'brain'—but my father was less enthusiastic. He had strong reservations about the implications of the 'necessary sacrifices', and all the hard work this might entail for his eight-year-old daughter. Big Alida seemed happy enough to continue her weekly classes at the Academy for enjoyment. But I was exempted from household chores, and this rankled. The whole situation was quite outside my parents' experience, and they decided to leave the shaping of my dance career in the hands of the experts. Madame Borovansky had already made it quite clear that my development as a dancer was her responsibility, and that she did not tolerate interference from lay people, parents or no.

Indeed, as I soon found, both Madame and her husband, who was director of the Borovansky Ballet Company, enshrouded ballet with mysticism. 'The theatre is the dancer's church', Monsieur would say,

Alida, aged eight, in full regalia: this photograph was taken at the Borovanskys' house.

'and must therefore be treated with the utmost faith and respect. Ballet is your religion, the class your liturgy. Nothing short of total commitment will suffice'.

The next year I was awarded a scholarship, which entitled me to free classes for the duration of my training. Naturally I was expected to do justice to this honour. 'You must do as many classes as possible', I was told. When I fell about in my third consecutive lesson of the evening, too tired to take in anything more or work my muscles properly, Madame would praise me for my stamina. In her eyes the quantity of work was more important than the quality.

I continued to progress at breakneck speed, and before I knew it I was in the top class with the professionals, sharing a barre with such luminaries as Kathleen Gorham and Peggy Sager. I churned out my balletic tricks with naïve promiscuity. I knew that Madame brought people along to the Academy to watch her prodigy. The classroom was my stage.

Though I could execute the most difficult steps with apparent ease, my skills were largely imitative and instinctive. No doubt it was cute to see this frail little girl with enormous dark eyes executing *fouettes sur les pointes* and assorted *batteries en l'air*. But, as one of the more astute professionals tried to warn my mother, it was dangerous to bypass the fundamentals. Though I slogged away relentlessly, sometimes until late into the night, I had no idea of the basic structure of the language I appeared to use so fluently.

2

Pure Theatre

Our first impressions of Melbourne had been extremely favourable. My parents gaped as they drove down St Kilda Road in Uncle Nico's long American car. They couldn't believe that the superb white mansions on either side were private homes. Perhaps the streets *were* paved with gold!

Our new home in Grant Street, East Malvern, also met with approval. Auntie Marie and Uncle Nico had found us a substantial double-storey red brick house, large enough for our two families to share. The street was lined with flowering gums, and all the houses seemed opulent and gracious.

The first thing we children did was to explore the formal English garden with its trellised red roses, fruit trees, symmetrical flower beds full of tiered colourful graded flowers and what seemed to be mile upon mile of green lawn. Our parents had been used to houses and apartments built straight on to the street, but this house had a sizeable front garden and a huge back garden, complete with a sprinkler system. I felt like a princess in a magic new world.

My father quickly established himself as the leading diamond-cutter at a Dutch factory, and Uncle Maurice found work as a storeman for a Dutch carpet warehouse. Melbourne was a good place to begin the healing process, and the adults of our families worked hard to create a secure ambience for their children.

I could not imagine life without my extended family. Our lack of space and privacy was never seen as a disadvantage. On the contrary, judging by the constant stream of visitors, our families thrived on all the noise and activity. Big Alida and I shared a single bed for the first few years, but this was not considered a hardship. Indeed, as my nights became increasingly anxiety-ridden, a cuddle or a game with Big Alida did a lot to comfort me.

I was always glad to get home from school. Those first years at Grant Street were filled with optimistic energy and a great deal of Continental histrionics. The dining room was the focal point of our household, and it was there that our family dramas were played out. The hub of this room was a large oval dining table, which accommodated up to twenty people. The dining room soon started to look the worse for wear. The door was eventually slammed right off its hinges, our chairs collapsed, and the magnificent oak table bore the scars of countless games of ping-pong on its polished surface. Even the wallpaper couldn't stand the ravages of time and the residue of tobacco and cooking, but the huge strips of discoloured paper that hung down over our heads only made the dining room seem even more festive, rather like a sheikh's tent.

The dining room was not only the place where we ate our meals; it was also the room in which we listened to operas, classical music, Sophie Tucker, talent quests and later, due to Harry's influence, 'Rock around the clock' on our proudest possession of all, the radiogram.

Our one concession to Jewish tradition was the Friday night meal. Afterwards the family gathered around the table for a noisy card game, which sometimes went on until the early hours of the morning. Friday night was also sweets night. Big Alida and I were given small plates of assorted sweets, which we would take to our special place under the table, surrounded by an array of legs and feet. As the tempers rose in direct ratio to the mounting stakes on the table, Big Alida and I learnt to interpret body language, specializing from the knee down.

But the greatest dramas took place at meal-times. My mother always brought the pots and pans on to the table, unless we had Australian guests. She sat at one end of the table, hidden behind an enormous tureen. My father sat at the other end, silently surveying all that went on. Auntie Rosa and Uncle Maurice could usually be relied upon to have a spectacular disagreement. Harry and I sat opposite them, in the ringside seats, but Big Alida was sandwiched in between her parents. As the altercations sometimes erupted into physical warfare, her place was not an enviable one.

My aunt and uncle were a most unlikely-looking couple. Rosa was corpulent, and a head taller than her husband, who was diminutive but athletic and extremely vain about his appearance. A typical scene would run like this. My mother would begin to ladle the soup into large bowls, and Auntie Rosa would pass them around the table. When it got to Uncle Maurice's turn, the conversation would freeze. What would it be today? Too hot or too cold? The soup was always one or the other. 'It's too cold, is it?' my aunt would scream, turning lobster-red. 'You don't like it? Well, how is this, then?' and she would empty the contents over his head and career out of the room, slamming that much-abused door. Uncle Maurice, panic-stricken, would race up the stairs in hot pursuit, almost begging for forgiveness, while the rest of us sat eating the meal, pretending nothing untoward had happened. At times we had to duck the soft-boiled eggs that Auntie Rosa threw at him. Harry and I knew better than to laugh. In any case, after a few minutes my aunt and uncle would return, and the whole family would continue their meal, take tea and chocolate, then settle down to an affable card game as if nothing had happened.

My parents preferred to argue in the privacy of their bedroom, but we always knew when things were not harmonious. An exchange of sign language would flash across the table, heralding the outburst that would erupt when we children were out of earshot.

Food was a contentious issue. For my father, having more than enough to eat was a primary symbol of well-being, and having a well-spread table was a matter of personal dignity to him as the breadwinner of the family. He kept urging my mother to put copious amounts of food on her plate, but my mother had always been proud of her trim figure and liked to keep up with the latest clothing fashions. Her attempts to serve herself small helpings were a constant source of friction. My mother would often hide behind the soup tureen, but sometimes my father's insistence to eat up became too much, and then we would be treated to her Bette Davis act.

My mother had aspired to a career on the stage, but in the 1930s the theatre was not considered a suitable place for a girl from a respectable family. The theatre's loss was our gain.

Mother had been a chain-smoker since the end of the war. We thrilled to hear the striking of the match and the first deep inhalation, for we knew what it presaged. She would light a cigarette with dramatic panache, narrow her eyes to menacing slits, and, jumping from her chair, would make as if to abandon us to our unsympathetic selves. But a good actress never leaves her audience while the going is good. Exploiting the situation to the hilt, she would strut around her chair, watching herself in the mirror all the while; and then, with a final exaggerated flounce of resignation, she would plonk herself back at the table to resume her meal in peeved silence. Harry and I were filled with admiration for her talent.

Our neighbours could hardly have failed to notice the noise level, but they never complained. On the contrary, one of our neighbours, Mrs Benson, a white-haired widow, told us that she was delighted to have such perfect neighbours. 'The only sounds I hear are of that marvellous opera singer', she said, 'and when he sings I always stand with my ear pressed against the fence'. Our neighbours on the other side were either deaf or excessively polite.

We children were involved in almost everything—social gatherings, visits to other people's homes, cinema outings and tram rides to St Kilda beach. As we always felt free to express our opinions, there were often some very heated arguments as every member of the family threw in his or her pennyworth. For someone destined to a life in the theatre, it was excellent training to grow up in a household where almost the entire spectrum of human emotions could be covered in the space of half an hour. In fact, I need never have left home. The Glasbeeks and Goslers were pure theatre.

My mother was the second youngest of a bourgeois family of four children, two boys and two girls. My grandparents had worked tirelessly to build up a thriving delicatessen in a middle-class, Christian neighbourhood in Antwerp. It was in the Gosler family that we find the first presence of theatrical blood, a fact that my mother imbued with mammoth significance. As well as tending the shop by day, my grandfather was a soloist at the Antwerp Opera House in the evening. Uncle Maurice, the younger son, also became an opera singer, but like his father he learnt another trade as a financial backup; he became a butcher. Mother was considered to be the scholar of the family. After completing her schooling at the age of eighteen, she won a scholarship to the Conservatorium of Drama, and was apparently an exemplary student.

My father had no such opportunities for higher learning, although, as the bright child of the brood, he was allowed to extend his school years until the age of eleven, whereas his eight siblings were required to leave school at the age of eight. He was born into an impoverished Sephardic family in the crowded ghetto of Marken in Amsterdam. Life in Marken was not about planning futures but rather about accepting each day as it came, and trying to earn enough for the next day's food,

Uncle Maurice poses for the camera with Alida on his shoulders, Blankenberg, 1946.

rent and second-hand clothing. Yet many years later, in more affluent times, I would watch my father's whole countenance glow as he cast his mind back to his youth in Marken. The physical conditions were harsh; seven children slept in the gap between the rafters and the ceiling of the family's two-roomed flat. Though his mother kept the household scrupulously clean, the flat was often infested with vermin. Yet life in the ghetto was obviously vibrant. I found it hard to imagine my self-conscious father dancing in the streets to the sound of a barrel organ, but dance he did, along with many of the other young lads about town. Judging by my father's lack of bitterness, the strong sense of solidarity and collective identity in the ghetto must have compensated for the lack of material wealth. I am sure it was in Marken that socialist principles became an integral part of my father's life.

We migrants of the 1950s arrived in an Australia that was still deeply xenophobic. Like it or not, we were all wogs, and our curious customs, unintelligible languages and barbaric eating habits were seen to be undermining the superior British culture. In our neighbourhood we were spared the virulent wog-baiting associated with ghetto life, but some of our habits were still regarded as outlandish.

My girlfriends turned up their noses when they saw me drink yoghurt, eat steak tartare and scoff pickled herrings—raw fish! We in turn regarded Aussie food as unwholesome, uninspiring and miserly to boot. My mother occasionally tried to cook Australian dishes for the sake of her children, with some disastrous results. I remember her first roast rabbit lying with its little legs extended bolt upright, in an advanced state of rigor mortis.

As if seven people were not enough to feed, there were always numerous ring-ins. The nearest shopping centre was a good mile and a half away, so shopping expeditions were major undertakings. Laden down like peasants, barely recognizable under a mass of string bags filled to capacity with meat and vegetables, my aunt and mother were constantly being asked whether they were catering for a boarding house.

Our attitude to hygiene also set us apart. Fastidious cleanliness is an integral part of Dutch life. In Antwerp or Amsterdam the pavement in front of the house was scrubbed daily, and bedding was hung over windowsills to air. In Grant Street Auntie Rosa aired the Goslers' bedding at the front windows, while my parents' bedding was draped over the Hills hoist at the back. We wondered why passers-by would stop and stare; when we children discovered that they were not stopping to admire our conspicuous cleanliness, we pestered Auntie Rosa to put an end to our embarrassment.

Auntie Maria and Uncle Nico often came to visit. The excitement began as soon as they arrived in their car, which I believed to be the envy of the entire street. Then the unpacking ritual started. I hovered close to my aunt, for her suitcases always contained lots of gifts for the children—jewellery, ornamental knick-knacks, and other gloriously impractical fripperies. At that time Auntie had adopted the Lana Turner look. Her pointy breasts were accentuated by low-cut jumpers, pulled in with a wide belt. She exuded her own scent, a sensual French perfume that permeated her clothes and furs. I prayed that I might grow up to have a perfect figure like my aunt and inherit her immaculate sense of style.

Though hailing from the same ghetto as my father, Uncle Nico was the boy from the back streets who had made good. I thought he looked like a cross between Phil Silvers and a Chicago mobster, though he was extraordinarily vain about his appearance. Only the best tailored suits and silk monogrammed shirts and pyjamas would do. Ignoring the disdain of Aussie ockers, he cosseted his manicured, lily-white hands and daubed himself with expensive after-shave lotions (purchased on the Continent, of course). Uncle Nico was a successful travelling salesman, selling carpets throughout the remote country areas of South Africa, New Zealand and Australia. No one could recount a yarn more eloquently and charmingly than he. His stories of his sometimes dubious transactions with the forthright 'cockies' were tales of a world quite outside my family's ken.

On his visits Uncle Nico liked to run card games for his moneyed Dutch-Australian cronies. My parents graciously took a back seat while huge amounts of money were won and lost at our dining-room table. Sometimes Uncle Nico lost more money in one night's game or a misplaced flutter on the Saturday races than my father earned in a month. Cousin Gerrie and his wife and two small children were also frequent visitors. More often than not the Sydney relatives would all arrive at once, and then our life would be just one hectic party.

And then there was Harry, who wandered in and out of our house like a wayfarer, dragging in his wake a trail of friends as loquacious and vigorous as himself. In later years those acne-covered, awkward youths were transformed into clear-skinned, bleary-eyed young scholars, bent on trying to fit some study into a heavy schedule of dating.

The adults in our family sorely missed European city life. They longed for the sidewalk cafés, the opera and the theatre; they missed the interaction of people living in a small, densely populated area. The cinema was a poor substitute, but twice a week all seven of us walked the few miles to the Crystal Palace or Waverley Theatre and back. The programme did not matter; the important thing was the family outing. Sometimes we were the only people in the auditorium, and then we created our own atmosphere with noisy gusto. When my father's only surviving sister came from Amsterdam with her husband, son and daughter-in-law, we sometimes filled two rows in an empty theatre. The situation was made even more comical by the fact that our newly arrived relations could not understand a word of the dialogue.

When I was little I always went along in my pyjamas and dressing gown, so that I could slip off to sleep when the movie became too boring. For me the real magic began when we started out on our long journey home. From where I sat, perched on my father's strong shoulders, the moon and stars seemed to keep pace with me, and the street lamps cast mysterious shadows on the pavement, which echoed six dissonant sets of footsteps. I wondered how many children were already asleep in the bedrooms that lay behind all those dimly lit windows, and I felt privileged to be treated to an outing in the elusive night-time world of adults.

When I was too tired I would call down from my lofty perch, and my father would wrap me in his arms so that I could nestle my head in the cosy nook of his neck. Then I would sleep peacefully for the rest of the journey, safe and loved, in an enchanted world.

Back at the studio, I thoroughly enjoyed being a little adult. I never felt bored. When I danced it was as if the spirit of the music had entered my body. I used the formal classical steps I had learned, and filled the spaces of my knowledge with movements of my own invention. I suppose that in the purest sense I was a fake, but no one seemed to notice—or else they did not care.

If my dancing brought me special attention, it was simply a reward for doing what I truly loved. Dancing was my response to my greatest love, music, and music took over my soul to the extent that there could not be room for even a tinge of guile or deception. Music gave me the opportunity to link into a mystical universality that defied all logical explanation.

I had my first experience on the professional stage as one of two pageboys in the last act of the *Sleeping Beauty*. I helped to carry the queen's train as she strode to her throne, then stood motionless by her side as she watched the wedding festivities. But I was smitten by the smell of the greasepaint, the air of excitement, the applause, the sheer beauty of all these graceful beings.

At the end of the year I was cast in the leading role in *The Matchgirl*, Madame Borovansky's adaptation of the Hans Christian Andersen story, which was to be performed in the Academy's own postage-stamp-sized theatre. The rehearsal period was long and gruelling, but the closer the performance date, the greater the general hysteria, the more I threw myself into the dramatic range of such high-velocity living.

Although I was only eight, I danced the entire ballet *sur les pointes* and, I am told, moved the audience to tears with my interpretation of the pathetic, vulnerable little Matchgirl. The ballet ended on a note of triumph: the Matchgirl, left to die in the snow, was magically transformed into a golden star and lifted to the top of a magnificent Christmas tree. I can still feel the surge of excitement as the music mounted to its climax and I, only I, was the queen of the stage.

The next year I was cast in the leading roles of two Borovansky ballets on that small stage. In *The Nightingale and the Rose* (inspired by a Lorca poem), I danced the part of a little nightingale who sacrifices her life for the cause of true love. The nightingale's final fluttering steps in her dying moments brought tears to my eyes. At curtain down, even the applause took a long time to jolt me back to reality.

In contrast, my role in the second ballet, as the Joker in *The Card Game*, was a lively virtuoso character. I enjoyed the opportunity to show off my precarious pyrotechnics, but I far preferred the schmaltz of the doomed but heroic little nightingale. To wallow in thirty-five minutes or so of string-inspired melancholia was just my cup of tea.

It was in this concert that Monsieur Borovansky first saw me perform on stage. Apparently he bounced around the audience in that tiny hall, loudly extolling my talent. In his speech at the close of the performance, he prophesied that I would be the next Anna Pavlova, a prophecy that was to be both a blessing and a curse.

Monsieur's presence at the Ballet Academy had an electrifying effect. 'You, you big blowfly', he would scream at some hapless girl. Or 'What you do, you silly doughnut?' to a girl who was having problems keeping her weight down. But, though he terrified people with his outbursts, he dedicated himself to his art with absolute integrity. If Madame Borovansky was the epitome of the blue-blooded aristocrat, Monsieur was the archetypal Czech peasant, bald-headed and squat. She would glide around the studio like a cold, elegant viper, while Monsieur charged in head-on like a bull. Yet his unrefined exterior disguised a cultured and artistic man. He was an adept painter, an expert deep-sea fisherman, and had a reputation for womanizing that would have given Casanova a run for his money. And Monsieur Borovansky was the true founder of ballet in Australia.

3

The *Wunderkind*

I was now trying to live two very different lives, as Alida the wonder child and as Alida the schoolgirl. At Lloyd Street Primary School I did my best to fit in, but that mystery substance, school spirit, evaded me. School was a place for obligatory learning. Physical activities, however, were a different matter. I enjoyed the challenge of competitive running, and winning gave me the instant gratification that I was already addicted to.

In time, as my ballet training became even more heavy-handed and uncompromising, Madame Borovansky insisted that I abstain from all sporting activities except swimming. Presumably she was protecting my delicate muscles from being injured or over-developed. This was all very well in theory, but my legs were already far too muscle-bound for a child of my age. Madame simply believed in the overriding virtue of hard work, and disregarded the caution required for exercising a young, growing body. Still, we followed Madame's instructions to the letter. My mother wrote to the headmaster to obtain special dispensation from all sports, and permission was quickly granted.

My headmaster, Mr Wright, was an avowed balletomane. Although well beyond middle age, he had a very young daughter who also attended the Borovansky Ballet Academy. He was therefore aware of my reputation as a child prodigy, and extended the same kid-glove treatment to my schooling at Lloyd Street. This sometimes caused me embarrassment, but most of the time it was a bonus to be able to evade maths and other irksome lessons. Mr Wright would summon me to his office over the public address system, and I would gladly leave my colleagues stewing over their maths and grammar in order to give our worthy headmaster his regular ballet classes. It was amusing to see this conservative pedagogue hopping around the office, trying to memorize my instructions so that he could help his daughter with her practice at home.

My mother also became a well-known identity around the school. Every day at precisely 3 p.m. she would be waiting patiently at the school gates, with that fluffy white tutu hanging over her arm like an upside-down chook. If I forgot the time, one of the teachers or students would relay the message that my mother had arrived to collect me for my ballet lesson. The school had come to accept my comings and goings as part of the normal routine.

In order to prove that all the fuss I had created was not just due to a cleverly constructed myth, I felt it necessary to make some gesture to show that I could really dance. At annual speech nights I performed a solo, choreographed and carefully rehearsed by Madame Borovansky. As the roving ambassador for the Borovansky Ballet Academy, I was expected to do justice to the Academy's reputation. The rehearsals were taken very seriously, and meticulous attention was given to the smallest detail of costume and coiffure. Mr Wright allowed me to take off as much time as I needed to perfect my solo. The morning after the performance, he insisted that I sleep in, and chauffeured me to school in his Wolseley, an hour and a half later than the rest of my colleagues.

Although it was now a foregone conclusion that I would continue in the ballet world, no one in my family had any notion of how rapidly I would be pushed into pre-eminence. In 1955, when I was eleven, it was announced that the Borovansky Ballet was to mount a lavish production of *The Nutcracker*, premiering in Sydney, and David Lichine, the renowned American choreographer, had been commissioned to choreograph and direct it.

I was overjoyed when Madame Borovansky announced to the class that I had been chosen to dance the leading role of Clara. It all seemed like a dream. To be allowed to share the same stage as the heroes and heroines who had been my role models, to work side by side with them, was to tread on enchanted ground. But when two train tickets to Sydney materialized—one for my mother, who was to be my chaperone, and one for myself—I could see that the rest of the world believed in this whole incredible series of events.

It was a mark of how honoured my family felt that they permitted this disruption to the running of our household. Under normal circumstances my father would never have tolerated Mother's absence for such a long time, and my mother knew it would be emotionally difficult for him to be without her. He was not an outgoing man; though he would put up with our absence with his usual silent stoicism, at heart he would be pining for his wife and daughter. Still, he would never stand in the way of his children's development, no matter how adversely it affected him. He knew his children had their own destinies.

My headmaster was ecstatic to hear the news, and assured my mother that, as I was a very good pupil, it would not matter at all that I would miss a couple of months' schooling. My form teacher, Mrs Tyrrell, was equally supportive, and went to a great deal of trouble to write out the prospective syllabus, which she said I should do only if I had enough time. I was definitely the flavour of the month. The teachers behaved as if my good fortune was a direct reflection on the school. But, best of all, my peer group began to treat me with new respect. Even the school bully planted kisses on both my cheeks, handed me a good-luck present, and told me how much she would miss me. On my last day I was presented with a marcasite brooch, bought for me by my sixth-grade friends, and I was given a formal send-off at a school assembly held in my honour.

From the beginning of the rehearsal period it was clear that David Lichine and Monsieur Borovansky were not going to see eye to eye. They squabbled like children. Their rivalry obviously stretched back to the days when they danced with Colonel de Basil's Ballet Russe de Monte Carlo. Lichine, formerly David Lichtenstein, was a rather pompous man, one of those former *premiers danseurs* who refuse to lay aside their Siegfried cloaks. By all accounts he had been a brilliant dancer, and even though he was thickening with middle age you could still see that he had been an extremely beautiful young man. Indeed, it was said that he had been as much a matinee idol as a *danseur*.

Unfortunately for me, I became the meat in the sandwich, as one of the main issues they bickered about was how the role of Clara should be presented. Monsieur Borovansky wanted to highlight my precocity, but Mr Lichine had other ideas. He felt that the choreography for Clara should be kept low-key, more dependent on mime and the inherent appeal of having a cute little child as a central character. He did not want Clara to have any long solos. The real dancing, as far as he was concerned, should be left to the adults. But Monsieur got his way, and begrudgingly Lichine let me dance *sur les pointes*, and choreographed a little solo for me to show off my *fouettes*. Naturally all this did not help my relationship with Lichine.

The disruptions continued, and the rehearsals almost ground to a halt. Eventually Lichine banned Monsieur from rehearsals altogether, and after that things progressed much more smoothly. Lichine's choreography was pure Hollywood. The initial ideas were excellent, but he tended to drown his choreography under a layer of cuteness and slapstick. Performing children are a certain crowd-pleaser, but Lichine programmed wide-eyed Shirley Temple look-alikes whose antics almost strayed into the realms of musical comedy. Boro eventually saved the production from disaster; as soon as Lichine departed, he dispensed with huge chunks of gauche choreography, and toned down Lichine's wilder lapses.

Monsieur's behaviour towards me was unpredictable. I think he was ambivalent about how best to develop my talents as a dancer—to drive me as hard as the adults, or to treat me like a little girl. I suppose I didn't help matters much, for I liked to be thought of as a little adult, and behaved like a little adult. Then, at the least provocation, I could burst into tears and reveal all the emotional immaturity of an eleven-year-old.

At times Boro was infuriated by my refusal to be just a child. I found it easy enough to switch into a mood of wonderment, as in the transformation scene when the cot on which I sat began to move magically around the stage, while the living room was transformed into a snow-covered forest. I found it easy to be spellbound when the Christmas tree suddenly grew through the ceiling, up, up to the sky. I found it easy to appear totally enamoured of my prince. But I did not find it easy to play with dolls. It seemed ridiculous and demeaning for a girl of my age. 'For God's sake', Boro yelled, 'play with those bloody dolls! You're a little girl, not an adult. You *should* like dolls!'

Most of the children were terrified by his bellicose ways. Whenever I heard him striding through the corridors yelling some dancer's name, I felt sorry for the unfortunate creature who was about to suffer his temper. Once I saw him fire a dancer on the spot for arriving late for a rehearsal. Another time I heard him yell, 'I don't care if you're a bloody pansy offstage, but on stage you're supposed to look like a man, not a mincing fairy!'

But if Monsieur was pleased he was never reluctant to praise, and if the recipient of this praise were female a pinch on the bottom or an ardent bear-hug could be counted as high praise indeed. He seldom vented his temper on me. Indeed, he was proud of my achievements, and showed off my precocity whenever the opportunity arose. In turn I loved him for his refusal to compromise artistically. I knew that he would judge me on my merit rather than my age.

A bad dose of pre-opening-night jitters finally put paid to any notion that the past six weeks had been a dream. Having to wear a costume of velvet and swansdown in the sweltering Sydney heat was the least of my worries.

In rehearsal the dimly lit stage at the Empire Theatre had been merely a laboratory, a place for fixing one's mind on the choreography, a place for ironing out stutters that might inhibit the flow of magic from the deep. But now I was in a state of sheer terror. I spent the whole day consumed with fear of falling flat on my face, or having a mental blackout, or forgetting my steps. At the on-stage call I found myself wishing the theatre would burn down. But then the orchestra began to tune up and, standing in the wings, I could hear the seductive buzz of anticipation from the audience. There were frenetic flurries backstage as the stage crew made their final adjustments and the wardrobe ladies sewed on last-minute hooks and eyes. A burst of applause as the conductor entered the auditorium. Silence, a few taps of the baton, and the music swelled to fill my innermost corners. 'Chukkas!' the stage manager whispered, and I was on. After a few steps on to the stage, the panic felt terminal. Then, miraculously, the dry retching stopped, the other children made their entrance, and I slipped into the role of Clara.

After the performance I had only just had time to extricate my blistered feet from my shoes when, to my alarm, I was summoned to Monsieur Borovansky's office. I was still too high on adrenalin to know whether I had bombed or succeeded. Certainly I had experienced an unforgettable excitement as the company joined hands for the final call, to thunderous applause. And when I stepped out solo for my own curtain call, the thunder had risen to a deafening roar. But in the end the only opinion I cared about was Boro's.

I walked down the corridor in an acute state of the blues. Perhaps the performance had not gone as well as I had thought. Had I been too much the adult and too little the young innocent? That was it. I was surely going to be reprimanded.

Monsieur was already standing at the doorway of his office, wearing a stern countenance, which did not augur well. Without further ado he pulled me up on a few minor points. While I waited for the real thunderbolt, he walked menacingly towards me Quasimodo-fashion, deliberating each step, shoulders stooped, hands clasped behind his back. I was terrified, so intent on avoiding his eyes that my chin seemed to weld itself to my collar bone. It took some pressure from Monsieur's cupped hands to raise my face to meet his. To my astonishment, his eyes were twinkling. At once Quasimodo changed into that familiar beaming Humpty Dumpty. The joke had been on me.

Planting a noisy kiss on my forehead, Monsieur asked why I was looking at him with those huge, tragic eyes. And then my sustenance finally came. 'You were excellent', he said. 'I am extremely happy with you.' He handed me a small gift-wrapped box. I quickly fell into my expected child-like role, and peeled off the wrappings.

My present was a crucifix. A crucifix with a real diamond in the centre, on a beautiful golden chain.

There was no reason that Monsieur should have realized that we were Jewish. We certainly never publicized the fact. But my family was extremely superstitious, and often interpreted trivial happenings as ominous portents. Although we were not religious, any symbolic betrayal of our Jewish heritage was a profanity.

The crucifix was accompanied by a letter, a sentimental tract predicting a great future for me, and warning me not to forget Madame, who, as he put it, had first discovered me.

A few days later I was called to Monsieur's dressing room again. This time he was meek and apologetic. 'Madame tells me you are a little Jewish girl', he said. 'I'm sorry, I didn't know. Please let me exchange the gift for something else.'

Now it was my turn to feel embarrassed, as my insecurity about my Jewishness rose to the surface. 'Oh, we're not religious', I said. 'I would like to keep the cross as a memento anyway. I am very happy with it.'

To make amends, he bombarded me with questions. 'Do you like gefillte fish? Do you go to synagogue?' and a whole host of other nonsense, all of which to my mind was rather like asking an Eskimo if he enjoyed sunbaking.

There was evidently a law that forbade children from performing for any length of time without an alternate cast, but the rule was waived for *Nutcracker* on the pretext that the company could not find anyone else capable of dancing my role. The other children in the ballet all alternated, but I danced almost every performance, matinee and evening, for the entire six-week season. Eventually my understudy was groomed for a few matinee performances, but Monsieur wasn't terribly enamoured of her, and the impending threat evaporated into thin air. I was more than pleased to carry on with my heavy workload. To me it wasn't work; it was the ultimate egotistical ecstasy, and most definitely not for sharing.

My father, however, was concerned about my workload, and sceptical enough to suspect that I was being exploited. Conditions backstage at the Empire Theatre were archaic. Indeed, it was surprising that the child welfare organizations or the Health Department did not condemn the children's dressing room out of hand. It was a dank, squalid and gloomy basement, home to several families of very well-fed rats, more like a Dickensian workhouse than the glamorous home of showbiz.

Fortunately, as I was required to do a very quick costume change for the transformation scene, I was allocated a small space in the prop room. But I *was* on my own, and delighted not to be lumped together with other children. A vivid imagination and some delusions of grandeur turned the squalor into charm and glamour. I discovered a rather dilapidated dressing table and mirror, complete with surrounding lights, standing forlornly among an array of disused props and stored scenery. I added a Queen Anne velveteen chaise longue that had definitely seen better days, placed a silver star on my door, and could not have been happier. Considering the length of time I spent in those gloomy surroundings, it was just as well.

On matinee days I hardly ever saw daylight, arriving at the theatre before ten in the morning for the company class, then staying in the dressing room in the short respite between performances to do my school work. When I finally emerged at 11 p.m. it was hard to regain a grip on reality. But no one could have persuaded me to catch some more sleep and miss that early morning company class. For me it was just another performance, without make-up or sets. It gave me the opportunity to show off my technical precocity to the select audience of the ballet company itself.

I was the only child in the class, but this did not faze me. I saw this as a real chance to pitch myself against the best of the Australian ballet world. There were some luminaries with whom I would never presume to compare myself. Kathleen Gorham was one such ballerina. To me she was more fairy than human, an ethereal creature with her own magical aura, both on and off the stage. I modelled my whole persona on this quintessential ballerina, hoping only that I might grow up to dance and look as beautiful as she.

These aspirations had not sprung up entirely without reason. Many people had already remarked on the similarities between Kathleen and myself. Kathleen's dramatic talents were diverse; in a ballet like *Pineapple Poll* she could enchant her audience with her natural comical ability, but she could move people to tears in tragi-dramas such as *Corrida* and *Giselle*. And she was a home-grown star, a role model for would-be ballerinas throughout Australia. Her first instructor had been Leon Kellaway, a superb teacher who had also taught me at the Academy and was now playing my doddery old grandpa in *The Nutcracker*. Like Monsieur and Madame Borovansky, he had been a member of Pavlova's company. Indeed, Monsieur had several members of Pavlova's company working for him as character dancers, teachers, artistic advisers and mentors.

Many years later one of the ex-Borovansky dancers reminisced about the impact I had made on the company. 'We didn't all love you', she mused.

> In fact, some of us came to loathe you. There you were, this tiny tot with enormous eyes, bouncing into all the most technical *enchaînements* effortlessly, while the rest of us moaned and groaned. But the ultimate show-stopper was those twenty-four *fouettes* both to the left and to the right. We all could have killed you for those.

My life was not all work. There were other less manageable agonies to contend with. I was passionately in love with several of my princes, but, though they were sweet and considerate to me, even at the age of eleven I could tell it was not the real thing.

This time was also an eye-opener to less conventional sexual mores. There was much hilarity and giggling, and some very demonstrative body language, among male dancers in the gloomy wings. Here was a mode of sexuality quite outside the neatly packaged sex education my mother had given me some years before. When I asked my mother why these men were behaving so amorously she explained the facts, as she always did, in a very straightforward manner, and that was that. Now that I had unravelled a little more of the mystery of the theatre world, I felt all the more drawn to it.

In the end this production of *Nutcracker* was sheer magic. It was pure escapism. People came out of the theatre feeling carefree and uplifted, having been transported into a mythical kingdom. Even the sceptics could not help being moved; despite their intellectual reservations, they invariably found themselves swaying to and fro with Tchaikovsky's simple, gloriously melodic music.

The critics were unanimous. 'A star is born', said one reviewer. 'Monsieur Borovansky predicts that Alida Glasbeek is destined to be another Anna Pavlova', another reported. I was interviewed by the press, photographed for colour spreads in the *Women's Weekly*, and, much to my delight, recognized on the street. 'That's the little girl who dances Clara', someone would whisper, pointing in my direction, while I walked on, feigning nonchalance.

To me it was a fairy tale come true to be up there on the stage, a nightly part of a wondrous magical happening, feeling that hypnotic sense of power to excite, sadden, soothe and chasten. I thrived on the desultory activity in the backstage gloom, and the pomp and glitter out front. I believed I was tailor-made to take on stardom headlong, and from where I was standing I couldn't see too many pitfalls.

Even the duties associated with being a celebrity only added to my self-importance. 'Oh dear, look at all those people at the stage door', I would sigh, eyeing off the patient crowd. I could have resorted to the side door, but with an air of brave martyrdom I would opt for the stage door, feigning surprise at all the interest. Amid gasps of 'Isn't she tiny?' and 'Oh, the poor thing looks so exhausted!', I stoically signed the autograph books, programmes and slips of paper that several generations of hands were thrusting under my nose. I remembered to smile and chat to my admirers whenever I could. A pro, after all, never forgets her public. And I loved every moment of it.

I adjusted to that strange twilight world as if I had been born to it. When most other children were preparing to go to bed, I would leave my aunt and uncle's Elizabeth Bay flat and make my way to the theatre to begin my day's work, and in the early hours of the morning I would be happily sipping iced coffee at a café on Kings Cross, unwinding after the evening's performance. There was nothing quite like the excitement of big city life after dark. Kings Cross was the most cosmopolitan and bohemian spot in Australia, a haven for artists, post-war European immigrants, and the women of the night, who fascinated me most of all.

The *Wunderkind* 35

The *Nutcracker* magic: Alida with her Prince, Royce Fernandez, in the snow scene, Sydney, 1956

A tiny ballerina and her fans, Adelaide, 1957

Auntie Maria and Uncle Nico's flat was on the fourth floor of a rather stylish art deco building, which had an idyllic view of Rushcutters Bay with its hundreds of little yachts and launches. It was only a few doors down from the Macleay Street park and the hub of the Cross. There could be no greater contrast to life in suburban East Malvern, but, far from feeling cooped up, I began to feel at home in this high-density area with its richly varied people. There was a small group of Dutch Jews who lived in Sydney's eastern suburbs. Most of the men were carpet salesmen like Uncle Nico, and when they weren't on long trips into the Australian outback they would spend most of the day in one of the cafés on the Cross, drinking coffee, playing cards and gossiping. I loved to go with Uncle Nico and listen to their colourful stories about their poorer days in Marken; though they were all far more affluent now, I don't think their outlook on life had changed much. In the afternoons they would move to the terrace of the Rex Hotel, another fashionable meeting place, where the women would join them for cocktails and rich cakes.

After the performance we would often go out for supper, especially if Uncle Nico and Auntie Maria had been to see the show, and then nothing but the best spot in town would do. We would arrive laden with bouquets of flowers, exciting comments from all quarters of the restaurant. If it appeared that no one recognized me, Uncle Nico felt it his duty to rectify this oversight. For an hour or so everyone in the place would be given a rundown on my experiences so far, and all the complimentary predictions for my future. Then he would order drinks for the house, and a banquet for our table. He enjoyed making it clear that money was no object; often he would pull out wads of notes, which never failed to impress his audience. He was the most unlikely theatregoer, with his flashy, urbane clothes, diamond rings and brash presentation, but people were won over by his showmanship, his engaging conversation and his spontaneous generosity.

New Year's Eve was an unforgettable experience. The festivities began at the theatre. Even as the audience began to arrive it was clear they were intent on enjoying themselves. The cast and stage crew were all in high spirits. Every dancer was braced for the practical jokes that would be scattered throughout the performance. Bottle tops descended from the heavens, like chunks of ice amongst the falling snow. Props were interchanged, and dancers switched roles to hilarious effect. The *pièce de résistance* was Paul Grinwis's appearance as the *bonbonnière*. This was always a humorous divertissement, performed by a man sitting on the shoulders of another man, disguised by a huge skirt, from which teams of children emerged to perform a little dance. Paul was a master of these drag-queen roles, and had us all in stitches. It was very hard to pull ourselves together to finish the last act. The audience entered into the spirit of things, and on the final curtain call, amid a chorus of raucous 'Happy New Years', the cast was showered with streamers and flowers.

Auntie Maria and Uncle Nico were at the performance, and after supper we walked from the city to the Cross to take part in the celebrations there. The streets were so packed with people that it seemed pointless to defy the main sweep of the crowd. The pips of midnight sounded, and everyone went mad. Car horns honked, people kissed, blew whistles and linked arms with total strangers to sing a rousing if unmusical rendition of 'Auld Lang Syne'.

At 2 a.m. we struggled home through knee-high streamers, while the revelry was still in full swing. No New Year's Eve since has been quite able to measure up to the magical impact of that night that ushered in 1956.

Soon afterwards my father arrived in Sydney to spend a couple of weeks with us. Though he had never said outright that he had missed

Monsieur Borovansky and Alida at the ballet's Christmas party, Sydney, 1956

us, it was obvious from his appearance that he had been pining away. In reality he wasn't happy with any part of this business. He was suspicious of theatre people, with their extravagant displays of affection. He harboured the usual prejudices against ballet men and their ilk, and could not understand why my mother and I were obviously enjoying what seemed to him to be a bizarre lifestyle. Maybe he also felt a sense of impending loss.

His anxieties were exacerbated when I came down with the Asian 'flu, but staggered on to the stage, drugged to the eyeballs. So conditioned was I already to the sanctity of the theatre that I did not think it at all extraordinary that I should perform with a raging temperature, simply because my understudy was also sick, and Monsieur felt that I would make a better botch job than she. For about a week I swigged back foul-tasting quinine in order to make it through my paces. Months later the mere mention of quinine would still conjure up that horrible taste.

In my eyes Monsieur Boro was infallible. If my art required that I should suffer, well, so be it. If Pavlova's toes bled while she danced, then who was I to quibble? It was all rather chivalrous, I thought, rather like an endurance test, proving that dancers could transcend the pain and enter a spiritual plane reserved for true 'artistes'. I had very little sense of humour regarding my chosen career. Indeed, I expected everyone else to be as overawed as I was.

Apart from Beth Gray, the girl who played the role of my brother Franz, most of my friends were adult members of the company. My mother and I were often asked to join a group of dancers for a day at Redleaf Pool. I generally had no difficulty in relating to the adults, and even threw in my pennyworth when they got on to gossiping about other members of the company. Nobody made any effort to censor even the most explicit sexual titbits; either they overlooked my age, or they assumed that I was in the know about such things. In fact I was not, and those afternoons at Redleaf were very educational.

By any standards the Sydney season was a long, hard slog, but I dreaded the thought of having to leave this self-sufficient, secluded island state with its own jargon, traditions, superstitions and uncommon people. What did I have to look forward to after such a life?

4

Old Roles, New Rivals

I returned to the Melbourne studio as a celebrity. Madame gave a ponderous lecture pointing out that it was she who had created this natty little product. The fact that I had anaemia was considered a minor side-effect. I was in desperate need of a rest, but I would not take time off without Madame's permission. Predictably Madame announced that she didn't need to be told by a doctor, she was going to insist that I take a rest. 'Out', she said magnanimously, pointing to the door. 'Out you go and don't come back to classes until there is some colour in your cheeks. Mum Glasbeek, make sure she walks along the beach every day and eats plenty of red steak and vegetables.' And she proceeded to lecture my mother on the rules of child-rearing with all the dogmatism of one who had never experienced the task at first hand.

Steak was the magic potion for all athletes in those days, and my mother did as she was bidden. I was treated like a rare and exotic orchid, to be handled with extreme care. All this would have been very nice if I hadn't begun to believe it myself.

Life returned to its normal pattern all too soon. The fear of being toppled from my pinnacle was enough to keep my nose to the grindstone. That overwhelming feeling brought on by the sound of tributary applause would be with me forever. There was no going back. It just was not possible to contemplate any destiny other than stardom.

Although most seasoned performers might consider replying to fan mail an irksome task, I found the fact that people were still displaying an interest in my *Nutcracker* persona a most welcome and reassuring relief from ordinary life. Not all these correspondents were invisible admirers, however.

My friendship with the Kinmont family began in this rather lop-sided manner, but developed very rapidly into a warm, long-standing relationship based on mutual respect. I first met the three Kinmont daughters while signing autographs at the Empire Theatre, and they announced that they were my number one fans. Henceforth I searched for their faces at the stage door after each matinee for the rest of the Sydney season.

I was invited to spend some time with them during the summer holidays. Their home in Kirribilli was a beautiful old mansion with sweeping views of Sydney Harbour and more rooms than I could possibly imagine any non-Royal family owning. These holidays with the Kinmonts opened up a whole affluent existence beyond my ken.

At the same time, I made a very special friend at school. Lynne was a girl from a dinky-di Aussie family, a family not at all predisposed to the alien mores of the world of theatre. We giggled about deliciously unballetic things, compared her burgeoning tits to my unburgeoning ones, overindulged in Continental foods, and tore teachers, friends and foes to shreds—a pastime we enjoyed less out of malice than for the opportunity to develop our skills in bitchy banter. I needed Lynne's close and steadying influence. When I look back now, I marvel at the maturity she manifested in tolerating the variable moods of her anxious little ballerina friend.

In the space of just a few months, one can lose one's hold over the ballet world and succumb to becoming a regular human being. No one is very interested in a dancer who once performed. But fortunately, after only a short time in civvies, I was called to action once again. My mother and I were off to Adelaide after a period of rehearsal in Melbourne. This time, however, some of the gloss would be missing. I was no longer the singular *Wunderkind*. I would have to learn to share some of the adulation with a second child. Anna Fraser was cute, innocent, a little girl with even larger eyes than mine. I knew she would be far more endearing to the rest of the company than I could ever be, for she had an apparent simplicity that adults found comforting after my disconcerting precocity. So it was with considerable trepidation that I accepted this delegation of my workload.

It was left to me to teach Anna my own precious role. Clara was a character portrayal that I had developed from only the most rudimentary beginnings. Lichine had taught me the steps, shown me the basic stage directions and sketched out a faint character outline, but the substance was all drawn from my own inner resources. I had made Clara come alive, and now I had to stand by and watch someone else come along and pick up the finished product.

Naïve, good-natured little Anna copied my version to the letter, which annoyed me more than if she had presented an interpretation of her own. All the nuances that I had slowly added as my understanding of the role grew, all my gut feelings, were now written into the choreography, to be stolen by others as if they had never been mine at all.

Many dancers commented on how well she had learnt the role. This was the ultimate insult. Now I saw the company dividing into two camps, those who supported Anna and those who remained loyal to me. Publicly I was co-operative, even friendly, but privately I was tormented. I constantly urged my mother to reassure me that I was the better dancer. I could not be magnanimous about Anna; I hoped she would always continue to be second cast, a second-class citizen.

The Overland, still a relatively new train, seemed sheer luxury. I was thrilled with our cosy little self-contained compartment, and fiddled with the gadgets for most of the night. I think I must have opened and shut the natty little toilet a hundred times!

Compared with the child stars of the American film world, we ballet kids had few luxuries. There was certainly no risk of creating spoilt monsterettes. My appointment as Clara was seen as an honour, and neither my mother nor I thought in terms of payment. It seemed ungrateful to even contemplate complaining. Respect for money had not yet crept into the Australian theatre world. We didn't think twice about the fact that J. C. Williamson's didn't provide their little breadwinners with all the necessary creature comforts. It was enough that they always remembered to deliver huge baskets of flowers to the stage on opening night, with a special handwritten thank-you note from Claude Kingston on behalf of the management.

Even so, our arrival in Adelaide was a trying experience. We were left to find our own way to our digs, and it was a Sunday. Adelaide had not acquired its reputation as the city of churches for nothing; it seemed the entire population was either asleep or at church. Fortunately we were with Beth and her mother, who helped make what could have been a depressing situation into a humorous one, even if in the vein of black comedy.

Beth Gray was an easygoing person, and good company. Chosen to play the part of my brother because of her impish face, big ears and gangly limbs, she was a tomboy off-stage as well. Her mother had a direct manner and a raucous sense of humour. The theatre world was as much of a novelty to them as it was to us. Beth's family was Aussie working-class, with an endearing warmth and earthiness. Probably Beth and her mother were both grateful to escape their rather tough existence in Leichhardt.

After our long train journey my mother and I were eager to settle into our digs and rest before the rehearsal next day. We were also looking forward to our reunion with Beth and her mother, who were booked into the same place.

The taxi drew up outside a grey timber lean-to. 'My God', I said, 'I bet Shirley Temple's accommodation was never like this!'

An old lady opened the door, and showed us around the lodgings with a gracious smile. Beth and her mother were already there, crumpled and forlorn, sitting on a filthy couch. My mother and I burst out laughing at the sight. Obviously we would have to find somewhere else, but it was Sunday, so we were stuck for the night at least. Our 'bedrooms' were cold, dank closets. The floors were covered with broken lino, which in places revealed tattered newspapers spanning at least forty years.

'At least we've got a window', my mother remarked. 'You're lucky, because we haven't', Mrs Gray yelled through the paper-thin wall. Later we opened our window to find ourselves gazing at an open-mouthed, toothless lady sleeping in the adjoining room. Drawers full of mouse droppings soon put paid to any idea of eating in, so we went to bed with the noise of our rumbling stomachs accompanying the sounds of rampaging rodents.

The next day the Salvation Army took us in at their 'People's Palace'. The wool sales were on, and not a vacant room was to be found in the city. Looking more like bedraggled refugees than mini-stars, we were amused to find ourselves the sole occupants of an eight-bed dormitory, where Beth and I spent most of the evening bouncing from bed to bed. My mother worried that I might catch some terrible disease from the communal bathroom. She insisted that I put a towel down on the tiled floor before showering, and suspiciously examined the ancient taps, which popped and steamed like angry demons. Finally, after failing to find a neutral corner, we fell asleep under the serene gaze of Jesus.

Eventually we found some self-contained flats in Glenelg, but the mistake with our original accommodation was costly. Having paid several weeks' rent in advance, we had to live frugally. We did, however, receive an opportune invitation to tea at Government House. We all decided to skip a couple of meals to make sure we got the most out of this free meal.

I arrived at Government House in a borrowed white dress, hoping that everyone would think that I was at ease in such sumptuous surroundings. My mother and I chatted nonchalantly, avoiding looking too eager, as the waiters appeared holding huge silver platters, which we assumed would be filled with mouth-watering edibles. I assumed a slightly bored look, as if attending these functions was an excruciating duty. But there was no banquet. The platters were filled with the tiniest savouries, and they were whisked around at such speed that we would have had to chase the waiters and wrestle them to the ground to get more than a cracker. Most of the people in the room were standing around, taking occasional sips from their champagne glasses, looking over the shoulders of the people talking at them. The few who were eating nibbled away with such restraint that they were able to put the remnants of that ridiculous little savoury on their plate several times before putting the last morsel into their mouths.

A few nights later the Governor and his wife came to see the performance, and I was photographed with them backstage, again wearing the little borrowed white dress with the pink satin sash tied around my waist. Several governors and several banquets later, some of the gloss had worn off. The people at the zenith of the social scale, I discovered, were no better and no worse than anyone else. And it didn't take me long to recognize that there were people who specialized in collecting people, especially little celebrities like myself. While I was flattered to be numbered amongst those collectibles, I didn't confuse such flattery with sincerity.

But above all I didn't want to share my glory with anyone else, and especially not with the perky, long-lashed, high-instepped Anna with her rich family—she even had a black maid called Ruby! By now I understood management attitude to box office. The most popular performer is reserved for opening nights, and more often than not for last nights. When I heard that Anna might be offered the last night, I was devastated. Could it be that I was regarded as second best? I felt Monsieur had abandoned me. I was still fairly confident that my performance had the edge on Anna's, but the gap was narrowing. I had someone breathing down my neck, and I didn't like it.

Eventually a compromise was reached: Anna danced the last night, but I was summoned to the stage for the final curtain call. As I walked on from the wings, carefully made up, my hair in ringlets, and took my

Old Roles, New Rivals 45

Meeting the Governor in that borrowed white dress, Adelaide, 1957

curtain call among the tangle of streamers, I smiled inwardly. It was *I* who was taking the final bow.

It was opening night at Her Majesty's Theatre, Melbourne. The on-stage call had brought down only the most zealous dancers, who were flurrying about with misguided urgency. I made the rounds with all the others in a last-ditch attempt to familiarize myself with the stage. Out there, beyond the fire curtain, I could hear the cacophony of thirty-one unsynchronized instruments, defiant voices rejoicing in their last moments of anarchy. Applause! The human gabble calms down, and the conductor enters the orchestra pit. Three taps of the baton and, miracle of miracles, the instruments play as one; the genius of Tchaikovsky reigns.

I knew they were all out there in the auditorium—my relatives, friends, ballet colleagues, and would-be usurpers who would condemn my performance from the start. And tonight my most forthright critic, my brother Harry, would see me dance Clara for the first time. I was scared stiff.

At curtain down the audience boomed its approval. The full cast was still standing on the stage, scattered with flowers and streamers, when the auditorium lights came on to erase the line between fantasy and reality. The audience thundered on and on. I scanned the house for familiar faces. And there, sitting in the front row of the dress circle, were my parents, beaming like two Cheshire cats. I continued to curtsy and acknowledge the audience at large, but only my family mattered. It was my parents I was thanking; the applause was for them as well. I wept with the joy of all that good fortune.

My apprehension returned when I pushed my way through to the dressing rooms. I hadn't seen my brother yet. For once I scarcely heard the flattering remarks of the ballet VIPs. One by one I thanked my relations and friends for their kind comments; it seemed that a never-ending stream of acquaintances had popped up from all over Melbourne. I was farewelling the last of them when I noticed my brother, wedged up between baskets of flowers and costumes, calmly surveying the histrionics.

He waited for the last person to leave before he made any move towards me, and then silently he planted a kiss on my cheek, gently squeezed my arm, and said, 'You were tremendous, Puss. You are really super-talented. Though I say it reluctantly, I think you have the makings of a great dancer'. This was the judgement I had hardly dared to hope for.

Next stop was Brisbane—a far more pleasant experience than Adelaide. I loved the steamy heat. While most of the other members of the company flopped around lethargically, I felt relaxed and supple.

Brisbane in those days was rather a romantic place, touched by a Wild West atmosphere. It was as if the entire population of this laconic city had sprung straight off a Drysdale canvas: tall, sinewy bushmen and their honest-faced female counterparts. Evidently the climate was so enervating that the natives scarcely dared move their lips to speak. The Aussie drawl had always been a problem for my parents, but here the mumbled utterances were almost impossible for my mother to translate.

Our landlady, Mrs Peterson, was an elderly widow who had lived most of her life in the ramshackle timber house where she now took lodgers. My mother and I were filled with a sense of adventure, but on our first night in Brisbane we were tired out by the tedious bus journey home. By the time we arrived at Mrs Peterson's door we wanted nothing more than to fall into a soft, clean bed. We were welcomed by the most evil-looking army of cockroaches I had ever seen. They swarmed over the floor like a sinister black sea. My mother yelled and screamed, massacring scores of crackling creatures underfoot in a bid to reach the light switch. We spent the night sitting like frozen frogs, with our knees clasped under our chins.

My mother did her best to reassure me that this was a freak situation, and that Mrs Peterson would prevent it from happening again. She was a Queenslander, after all, and if this was a nightly event, surely nobody would stay in such a vermin-infested city. But when my mother recounted our nightmare Mrs Peterson threw her head back and rocked back and forth with laughter. 'You poor dears!' she said. 'We see them all the time up here. Better get used to those clicking little feet!' Then, after a moment's reflection, 'You know, I think I'd miss them if they disappeared'.

By this stage Anna and I had become friends, surface friends at first, for we both realized the need to work through our animosities under a veneer of friendship. We had stayed overnight at each other's homes, and I had shared private lessons at her expense. People were touched to see such a sweet little friendship blossoming where instead there could have been a nasty rivalry, mother versus mother, child versus child.

The charade was to go on for many years. As our rivalry grew more intense, egged on by Madame, so our friendship became more necessary. Anna's mother had been a well-known showbiz personality. That, and being rich, seemed to me to give her an unfair advantage. I noticed with some jealousy the feeling of kinship that Anna's mother inspired in all dancers. She was perfectly at home backstage. Theatrical clichés rolled off her tongue with irritating naturalness. Even her relationship with Boro and the management seemed to be on a more equal footing.

Anna had returned to Australia from Los Angeles with a slick American accent and a genuine claim to sympathy, as her father had died. She had beautiful eyes, long, articulate legs (ooh, how I hated them!), and just the right amount of talent—enough to be noticed, but not enough to be threatening. So there was nothing for me to do other than to stay right out in front.

In that world of smiles and forced flattery, the anxieties have to seep out somewhere; in my case it was my poor mother who had to pay the price for my public self-control. When I came home after a day of bottling up my insecurities, the lid would fly off at the first glimpse of my mother. Wasn't it her duty to see that her daughter remained securely on top? Only to her could I reveal my discomfort, but by tacit agreement I don't think either of us ever uttered the word 'jealousy'. And the simple fact was that I *was* jealous, fearfully jealous, for by now the stakes were far too high for me to move over for other rising stars.

There are many ways of undermining the paranoiac's tenuous confidence, and Anna challenged my superiority in ways that I could do nothing about. Not only had J. C. Williamson's again brought her along to Brisbane to 'ease my workload', but she arrived with the formidable Aunt Ruby. Devastated though I was, I couldn't help being impressed; secretly I felt Anna had achieved quite a coup. It was altogether frightfully toffish, ersatz Hollywood.

Brisbane, it transpired, was to be my swan-song in the role of Clara. My parents refused to let me join the company for one more tour in New Zealand. I was now at high school, and my parents wisely realized that it would not be so easy to catch up on missed study now. So I

The travelling circus: from left, Beth Gray and Mrs Gray, Carmel Nolan and Mrs Nolan, Anna Fraser, Alida, Mrs Glasbeek and the inimitable Aunt Ruby

experienced my first taste of dispensability at the ripe old age of fourteen years, just three years after I had created the role of Clara. It was a bitter pill. I was obliged to abdicate my position to a younger heir-apparent.

There could be no denying that Clara had changed my life. Because I reached such heights at such an early age, the weight and balance that might hold me to some kind of steady course in life had been altered irredeemably. It would take me a ballet lifetime to get over the experience. Perhaps my only real period of creativity began and ended in those naïve days.

As a child earmarked as 'special', I had been allowed to travel in a sphere of my own, gloriously free of the indignities of childhood. I had also been spared the constraints on natural spontaneity and intuition that seem to go hand in hand with adult sophistication. Never again would I feel so wholesome, and never again would I be quite so invincible, for as an adult dancer I would always be fair game for the criticism that had gently eluded me as a child star.

5

Number 358

After all the glitter of the *Nutcracker* years, I faced the glum prospect of having to adapt to normal life again. There would, however, be some changes. I had passed the entrance examination for MacRobertson Girls High School, and was rather excited at the prospect of tramming in to join that privileged coterie of students.

For some time now I had been watching as my girlfriend Lynne metamorphosed into a shapely young woman. It seemed an indecently short time since she had whispered in my ear that she had purchased her very first bra. She had kept me informed of her progression from 32A to B, right up to a most remarkable 36B, and all the while my chest showed not the slightest indication of changing.

I think I showed considerable generosity in sharing all those horrendous tit-and-bra jokes with Lynne as we washed under the giant shower at Grant Street. It seemed I was fated to skulk around, flat and uninteresting, plainly not long off the drawing-board. I was relieved when all this inequality began to change. The seams of my costume were stretched to bursting point, proof enough of my imminent womanhood. But it was all a façade, and would remain so for many years to come. All those years of strenuous exercise had already done their damage. While most of my peer group had already begun to menstruate, I showed no sign of following suit.

The perpetrators of the MacRobertson Girls High School uniform must have been sacerdotal prigs. The original design had two underlying principles: a definite anti-fashion statement, and an attempt to

No longer centre stage: Alida (far right, second row from back) at Mac-Robertson Girls High School, 1958

enshroud all those budding female bodies in a shapeless envelope of the drabbest grey imaginable. I suppose this was all part of the school's desire to act as custodian of our collective virtues, in case we should transgress the school motto: '*Poten Sui*'—self-control. Still, some girls managed to put all the bumps and bulges in the right places. The founding mothers would have turned in their graves to see how voluptuous the girls could look in those ridiculously suggestive short skirts, with their green velvet pudding-bowl hats tilted brazenly over one eye.

On our way home Lynne would draw an enviable cascade of wolf-whistles, while I was probably dismissed as her kid sister. Certainly the grey did absolutely nothing to enhance my sallow complexion. The tunic hung on my skinny body like a dowdy sack; with grey stockings, black lace-up shoes, gloves and pudding-bowl hat, my entire persona seemed to be swallowed up by the uniform, leaving me looking like a pathetic little rat.

My immature appearance did have one side benefit, however: I could travel half fare for most of my high-school days. But my deep voice belied my apparent youth, and my friends would collapse with laughter at the tram conductor's perplexity as he tried to work out whether that anomalous voice asking for half fare actually came from me.

At MacRob academic achievement was the most important goal from the start. Although they came from mixed backgrounds, it was always assumed that the students had one aim in common—to progress to tertiary education and an eminent academic life. It wasn't too long, however, before my mind began to stray from those dreary lessons, colouring-in rainforests on my perpetually inaccurate maps. It was difficult for me to get serious about the traditions of the previous generations of Palladian scholars who were held up as role models. At the beginning and end of the school day I had to trundle across the pedestrian crossing with a gaggle of dismal little grey carbon copies. I am Number 358, I would think glumly as I got on to the tram and pressed my nose against the window separating me from the outside world, only vaguely aware of all those ghastly, buxom young women tearing around the oval playing hockey.

The pressures were on at the ballet, too. Students who had seemed talented but not world-shaking were now taking giant steps forward. Having been allowed to evolve along more normal lines, these upstarts were suddenly neck-and-neck with me, some even daring to surpass my technical skills. My natural skills, especially my pirouettes and elevation, were still going as strongly as ever, but in many areas it seemed my pedagogues had assumed that I already knew it all, ignoring the need for patient, well-regulated guidance and sheer hard slog to lay down a solid foundation.

I had become a complete perfectionist. Madame Borovansky came to dominate my life, and to a large extent my mother's. Our need for Madame's approval grew with our dependence on her guidance. Indeed, all the students and their parents seemed unduly flattered if Madame cast an approving glance their way. It was as if we should all be grateful that she should trouble herself with us in the first place. To meet with Madame's disapproval, however, was to be cast into a dreadful void. My moods depended entirely upon my ballet life. I would be soaring one minute and wallowing in depression the next, all because of the whims of one woman!

For the ballet students adolescence was a period of serious reckoning. All those adolescent physiques were scrutinized, and dismissed or accepted according to the stringent prerequisites of classical tradition. But it was also a time for separating the dilettantes from those who had more serious intentions. There were no institutions that combined academic study with serious ballet training, so ballet students often left school at the minimum age in order to attend as many ballet classes as possible. In my own family, however, education was held in high regard, so I tried to keep the candle alight at both ends in a desperate bid to excel both at school and at ballet.

But adolescence presented me with a greater challenge than most people. In undermining my identity as a child prodigy, it threatened to negate everything my life had stood for so far. I felt I had stumbled into a state of limbo. I was losing my specialness, and I feared that my life would come tumbling down around me.

I felt totally ill-equipped to change the situation for myself. I needed some positive, down-to-earth guidance. My skills were still intact, my creativity had not diminished, but my artistic development was frustrated and limited by the superficiality of my technical knowledge. I began to panic, sensing that I had come up against a brick wall. From the age of seven I had received nothing but encouragement and adulation. Why, I asked myself, should it stop now? It seemed grossly unjust that I should be forced to stand aside and watch all those less inspired plodders trespass on my terrain.

For me the classroom had always been a stage. I was clapped, insulted or patronized, but remained always the show pony, adept at covering up her technical shortcomings. I longed for time and space to stop all this tomfoolery and work on my technique, but by now there was no question of going back. My reputation preceded me; even in the classroom, I could never afford to risk a moment of clumsiness or ridiculousness in the hope that such a moment might eventually bring higher fulfilment. I was locked into a pattern of emotional and artistic dishonesty. Even my teachers were dependent on my continuing ability to impress, for they would not take kindly to acknowledging their own inadequacies. They had made me the Academy's flag-bearer, they had publicly set out to turn this cygnet into a swan, and I could not be allowed to fail them.

But, just in case, the teachers took out insurance. Taking Madame's cue, they persistently pointed out that I was not the only talent in the ocean. Suddenly some other student would be pulled to the front of the class as an example for us all to behold. It was obvious what all *that* was about.

I began to fear classes, and secretly wished that somehow I might be absolved from the awesome responsibilities that were descending on me. I began to envy the more carefree existence of my peers, full of the pains and joys of love and dating and dressing up, and days and days of unadulterated indolence. Yet there was no question of giving up. To want to miss class was one thing in theory, but in reality I was far too anxious, far too fearful of slipping behind the others, to take such liberties. Come what may, I just *had* to remain a star. There was no other reassurance, there never *could* be any other reassurance; I had to be best. This psychosis did not stop with ballet, but soon filled every area of my life.

Having determined that the raw materials were no longer enough, I urgently needed some direction—not to imitate those legends of the past like Pavlova, but to find my very own line of passage. More than at any other time, I needed to be guided towards self-fulfilment by an imaginative and dedicated teacher.

Some years back, when Madame had first made her pronouncement that the Glasbeeks had a prodigy in their midst, she had prophesied that when I reached my teens I would have to go further afield for guidance, as she felt by then I would have outgrown her capacity to help me. But now she preferred to disown this statement when I reminded her of it. Mother and I did not press the issue; our judgement was obscured by our sense of loyalty and gratitude to Madame and her studio. The Academy was the centre of my universe, and the Borovanskys were going to make me the Pavlova of the Antipodes.

But when I sought some real instruction, some insight into the scientific development of my technical skills, the answer was always alarmingly pat. 'Don't worry, darling, it will happen in time. Just keep practising, and your leg will go higher.' That was like saying that if a blind man keeps walking around with his eyes open he will eventually see. Regardless of how hard I pushed and shoved, the leg wouldn't budge an inch higher. So, though I continued to work like a Trojan, I improved very little. The thrill of testing, numbing endurance had long since diminished. To work simply for an improved approval rating, like a performing monkey, seemed altogether too foolish. In truth, the time had come when I needed to experience the satisfaction that comes from pitching oneself solely against oneself.

It must have been evident that I was changing from a confident, precocious child, basking in the warmth and security of my family, to an adolescent riddled with self-doubt and insecurity. Harry and my father realized that my tears and tantrums were a measure of my fears and helplessness rather than a natural manifestation of an artistic temperament. But I did not take seriously Harry's brotherly advice to develop alternative interests and adopt a less serious approach to ballet and to Madame's authoritarianism. I continued to believe that ballet was my destiny, knowing that I couldn't expect my father or Harry to see it from my point of view.

And there were never any doubts in my mother's mind, absorbed as she was with the trials and tribulations of her extraordinary offspring. My pain was hers, my joy hers. She was my solace and buffer board, as well as having to bear the brunt of my own introverted hypercriticism. I looked to her to make right the wrongs of my world and carry the cross of all my anxieties.

Madame's attitude towards me oscillated between genuine affection and downright vindictiveness in the name of discipline. Conditioned to crave approval, I felt my world collapse when I found myself out of favour. Had she found a new contender for her attention? Was her enthusiasm waning because I had lost my touch? Inconsolable, I would beg my mother to go and see her. Torn between her instinctive desire to ease my pain and her reluctance to be seen as the stereotyped ballet mum, my mother always obliged, and nerved herself for a chat with Madame, which was rather like asking for an audience with the Queen. Conversation with Madame never even pretended to be egalitarian. Madame presided, while other people listened attentively. Still, my mother always managed to edge into the action; following the script I had invented and rehearsed with her for several days beforehand, she would give vent to all *my* grievances in one fell swoop.

To be ignored in class was to be damned, thrown into oblivion—a sure mark that the teacher was too bored with you to waste her precious bitchery on such a non-talent. To be singled out for an exclusive dose of vitriol was the biggest morale booster in the business. How lovely it had been in the good old days when all that continuous stream of sarcasm and bitchery was meant for me alone!

In the ballet world you had to suffer: bleeding toes, aching limbs and an injured soul were all an integral part of the grand myth. You had to be scourged and disciplined before you could—or was it would?—be allowed to emerge as a creature of beauty. So we were all gradually inured to pain, and smugly delighted if we could punish the feet to the point of bleeding, or whip the old body to the point of dropping. After all, as Madame so often reminded us, we were in good company. Pavlova had danced until the blood stained her satin shoes red. Maybe, I couldn't help thinking sacrilegiously, it was out of such acts of martyrdom that the inspiration for the Dying Swan was born.

Fortunately there weren't too many starry-eyed people at 27 Grant Street, and introspection was almost impossible in a house that at any given time seemed full of people of assorted ages and sizes. As I became more Australianized I came to see what I had regarded as perfectly normal family behaviour as rather embarrassingly different, if not bizarre. We three children begged our parents to tone down their European gregariousness when our Australian friends came to visit. We were convinced that only a veneer of Anglo-Saxon etiquette would redeem us in the eyes of our Aussie acquaintances.

'Please remember to speak English, lay your fork and knife side by side on your plate, don't cross them after the meal, and for God's sake don't scream at one another', we pompously instructed our elders. The futile attempt to de-migrantize our parents became an almost constant harangue of 'don'ts'. But Australian friends flocked to our house, attracted by exactly this outlandish foreign behaviour.

Anna and I, still aspirants to the same crown, continued to stay at each other's homes. Anna never refused an invitation to stay with the crazy Glasbeek/Gosler household, and she never appeared to be at all overwhelmed by the mayhem. But I am convinced that the end of the weekend, or weeks in the summer vacation, must also have brought relief as she returned to a more peaceful environment. Lynne, however, remained my closest confidante, and she positively revelled in Grant Street's action-packed atmosphere.

My life was quite a strange mixture. Although I lived to dance, life at Grant Street was so full that I could not possibly abstain, even if Madame had demanded it. An extremist by nature in any case, I was so full of the desire to learn as much as I could that I could never hope to find equilibrium in ballet alone. Though my goals *were* primarily aimed at dancing, my life was peppered by a heavy dose of insanity. And insane was the only way you could possibly have described my family in action.

They had a rather mysterious interpretation of the use of space, suburban garden space in particular. They ran riot now they had a veritable park for their own exclusive use. Taking quiet cups of tea under the elm was definitely not for us. Indeed, I can't remember sitting around in the garden much. For us all this glorious space was a perfect setting for cavorting, noise-making and holding open-air concerts. It was not at all unusual to see us, including our middle-aged parents, practising cossack dancing, playing ball, or running through the sprinklers.

And then there was the weather. Melbourne's long heatwaves seemed to inspire the adults in our family with awe, particularly Uncle Maurice, an obsessed weather-watcher who insisted on announcing all the barometer readings and temperature fluctuations on the hour, by the hour. I especially remember one of those unbearably hot nights when we were into the second week of century temperatures. Our double-storey brick home was like an oven, especially upstairs, where Auntie Rosa, Uncle Maurice and Harry slept. Fed up after a string of sleepless nights, we decided we couldn't spend one more night in our stifling house, and planned to sleep out in the garden.

Not all our sense of ritual was thrown out. First there was dinner—hot soup, as usual—followed by a drive to the beach in the hope of catching a cooling sea breeze. We all crammed into Uncle Maurice's tiny but immaculate Ford Anglia, and took our place in the endless stream of cars heading for the bay. The traffic jams annoyed Uncle Maurice no end. 'Look at that', he would say. 'The cars are boomper to boomper!' And, if someone should dare to move too close to his highly polished bumper bar, he would shout 'Move over, you . . . you . . . you, Buddy', a word that he obviously believed was an insult of the very worst kind.

Desperate for some sleep, we gave up and drove home, to our makeshift sleeping quarters in the garden. The adult couples sought out a suitable spot to park their mattresses without impinging on each other's privacy. Big Alida chose a nifty spot by the rose trellis. Harry had wisely decided that he could do better at a friend's air-conditioned house, while Lynne and I found a magical nook under a bush.

At first, overcome with exhaustion, we all retreated to our respective territories. And then suddenly all hell broke loose. Uncle Maurice, having got over all those buddies going boomper to boomper, decided to serenade us all, crooning at the top of his fine tenor voice, while Mother pranced around the lawn in her clingy white satin nightdress, emulating Isadora Duncan, then a seductive French songstress of the 'thirties and 'forties, and an Apache dancer, then gave what appeared to be a mysterious, individualistic rendition of Homer's *Circe*. My father rushed into the house to fetch his mouth organ. The classical segment was followed by a smorgasbord of perky, rather smutty Dutch songs accompanied by off-key whistling and a great deal of uncontrollable laughter. Even Mishka (our dog was named after Madame Borovansky's dog—imaginative, weren't we?) joined in, yelping and howling and rushing wildly round and round the garden.

This revelling went on until we were surprised by the first rays of dawn. It was only then that we became concerned about the noise level and the possible reactions of our poor neighbours. 'God, the Australians must have thought we were having a bacchanal', my mother giggled.

Later that morning my mother, the nominated spokesperson for our little band of lunatics, was sent over to Mrs Benson's to enquire whether the noise had disturbed her. We were lucky. Dear Mrs Benson, an eccentric herself, brushed away my mother's apologies and confessed that once again she had been induced to press her ear to the fence. 'What's more', she added, 'if I had been young enough, I would have perched myself right up on the top branch of that tree just so that I could have seen the dancing as well as listened to your brother's glorious voice'.

During the *Nutcracker* season my mother and I had managed to obtain a complimentary ticket for Mrs Benson, so she could see me dance at a Saturday matinee. She became my most ardent devotee, for she had been absolutely carried away, quite literally believing the story from beginning to end.

The following spring, with *Nutcracker* now relegated to the back of my mind, Lynne and I were invited to see Mrs Benson's garden, which was in full bloom. Mrs Benson began to dance. 'Look, I'm dancing, I'm dancing, just like you in the snowflakes!' she cried.

The sight of this little old white-haired lady kicking up her Wellington boots and frolicking in the shower of blossoms that she was shaking overhead had Lynne and me in hysterics. Then, to cap it all, she suddenly stopped to say quite seriously, 'You poor child, I bet you were cold, having to dance in the snow every night'.

6

Out of My Depth

Back at the Academy I was told to focus my mind on flat tummies, toes and thigh muscles. Late nights, eating and boyfriends were anathema. It was as if we were being bred to reject life lest it tarnish our delicate senses. My mother colluded in this regime. She understood that, if at times I hated the routine torture of life at the Academy, I needed the beauty of movement I could only find in dance. She and I were already identifying with the notion that I should lead a life of greatness and dedication. It was the chance of a lifetime, and my mother and I were not going to fail.

We demanded the complicity of the other family members. Any joke directed at me or my vocation was promptly dismissed. My busy schedule at ballet and school left me less and less time for dishwashing or setting the family table, and Harry was excluded from such 'female' jobs, so the burden fell to Big Alida.

On nights when my mother couldn't come to watch my lessons, my father walked all the way to Caulfield, often in the freezing cold, to pick me up from the station. I really enjoyed these walks; time alone with my father was becoming a rare thing, as he was increasingly a bystander as I became involved in a world with which he had little sympathy. Yet he remained our benefactor, in spite of his reservations.

That insidious master, ambition, even inspired my mother and me to a degree of furtiveness against my father. So smitten were we with Madame Borovansky that we went to extraordinary lengths to spend time alone with her. We were prepared to pay for the privilege. Although it was some distance from East Malvern to Hawthorn, where

Madame lived, we would offer Madame a lift home in a taxi at our expense, on the pretext that we were going to visit our relations in Hawthorn.

Madame seemed a different person on those rides, bringing herself to open out a little. Though it was usually quite late, 9.30 or 10 p.m., and I was generally very tired, it boosted my morale to feel that I had been able to edge in a little closer to Madame the woman, in the hope of perhaps finding in her some secret vulnerability. Sometimes we didn't even have enough money to take the taxi on to East Malvern, but would pay off the cab just around the corner from Madame's house and catch a bus, then walk the last mile and a half.

In 1958, when my father was fifty-one, the diamond-cutting firm where he worked closed down. It was more economical to import ready-cut diamonds. My father spoke little English and he had no marketable skills other than diamond-cutting and tailoring. To a man whose entire ethos was bound up with his ability to provide for his family, unemployment struck a deep blow. He spent day after day queuing at employment offices, or turning up at the docks or car factories for casual labour, only to find that there was no work. It must have been demoralizing, but he kept his worries to himself. Perhaps he was protecting us, but as a result I wasn't as concerned or sympathetic as I should have been. It was only later that I realized his great strength and devotion at that time.

Eventually Dad got a job as an assembly worker at the Rootes car factory. It was demeaning, repetitive work, and to get to the factory in Fisherman's Bend he had to leave at 4.30 in the morning and change trams three times over a three-hour journey—a far cry from his previous status as a highly skilled diamond-cutter. His approach to work, however, altered little. He didn't expect anything for nothing, and was grateful that he had been able to regain his position as provider.

While my father kept his counsel, my brother Harry constantly reminded me that there was a world beyond ballet. He refused to accept that my ballet training was necessarily my prison. 'You have choice', he would remind me, and he rejected the notion that temper tantrums, posturing and broodiness were essential components of creativity.

I idolized Harry, and some of my happiest childhood memories are of my brother and his student friends filling the house with good-natured banter and laughter. I was in love with most of them, although the fact that Harry referred to me as 'that scrawny little rat' hardly

Student days: Harry (right) and friends, 1952

helped my chances. Mostly, though, I was just 'Puss', a more endearing nickname he had coined when I was a toddler, and the name by which I have been called by friends and family ever since.

The age gap was a big one; when I was still a girl of fourteen, he was already a young man of twenty-three, a university scholar whose every statement I quoted as if it were the wisdom of Chairman Mao. But we were often at loggerheads. He wasn't always right, and I was often infuriated by his ability to talk around almost any subject, even ballet. Mostly I stalked into my bedroom, refusing to acknowledge that Harry had emerged as the victor, but when our argument was about my behaviour towards my parents, I was secretly grateful that there was someone who could lay down some firm parameters.

I was out of my depth. Having been propelled so prematurely into an adult world, I now believed I had forfeited the child's inalienable right to fail. My self-esteem rose and fell according to the approval of others. I became obsessed with my appearance and my performance, both at school and ballet, and utterly dependent on the love and attention of others. I began to fear that I might never be able to be honest with myself again.

Someone had to bear the brunt of all this growing anxiety, and my mother was the main target. I screamed and yelled at her. 'Come on, answer me', I dared her. 'Am I too fat? Are my pirouettes still the best? Surely you noticed that Anna's leg was going up higher than mine?'

My poor, befuddled mother, so full of maternal love, fed me the answers she believed I wanted to hear, and ended up not pleasing me at all.

If she answered, 'No, darling, you are not too fat', I interpreted this as fobbing me off. But if she believed I wanted some objectivity, and replied meekly, 'Well, darling, you may have put on just a little weight', that offered me an excuse for an even more vindictive attack. If I had put on weight, it was her fault for feeding me too much. Then, my self-hatred spent, my anger would turn to tearful pleas. 'Promise me, promise me you won't let me eat too much tomorrow.' And all the time we both knew that *I* would determine just how much I would eat, and my mother would go along with my every whim.

I would scream at her to leave me to make my own decisions; then I would stand at the public phone in the corridor at school, begging her to join me at the studio, to do nothing more than just be there. And she would come and stand behind the closed door of the ballet studio, where she could not see the class. But it was enough that she was there. Then afterwards I would be overcome with remorse and self-loathing, and would pray that she understood that all these tirades of abuse were aimed as much at myself as they were at her.

Nothing seemed clear-cut for me any more. My ballet teachers were markedly more restrained in their attitude to my dancing. My daily schedule was preposterous. I was no longer enjoying classes, and I hated going to school. Any illness was a welcome respite from the pressures of having to go through the motions. But as soon as I recovered, panic would set in. It was a panic born out of guilt, and the insidious fear that I would slip out of the top bracket, both at school and at ballet, until eventually my absence would not be noticed at all. Enjoyment or no, back I'd always go.

Towards the end of the year, in preparation for the annual concert, we had to rehearse after class, and then I often wouldn't return home until 10.30 or 11 p.m. Even the weekends were not always free. Scholarship students at the Academy were expected to show their gratitude by earning their keep. We were 'volunteered' to come in to help with the junior classes on a Saturday morning, taking roll calls and making cups of tea. In the latter months of the year, Saturday afternoons and even Sundays were often spent indoors rehearsing for the concert, which was the most important advertisement for the studio itself. The time when I could float through my school work was now over, and high school alone would have been quite exhausting enough. But I couldn't think of success at ballet at the cost of failure at school.

I was becoming an insomniac. Sleep was a luxury I couldn't afford. As I had so much less study time than other students, I felt I had to grab every moment to cram my head with dates, theories and French irregular verbs. I took no pleasure in study, but just ploughed through it all, with nothing more than the examinations in mind. I would settle for nothing less than being dux of the school. I would wake in the small hours of the morning, bathed in sweat, my mind desperately trying to regroup the facts and figures that in my dozing I had carelessly diffused. As school examinations approached, my mother would come into my bedroom at 2 or 3 a.m. and find me studying furiously, reduced to a mixture of near-tears and determination.

With such a long list of worries I had no trouble finding something to make me sleepless on any given night. Soon I found myself regressing back to infancy: I needed my mother's smell and touch to lull me to sleep. Curled up like a baby, I would fall asleep, pressed into my mother's lap, with both her arms clasped around my waist for good measure.

I also had recurring nightmares in which I dreamt of being hunted down by the Nazis. I would hear the sound of hundreds of marching jackboots, and a blood-chilling German voice commanding us to come out of our building; I would see haunted, frightened people, gas chambers, and worst of all the barbed-wire fence separating my parents from myself. I would shake myself into stunned wakefulness, then, for fear of falling back into that same tormenting dream, I would rush into my parents' bedroom and beg them to reassure me that such a terrible event could never happen again. I believed their reassurances; from where I had crawled, sandwiched safely between my mother and father in their invincible bed, the world seemed safe enough.

My parents didn't speak much about the traumatic experiences of their war years. I was told only the bare facts they believed I should know without their having to relive too many of the memories they had fought to wipe out. But vanished aunts, uncles and grandparents have to be explained, and this they did in as factual and unembroidered a way as possible. My parents also needed to gain temporal and emotional distance before they could handle the details of the Holocaust. And so I lived with my own fantasies, built on spasmodic, scant references to things that were so terrible that not even my parents could speak to me about them. Maybe it was because I had never experienced these wartime traumas myself that I was so haunted by events that occurred before I was born. Nevertheless, the emaciated faces that I saw in my dreams became my reality, and in the end I found it difficult to believe that they were merely drawn out of my imagination. I had become part of the collective anguish of the survivors of the Holocaust. In my need to establish my own identity I somehow had to come to terms with my family's recent history.

My parents, having survived starvation, placed great value on food, so they found it impossible to understand my newest obsession—the fear of developing Jewish thighs. As if the burden of being born Jewish wasn't enough in itself, I was now consumed with fear that I would inherit what I had come to accept as a Jewish characteristic. I don't know where this ridiculous concept stemmed from, but sometimes the greatest propagators of such anti-Semitic myths can be the Jews themselves. In our family it was somehow taken for granted that most Jewish women developed heavy thighs, even if they had slim torsos. This was not a happy prospect for an aspiring young dancer. Most of our female Jewish acquaintances were not exactly streamlined, but if I had bothered to look around with less biased eyes I might have noticed that not too many of our Gentile friends were either. But I planted this additional worry in my troubled little mind, where it grew out of all proportion.

All my ballet contemporaries were passing from childhood to maturity. For some, this meant a charming softening of lines, a clever blurring of the unattractive edges, a blossoming that did nothing to spoil that look of innocent coltishness so desirable in ballet dancers. But for some the transformation was neither gradual nor gentle. There were girls who changed from looking like little stick figures to comical, podgy dumplings, through no fault of their own. In a milieu less fixated on the body beautiful, nature would probably have taken its course, and a balanced diet and some unexaggerated exercise would have helped these dumplings develop into slim, fit young women. For me, however, it was more a case of taking frenetic pre-emptive precautions.

I was very slim, but I knew my career hung in the balance if I didn't control that terrible genetic predisposition. And any worry pertaining to the ballet, no matter how minor, was sure to be exacerbated by the dance doyens. True to Madame's customary lack of subtlety, she ploughed in and delivered us a lecture on diet, just when we were all at our most self-conscious. When wearing a skin-tight leotard, it was difficult to hide those little knobs, which somehow seemed more provocative than a fully grown bosom. Each girl in the class felt that

Madame's directive was aimed specifically at her, and no doubt bemoaned last evening's indulgence. Guilty, guilty, guilty, silently resounded throughout the classroom as Madame detailed the list of prohibited foods. It was easy to pick the fanatics from the dilettantes. This was to be a parting of the ways between those who approached dance training as an enjoyable, healthy and beneficial pastime and those who were prepared to go to extreme lengths in order to aestheticize themselves for their chosen art.

The studio mirror took on an even more sinister connotation. Initially a teaching aid, it became like Big Brother, its reflection all-pervasive. No matter where you stood in the classroom, your image was beamed back at you, and denounced you without your having to dance a step. But mirrors play tricks of their own. Instead of putting the fear of God into all the paranoid dancers by reflecting us several pounds heavier than we really were, as our tyrants hoped, some mirrors did the opposite. To discover a slimming mirror was like discovering a pot of gold. Places in front of this ego-massager were heavily contested.

With her ill-timed maternal advice, Madame had rapped us all over the knuckles for succumbing to the worst sin in ballet ideology—over-eating—which, after her list of prohibited foods, might have been interpreted as eating anything at all.

'Dancers must be thin', she said, scrutinizing our overexposed bodies with those X-ray eyes. I made a mental note of every food I was to avoid, and added a few more for good measure. From that moment my mind was made up. If I was required to be thin, then I would make certain I was the thinnest, and I launched into my project with my usual obstinacy. I had all the arguments mapped out. If the other girls had a weight problem, then as a Jewess I had it tenfold. I started whittling down my food intake with a vengeance, a fervent vengeance aimed as much at my forebears for bequeathing me the prospect of those fat thighs as at the calories packed into all those appetizing titbits.

I soon became acutely constipated, a malaise that I was able to explain away as being a hereditary condition, for I had heard my parents say that Dad's family had a history of this problem. As the diet grew more stringent, my constipation worsened, and my mother took me to the family doctor. He prescribed a laxative, but to no effect. My problem was taken along to 'head office', where Madame expounded her *Reader's Digest* medical theories. When I complained that the current laxatives were having no effect, she suggested a far more potent brand. 'elephant pills', which we bought the very next day. Having received the official sanction, I began to consume these magical pills in ever-increasing quantities.

Constipation, the ballet dancer's primary occupational hazard, is one of the subjects most discussed in ballet changing rooms, and the remedies exchanged would fill a book of folk medicine. But the source of the problem is diet; dancers would rather suffer any amount of discomfort than risk putting on weight. In those days to diet meant to shun all foods high in carbohydrates, all fatty food, and, for the more dedicated of us, fruits with a high sugar content. We eliminated most of the fibre from our diets by trying to survive on a lettuce leaf and that much-vaunted piece of red meat, so it was no wonder that our poor bodies tried to go on strike.

My analysis of the situation was a frightening one. If the food I was eating was not being eliminated, then it must be going elsewhere, and that could only mean one thing. Even the diminishing amount that I was now eating was being stored in my body, and being busily turned into fat. Furthermore, although I was eating less and less, my energy level appeared to remain just as high, and gradually I could see the glorious result. I was becoming pencil-thin. To hell with what it was doing to my health; I felt ecstatically happy.

I loved the new ethereal me. It was ideal for my style of dancing, for I considered myself a romantic dancer in the Taglioni, Markova genre, and now with my pallid complexion and elongated limbs I drifted around to the dreamy music with just the right lithographic look. Once again I was held up as an example to follow; Madame saw my newly acquired super-slimness as proof that she was right, and as a tribute to her ability to command total dedication. For me it had been a long time between victories, so, encouraged by this favourable response, I determined to do still better.

No longer content with just one regular bowel movement daily, I swallowed handfuls of those wonder pills, and only felt happy if the result was a diarrhoea that extended throughout most of the school hours. My path to the body beautiful was becoming a painful one, for the diarrhoea was accompanied by severe stomach cramps. But the image now reflected in the studio mirror was pleasing, and pain seemed a small price to pay.

My plan required a certain amount of deviousness, for there was no way that I could tell my parents that all my nutrients were pouring out of my body. Instead, I told them that those wretched pills were useless; I needed to increase the dosage until my bowels returned to normal. What I also failed to tell them was that sometimes I could hardly control my bowel movements at all, so severe was the effect of the purgatives I ladled into my mouth. I wonder now at the naïvety of the adults around me. Even my teachers at MacRob seemed to find nothing unusual about this girl who had to go to the toilet at ten-minute intervals. And my sickly complexion stood me in good stead, for I was invariably given permission to go home whenever I asked to, a fact that was a bone of contention with Lynne, who, with her ruddy complexion and wholesome physique, had enormous difficulties persuading the teachers that she was sick even when she was.

At first the weight loss had been gradual, but suddenly I began to look emaciated, and the weight just continued to peel off. Now that I was close to achieving my goal, I worried that I would regain the weight that I had suffered so much to lose. Better to have a few kilos to play around with than to be on the borderline. 'Too thin, too thin', became a refrain that was music to my ears. I even believed that I danced better now that I was thin, as if I had released new and as yet unfathomed skills from their glyceridic prison.

The more obsessed I became about diet, the more I thought about food. My sleepless nights were filled with magnified images of platters overflowing with food. Starved, demented and anxiety-ridden, I would lie through the long, long night, studying, mentally rehearsing a variation, and planning my meagre diet for the following day.

I had now reduced myself to a breakfast of lemon juice and yoghurt, with the cream skimmed off, and coffee with skimmed milk. For lunch the menu consisted of two wafer-thin biscuits, without butter, and some prunes to help my exhausted bowels along still further. Eventually I even rejected the piece of fruit my mother had added to my ration. At first the apple was divided in half, then quarters, and then into thin slices, from which I would perhaps eat two or three daily. For my evening meal my mother would prepare a food thermos of fat-free meat and some vegetables, which I would devour after school before I went to study in the library. Soon, however, I resolved to do without even this, for the sake of ensuring an even more concave stomach for the night class. I was fast becoming the *cause célèbre* of the Borovansky Academy, but at great cost to my relationship with my parents and friends, for I had to sink to subterfuge to go on with this reckless behaviour.

My parents had always helped me when my restrictions had been confined to cakes, sweets and rich food, but this rollercoaster course

In the throes of anorexia, 1957

of starvation was anathema to them. My weight was now hovering around seventy-four pounds (thirty-four kilos). I feigned horror when people remarked on my emaciated condition; I was innocent of any complicity in this pathetic deterioration. My social life became more and more complicated, as dinners with friends were placed on my own list of ballet 'thou-shalt-nots'. I invented elaborate excuses, and if I found myself seated at a dinner table in the company of friends, I had to explain that my loss of appetite was due to my shrunken stomach, a result of a mysterious sickness. 'I am sorry', I would explain to my hosts, 'if I eat I will be sick'.

I could never bring myself to admit that I was, in fact, dieting. That would have been tantamount to confessing my problematic racial origins. Only blue-eyed blondes could eat whatever they wished and remain excruciatingly willowy. I never doubted that, if I ate normally, I would blow up to gigantic proportions and my ballet career would be shattered. There was a girl at the Academy who was living proof of my strange theories. She was a beautiful Jewish girl with an unlimited reserve of talent, but she had heavy legs, and no matter what she did—starve, envelop her thighs in plastic—she could do nothing about it. Monsieur was cruel to her, loudly proclaiming he could never put such a physique in a tutu, and telling her that she had legs like tree trunks.

I admired her artistry; she had the most expressive Levantine face and a unique softness of body and arm movement. When she danced, the music seemed to flow through her whole body, to emanate from her fingertips and create a lasting impression of beauty and serenity. But her build would deny her a place in an art in which she was one of the most proficient beings I had seen.

This lesson hardened my resolve to obtain a slim, *Gentile* body. My fatness had become my main topic of conversation with my mother, and it was she who had to take the blame for my defectiveness. 'You don't care', I would howl. 'You just want me to be fat, like the rest of our family.' Even as I raved, I could hardly believe the intensity of my venom. I was desperately ashamed of the pain that I was inflicting upon her; but all the time I was praying that someone would stop me before it was too late.

Ironically, my malnourished state gave me enormous psychological power. The demands I was making on myself were excessive, and the demands other people were making on me were excessive; I felt that, whichever way I turned, I could no longer meet any of these expectations. There was only one area of my life over which I could exercise total control, and that was in determining the weight and shape of my body. Unlike my career, my body was my own, and by using my spectacular weight loss to hog attention, I was controlling my parents' lives as well.

Father was devastated. So far he had tolerated the demands and excesses of my life, but to see me fading away in front of his eyes, supposedly for the good of my art, was more than he could accept. To diet at all seemed punitive, but to starve until one looked like a Belsen concentration camp survivor was preposterous. Nothing could be worth such self-destruction. He blamed my ballet teachers, who he felt sure must be insane. He begged me to eat, but my mind was made up. 'Be happy, popje', my father would implore, and I knew that plea encapsulated his life's philosophy. He had made it through the war, he had provided for his family. To have love, food, shelter, freedom, was everything anyone could ask of life. And here was I destroying myself, just because I wanted to be a ballerina.

My mother was just as bewildered; she understood all too well what real hunger meant. During the war she had sold the rings off her fingers so that her children might eat. But nothing could break my resolve. I was not tempted in the slightest by cakes or sweets, and this frightened my father more than anything. In his experience there wasn't a child in the world who couldn't be won with a square of chocolate or a biscuit. This exaggerated discipline, this obsessive, fanatical streak, would be my undoing, and with all his energy he tried to induce me to see life in his own terms, as a matter of a simple choice—to be happy, or to be unhappy.

By now my parents had little influence over my life as a dancer. Indeed, they had a tough time competing with the power of my ballet masters, let alone with the tyrant within me. I had my own internal government to answer to, and believed that if I let go on the issue of weight control my whole life would be lost. If anyone asked my mother why she did not force me to eat, she looked amazed at such presumption. 'My daughter has a mind of her own, and nothing will change her mind once she has determined to do something.'

There was only one person on whom my clever stratagems had little or no effect, and that was Harry. He was horrified both at my weight loss and at what the situation was doing to our parents. My parents sought professional medical help, but anorexia nervosa was not yet a recognized disorder. My loss of appetite was put down to depression, or described as self-perpetuating: the less I ate, the more my stomach shrank. My excuse that I couldn't eat without feeling nauseated was readily accepted. One doctor suggested that it would be better to eat and vomit so that I would at least get some nourishment. Harry went along with this, and refused to listen to my arguments. 'It doesn't matter if you throw up, some food will stay inside you', he would yell. Yes, in this instance he would yell, as he had lost patience well before I reached the five-stone mark.

But it was no longer just a matter of eating more or less. The underlying problems were far more profound than that. I had a far deeper malaise, a mixture of apprehension, despondency, fear and a genuine desire to stay the 'girl-child'.

The subterfuge continued, and my health deteriorated further. The more people gaped in horror at my emaciated body, the more self-satisfied I became; after all, an improved complexion or any other outward sign of improvement could only mean one thing—that I had put on weight.

Throughout my ballet career I had believed that a report of glowing health was synonymous with being overweight. Who ever heard of a dancer being described as wholesome, robust or bursting with health? The image I wanted was that of the ethereal ballerina, and I worked hard to cultivate the strained, wan look coveted by dancers the world over. A ballerina in fine form is a fragile creature, seemingly from another world, whose pale face is out of place in the harsh glare of sunlit reality, and whose overstretched, taut limbs look awkward and out of place disguised in ordinary mortals' clothing. But there is a fine line between a streamlined body that is aesthetically appealing and the thinness of a person who is wasting away. I went far beyond the bounds of aestheticism; I appeared not only very ugly, but also extremely ill. Yet I remained ambivalent about my appearance. My vision was not so impaired that I couldn't see the deathly pale stick figure reflected in the mirror, and I was often embarrassed at my own unattractiveness. But the terror of putting on too much weight was greater than the fear of social embarrassment. I believed that for someone with my predisposition for fatness the word 'moderate' could have no meaning. I was doomed to be either too fat or too thin, and I far preferred the latter.

I think I looked better in leotards than in street clothes. Somehow the distinct muscle formation of my legs and arms and diaphragm belied my true thinness, although my eyes had now taken on the exaggerated sparkle and slight protuberance that is common in anorexics. The eyes revealed the zealotry in my soul; in spite of my sickly appearance, I found that I had more energy than ever. In spite of all the warnings that I would lose my strength for dancing, I felt exhilarated by the weightlessness of my movements.

Outside the classroom, however, I felt dreadfully lethargic. When there was no music, no snapped directive bidding me to move, I just drifted around in an increasingly unreal world. Eventually I began to feel that I had separated into two different people, one hovering and watching with great curiosity the other strange being who was wasting away. Though the former was quite aware of the effects of such foolishness, she could not resist the desire to see the adventure right through to the end.

I began to find great difficulty in doing the simplest things. Whereas at first I had forced myself to do extra exercise to reduce my weight further, now I found I could hardly walk the short distance from the tram stop to school. Although I was constantly exhausted, I could not sleep, and I began each day drained, listless and cold. Oh, that terrible cold! Even at the height of the summer heatwaves I was shivering; no amount of clothing seemed to keep me warm. What a strange figure I must have cut, this bedraggled creature with two pairs of socks showing through her grey nylon stockings, and at least three jumpers under her white cotton shirt!

As a result of my deficiencies in vitamins and nutrients my skin turned pallid, and was covered with goose-pimples. My poor blood circulation produced excruciating chilblains on my fingers and toes, and my fingernails were permanently blue, despite Lynne's efforts to warm them up under the desk by rubbing my frozen hands in her warm ones. The thinner I became, the more frenzied my pace of life became. Everything was a race against time. I began to arrive at school early to study, a lone figure seated at her desk in the middle of an empty classroom, in an empty school. After school I would race to the public library for yet more study, even though my mother would sometimes enter the hall to find me slumped over my books, almost asleep. Then I raced to ballet for three or four hours of classes, after which it was home to more study.

My body had built up a resistance to the laxatives, and now required far larger doses to react at all. I was not satisfied until I was passing liquid. I was often in agony, suffering terrible stomach cramps and shooting pains in the lower back and coccyx. I also became expert at satisfying my taste buds without eating. I would bite off a tiny piece of food and swill it around inside my mouth without swallowing it. When I was at the height of my mania, I resorted to chewing it, pressing out every bit of flavour, and then spitting it out in a tissue under the guise of having to sneeze, or to pick up a dropped fork from under the table. It cheered my parents to see the food disappear from my plate. My mother dragged me from doctor to doctor. Fascinated by this unusual case, they suggested various well-intentioned remedies, but my mother returned each time knowing that what was required to precipitate my recovery was a change of heart.

The school examinations approached. Although I must have done six times the amount of work necessary, nobody could convince me that I had done enough. I was adamant that I would flunk every subject, and nearly drove my mother mad, calling her at all hours of the night to sit by my bed and hear my work. If it had gone on much longer I am sure I would have had everyone at home flying at each other's throats. The exams themselves were an anticlimax, as I had done far more work than was expected; contrary to my fears, I came top of my year.

But I paid a heavy price for my success. By now my health was so bad that my mother wrote to ask if I could be excused for the final weeks of term. The principal agreed, but I returned to school for the speech night rehearsal. There was no way I was going to let anyone else steal my limelight, even though I was only one in a line-up of many girls. The rehearsal day was a scorcher. Some of the girls were already sporting the tans they had acquired by sunbaking against the shelter sheds with their dresses pulled up above their knees, but I was still deathly white and cold, so cold that I stood against the wall, huddled and shivering, my arms folded over my chest for extra body warmth, like a little old lady. The principal, Miss Barrett, knew of my illness, but she was a firm believer in school spirit, and my appearance seemed to annoy her on this auspicious day. She suddenly flew at me as if she was going to attack me physically. 'Straighten up, you ridiculous child', she screamed, poking me in the ribs. 'You can't be cold in this weather. For goodness' sake, pull yourself together and stop this nonsense at once.' This unprovoked outburst left me flabbergasted. I felt ashamed of my pathetic appearance, and maybe even guilty at the knowledge that my illness was self-induced. The memory of that moment has stayed with me to this day.

7

A Foreign Body

When school finished for the year, work at the Academy began to intensify in preparation for the end-of-year performance. For the first time I had to accept that I did not have a monopoly over the plum roles. I had been given one leading role, but in another ballet I had been given a secondary role, which I accepted with undisguised disdain. Madame, having started me out on this starvation campaign, was now vilifying me for being too successful in doing what she demanded. Suddenly I was ugly, an extremist, even a rebel, and Mother and I were severely reprimanded for having spoilt Madame's most prized little possession. I was devastated.

I was cast in the title role of a ballet based on the Greek myth of Persephone and the Underworld, and I set out to make this my role by studying the myth in as much depth as I could. It was December, and by this stage my energy had all but left my five-stone frame. Most of the time I just lay in my bed, unable to sleep, blissfully removed from a reality that now held little interest for me. I had become quite impervious to my parents' pleas, and their voices seemed distant and strange. I felt as though the creature lying in the bed wasn't me at all, and that the other me, the real me, hovered somewhere near the ceiling, watching. It was an effort to lift my head off the pillow to read. Yet, like a robot designed to fulfil a specific task, I dived frenetically into classes and rehearsals, only to collapse as soon as the task was done.

When I wasn't dancing I dwelt in an eerie, misty no-man's-land somewhere between life and death. Perhaps if I hadn't had those dancing commitments I might have given in entirely to the euphoria of death's calling. But the performance must go on, and I managed to push myself into top gear, determined to dance better than I had ever danced before.

And it went splendidly. My energy wasn't even called upon. It all just seemed to happen: the music and the drama carried me through in what seemed to be an effortless journey through an imaginary world. I became Persephone, and her tragic life became my own reality, a world without critics, expectations and cynical opportunists. If my adversaries had thought that this little stick figure in her blonde wig would keel over or drag through the performance on her hands and knees, they were wrong.

After the performance, surrounded by flowers, well-wishers and subdued rivals, I felt exhilarated, truly happy, totally imbued with the magical power of the world of dance. If only that was all there was to dancing! I never felt threatened while I danced. There was an honesty in true dancing that was completely absent from the manoeuvring and self-aggrandizement that went on behind the scenes. If I was complicated and difficult to handle off the stage, in performance I became complete. My inner persona was revealed, my agonies, joys, sense of humour, love for my family—all of this was the true Alida, and all of this I laid open for the world to see.

My parents hoped that during the summer vacation, with the pressure off, I might relax and find normality a little more tempting.

The 'new ethereal me': Alida in *Persephone*, 1957

They were delighted when a young couple who had seen me dance Persephone asked if they might take me for some drives to the countryside. I was too weak to benefit much from these well-intentioned trips, for I couldn't find the strength to hold my head up as I sat in the back. All I really wanted to do was lie down and drift. I accepted that I was probably dying, but I luxuriated in the peacefulness that was lapping over me.

Uncle Nico and Auntie Maria came to visit us, and they were absolutely shocked. They blamed my parents for allowing me to starve myself until I looked like a concentration-camp inmate. 'The girl is dying', they said. 'You've got to force her to eat.' They didn't understand that no disciplinary methods would bend my iron will.

In the depths of despair, my parents took me along to an eminent doctor who was supposedly an expert on diet. The doctor saw the urgency of the situation, and told my mother that if I lost any more weight I would die. I would have to be fed intravenously in hospital under constant medical supervision. This threat set off all the alarm bells in my mind. There was no way in the world that I would allow any stupid nurse to make me fat. When we had left the doctor's surgery I decided it was time for an apparent change of faith. My parents were now at their wits' end, and ready to follow the advice of others, for they could see that I could no longer be held responsible for determining whether I should live or die. But still my mother preferred to believe that I would not exploit their trust in me, and gave in. I promised her that I would try to put on weight.

I think my mother was horrified at the idea of having her daughter attached to a whole lot of tubes and bottles in a cold, impersonal clinic. Perhaps the idea that the situation had deteriorated to such a state of urgency was something she found too frightening to accept. All along, she believed that reason would prevail, that I would take the initiative and begin to help myself.

I was reprieved from this punitive health cure and packed off to stay with my friends the Mollards at their beach home in Rye—but not without taking that all-important bottle of cascara. I had already anticipated that as a guest I would not be able to dictate my daily menu. I ate a token amount to keep my genial hosts happy, but stepped up my dosage of cascara to counteract the benefits of the additional food intake. In these primitive surroundings without proper toilet facilities, it was unadulterated hell. I had to walk a considerable distance from the house to the toilet, sometimes so crippled with agony I almost didn't make it. Even when I got there, sitting on a huge bin with a wooden seat in a dirty corrugated-iron shed infested with redback spiders was an experience in itself.

Mr and Mrs Mollard could not have been kinder, and appeared to accept my silly excuse for my lack of appetite. I still refused to admit I was on a diet and kept on with my act of bravado, feigning sadness at my adversity to food. At mealtimes my plate looked like a battleground, as I dispersed my food over as large an area as possible in order to make the quantity look less. What I had to eat, I swallowed with terrible forebodings of the sacrifices I would have to make later. Whenever I had the opportunity I would spit out a mouthful of masticated food into a serviette or tissue, then duck under the table, allegedly to pick up the zillionth thing I had dropped, and carefully put the offending food into my handbag or pocket. It must have been quite disconcerting to watch me bobbing up and down, but by now I was so engrossed in my all-out war against food that it didn't occur to me that I might have been behaving extraordinarily. In spite of all my promises to try and put on weight, when I arrived home my parents were greeted by an even thinner and paler apparition than before.

What a strange specimen I was, with my bonsai body, so underdeveloped and old at the same time! Although I was now fifteen, I had not yet menstruated. My mother evidently believed the joys of womanhood were imminent, and forced me to carry a wad of sanitary pads around with me whenever I ventured away from home, just in case. But I was to carry them around for quite some time. I did not have my first period until I was seventeen, and then it was another year before my second, which came when I was in London, well away from my mother's watchful eye, and *without* those sanitary pads.

Later that summer my friend Merry, the ballet-dancing member of the Kinmont family, came down to Melbourne to spend some time with us. We were close friends in spite of a two-year age gap. Merry also claimed to be on a diet, but to me her paltry efforts at food restraint were laughable. Maybe I was possessed by some dybbuk that drove me to extremes. Though I absolutely adored Merry, the fact that she was prepared to take that middle road towards her destination suggested to me that, in this regard, we were poles apart.

Merry and I went to the beach almost daily, she attracting wolf-whistles and admiring glances wherever she went, while I received disbelieving stares. My skinniness certainly did nothing for my ego as a beach girl. Even my exaggerated balletic duck walk could not explain my atrocious appearance. I wished I could carry a billboard announcing to the world that I was an extremely talented ballerina, and didn't they know ballerinas had to be thin? I accepted *their* bulges and cellulite with a degree of compassion, but the first thing I noticed about people was their bodies. When I was doing normal things in everyday circumstances I really felt my ugliness. It was then that I wished I could be just slim—in the way some people can be slim and look as if they haven't even been trying. But as much as I wanted to look a little more healthy, I knew that I couldn't allow myself to start out on that road. Once I began to eat normally, I would surely grow as fat as a house, and it would be better to die than to accept such a fate.

I tried to enhance my appearance by stuffing little balls of cotton wool down the front of my bathing suit to fluff out those miserably empty brassières. Unfortunately when I emerged from the sea those water-saturated cotton balls had slipped down to my navel, and they stayed there unnoticed until Merry asked me what those strange lumps were around my stomach.

Merry couldn't survive a day at the beach without some lunch, and as she was on a diet, she asked my mother to pack her a special slimming lunch consisting of Ryvitas and fruit. What a laugh—a slimming lunch! To me it seemed like a banquet. I had not touched a piece of bread or even a dry biscuit for months, but Merry even had butter, a thick layer of butter, animal fat, spread on the top of those biscuits. I knew that there was only one sure way to lose weight, and that was to stop eating altogether.

Around this time I began to take an interest in cooking. It was one way to enjoy food vicariously. I would spend hours in the kitchen preparing the most fattening, stodgy dishes I could invent, which I would then take immense pleasure in serving to my friends and family. Either they were trying to please me or they had undiscerning palates, but they seemed to eat everything I cooked, with considerable relish. I now had yet another talent.

I can't remember exactly when I decided to rejoin the human race. There was no sudden moment of revelation. Perhaps it was simply that I wanted an opportunity to remain in the game, and sensed that there might not be an audience waiting for me on the other side of the curtain. Maybe my love of my family outweighed the soporific allure of death. But somehow, ever so cautiously, I drifted back into conscious existence. Without going overboard, I fed my body just enough to remain on this earth. Even so, I could not bring myself to trust my tardy bowels, and I still swallowed handfuls of purgatives nightly.

At first all that seemed to happen was that my stomach distended so that I felt uncomfortably bloated, but little by little the rest of my body filled out, approaching closer to normality. Having worked so hard to reduce my body to skin and bones in the first place, I felt guilty at what I was now doing. I had felt secure feeling my bones; running my hands over my sharply defined frame, I had felt I was in contact with my inner persona. Now, disguised by a thin layer of fat, my body felt foreign. The little detached person who had hovered over me before returned, daring me to see how far I could go before my body blew up to gigantic proportions. Yet some inner control always stopped me from going too far. Any softening contours would have to be eradicated with a disciplinary regimen of purgatives and a bout of food deprivation. I was still in total control of my body. My life was still far too disciplined to succumb to the temptation of the illicit cream puff. And to me it was, and still is, the epitome of aestheticism to see a finely tuned dancer working the streamlined machinery of the human body with beautiful precision.

I took little joy in my thickening body, and with each mouthful of food I forced down my throat I felt guiltier. My change of attitude clearly delighted my parents, however, and their pleasure was some compensation for the risk I believed I was taking.

My life at the Academy was also far from satisfying. I was frustrated with the lack of training in technique, and bored to tears with having to concern myself with my fluctuating status *vis-à-vis* Madame. I continued to play my deceptive game in the classroom, skilfully diverting my audience's attention away from the limitations of my legs and feet by highlighting my facial expressions, musicality and *épaulements*. When it came to the lyrical, heart-rending schmaltz I excelled in I was right up in front, performing like crazy, indulging the music to the hilt and revelling in the sensuality of it all. But when we were given a dry, no-frills technical exercise I did my very best to become as invisible as possible, so mortified was I by my shortcomings.

Even as I kept to my rigorous schedule of ballet and academic studies, I began to have serious doubts. Was it worth crushing my youthful passions just for the thought of achieving something in the remote future? Harry's world of fun, ideas and talk began to tempt me more and more. When I wasn't dancing or studying, I was devouring books that I believed would be intellectually stimulating.

I felt disillusioned, frustrated, but still I clung to routine and habit. Gradually I realized that I no longer had a straight vision like my heroines of the dance. There was more to life than *pliés* and wintergreen ointment. It had all been so easy when I had regarded Madame as an infallible Mother Superior, but once I began to doubt her my universe started to crumble around me. Still I did not have the courage to make a clean break. Emotionally I felt beholden to Madame and her school. I knew the suggestion that I move on would not get a sympathetic hearing from Madame herself, and so I felt compelled to remain where I was, even though my commitment was less than sincere, and there was little satisfaction in living a lie. I was also beginning to learn that I could no longer depend on others to take me by the hand and direct me on to the end of the rainbow. In many ways I had resisted facing up to the fact that the people I had idolized were no longer living up to my expectations.

Around this time I became bedridden, having contracted glandular fever. In some ways it was lovely to have a legitimate excuse to be away from all the competitive tension, but I dreaded what would happen when I went back. My mother insisted that I stay home until I had completely recovered. But then we were honoured by a phone call from Monsieur Borovansky, a very rare privilege indeed. Monsieur told my mother that he was going to create a ballet for our end-of-year performance, and that he particularly wanted me to dance the main role. It was going to be a romantic ballet to Chopin music, and he believed that I was the obvious choice to interpret the ethereal Chopiniana style he envisaged. 'But', he hastened to add, 'if Alida is not well enough, I shall have to use someone else'.

His loud voice was audible from where I stood, so close that I had almost edged my mother's ear off the receiver, and when I heard those words I was simply horrified. I gesticulated madly and hissed urgent messages to the effect that I had just made a miraculous recovery. My mother dutifully conveyed my wishes, and the following Monday, pale as a sheet and wobbly on deliciously thin legs, I arrived promptly at 4 p.m. for my first rehearsal. Though my body may have been less than willing, the spirit of Chopin and Monsieur's beautiful choreography simply enveloped me and carried me off effortlessly. It was a *pas de deux*, evocative and pure, simple yet profound, and in performing this piece, choreographed specifically for my dance qualities, I danced not only because it would have been impossible not to, but also in tribute to Monsieur, who had restored my faith in dance.

After my performance Monsieur kissed me and reminded me that my graduation was now not far off. He said that he was greatly looking forward to working with me in his company. He would have accepted me in the company there and then, but he respected my desire to finish my secondary education.

Shortly afterwards, just as I was about to leave for Sydney to spend the Christmas holidays with the Kinmonts, I learned that Monsieur had died suddenly. I was grief-stricken, for we had lost the most exciting driving force in the early years of Australian dance. No one knew if another permanent company would be formed. The most frightening prospect was the feeling that the line of continuation had been broken. Monsieur's death was also a terrible blow to my prospects for the future. While he had been alive, my position as a prospective star of his company was secure. I could not be sure that Monsieur's heir would be equally captivated by my talent. I was well and truly on my own.

8

Russian Style

My holiday was a lovely respite from the uncertainty that now clouded my future. For two weeks I tried not to think of ballet at all, and simply revelled in the pleasures Sydney had to offer. In any case, it would have been stupid to think of hard work while I was living such a cosseted, luxurious life, in my own personal suite in the Kinmonts' rambling harbour-front mansion. I pirouetted and leapt about exultantly on the lawns, trying to look unaware of the movie camera that Jenny Kinmont was focusing on my 'spontaneous' dance. It was comforting to know that the Kinmonts at least believed that I still had a great future ahead of me.

There wasn't much to look forward to in 1960. I anticipated that I would have a heavy year at school, where I was entering my fifth year, and as far as I could tell there would be little cheer at the Academy. When I returned, Madame Borovansky seemed dejected and uncharacteristically subdued. Suddenly her Academy was no longer the centre of the ballet universe. Students were leaving in droves to try other teachers and more commercial styles of dancing, endeavouring no doubt to try to get work in the rising TV industry. There were rumours that a new company was to be formed around a nucleus of the remaining Borovansky dancers, and that it would be headed by Peggy van Praagh, a ballet mistress from the second Royal Ballet Company. But if this was true I didn't much like my chances. I was trained in the Russian style, and believed myself to be the antithesis of an English dancer. Holding little hope of working in another Australian company, I set my sights on Moscow.

Christmas with the Kinmonts: Felicity Kinmont and Alida with Clever the spaniel, Sydney, 1959

In the late 1950s and early 1960s an interest in anything Russian was regarded as most unpatriotic. The Cold War had gripped Australia, and the very word 'Russian' inspired terror. It was certainly not the time to publicize even mildly left-wing sympathies. My aspirations were therefore considered a little odd, even at home, where Uncle Maurice was surprisingly vehement in his anti-Communism, considering he had been a card-carrying member of the party in his youth. I was too politically naïve to care one way or the other. To my mind any nation that could produce artists of the calibre of Oistrakh, Ulanova and Vishnevskaya couldn't be all bad. Besides, I argued, my temperament required the expansive approach of the Bolshoi Ballet.

Although a change of teaching style was long overdue, I didn't want to desert the Academy; all I wanted was permission to attend a few outside classes, as many other Borovansky pupils were already doing. I had every right to go wherever I wished. I was sixteen and no longer a full scholarship student; Madame had to revoke the scholarships after Monsieur's death, as she could no longer afford non-paying students. But mustering up the courage to discuss this with her was a different matter. I suspected that she would be reluctant to let me go, not because she had my interests at heart, but because she wished to possess me.

I started to sneak along to the occasional outside class with some of the other leading teachers in Melbourne. But the classes were not the exhilarating experience I had hoped for. My disappointment lay not with the teaching but with myself, for the glaring ineptitude of my technique. These classes concentrated on pure, technical exercises, backed by dum-de-dah piano chords. If I had been given a true sequence of dance steps, choreographed to fit a tuneful melody, I could have convinced the whole class that I was indeed the superior little ballerina they had heard so much about. But give me a simple *plié* without a barre in the centre of the room, and I wobbled all over the place, angry, frustrated and humiliated that someone who could do the most advanced steps in the ballet vocabulary should find this fundamental step so torturous to execute.

I wanted to run for cover. After all, I had been fooling even the most trained onlookers up till now. What was to stop me from continuing on in this vein? But I did my best to swallow my pride, consoling myself with the thought that I would have the last laugh when, having ironed out the technical snags, I would be able to dance hell for leather.

Madame had been right when she said that no one teacher could be expected to be all things to dance. She and her teachers at the Academy had imparted a sense of artistry and a feeling for dance that I soon discovered was lacking in most other studios. Other cautious pedagogues could instruct me in the cold, hard facts of technique, but Madame Borovansky, Martin Rubinstein and Leon Kelloway had allowed me to experience dance. Perhaps, on reflection, it might have been better if I had acquired a technique elsewhere, then gone to the Borovansky Academy as a finishing school, to gain finesse and refinement and to explore the mysteries beyond technique.

It was a trying time, and more often than not I was so depressed that I felt like throwing in the towel. The more I learned, the more I realized I still had to learn, and the more inadequate I felt. In a sense, I lost the ability to dance for pure joy the moment I discovered technique. There would be many times when I longed to recapture some of the originality and natural dynamism that had been thwarted by discipline and mechanical toil.

Since the Borovansky Ballet disbanded, ballet in Australia had been at a low ebb. In order to keep a core group of dancers going, leading teachers had been rostered to take open professional-standard classes. In the past Monsieur had always picked his company members from Madame's academy or other approved schools interstate, but now dancers flocked to attend these classes in the hope that they might be chosen to form the nucleus of a company.

Peggy van Praagh, who had been invited to assist Monsieur in the running of his company before he died, was now given the go-ahead to form a new company. From the moment we came face to face, I realized I was not going to be her idea of the quintessential ballerina. She soon set about eradicating any hint of Borovanskyism from her new company. She clearly disapproved of the lack of discipline in the *corps de ballet*, and of the emphasis on character dancers with strong personalities. Though there was no doubt that the company needed to be whipped into a more cohesive shape and the standards of technique could do with some improvement, I think she rather missed the point. Though Monsieur's company did not have the uniformity nor the clean-cut qualities of the Royal Ballet, it did have a unique quality of its own. Some of the older members had direct experience with the Ballet Russe and the Pavlova companies, and Monsieur had wisely allowed their style and artistry to permeate the company. Individuality was a prized commodity, and with such a wonderful mix of mature dancers and young hopefuls, the character portrayals in all the dramatic ballets could be assured of having real human depth.

Peggy van Praagh aimed for a predominantly youthful company, with the emphasis on athleticism. Maturity was rooted out as a sign of decay, and now the audiences could expect to feast their eyes on symmetrical rows of neat little buns and neat little oval faces, long slim legs capable of slotting into hermetically sealed fifth positions, indicative of the hermetically sealed minds she deemed perfect for little ballet dancers. 'Lovely dancer, darling, but your neck's too short' was a typical comment when the young dancers paraded their wares for her critical appraisal. Instead of the bellowing European voice thundering abuse across the studio floor, we had the clipped English tones of the perfect English lady, far too polite to say what she really meant, but all the more cutting for her circumspection.

And so yet another branch of Australian theatre was brought back into the colonial fold. Though there was talk of finding a distinctive Australian style, for a long time the burgeoning company seemed to be just a rather poor copy of the Royal Ballet in the mother country, or at best a colonial branch of the London headquarters. Many Australian dancers left the country, and burst upon the European scene with an energy and vitality that was welcomed by company directors all over England and Europe.

Peggy van Praagh reluctantly included a number of Monsieur's principal dancers in her new company, as over the years people like

Kathleen Gorham had become household names, and were important for box office. I don't think Peggy van Praagh approved of Borovansky's star system, preferring to attract audiences on the company's merits as a whole. Monsieur had encouraged people to come and see their favourite dancers, and understood the public desire for an aura of glamour in the theatre. Now the helm of the company had been taken over by a member of the opposition, for in those days the Russian and English schools of dance were poles apart. Those of us devoted to the Russian style were horrified to see Peggy van Praagh hoe in to purify the ranks of any remaining elements of the old order. A company requiring nothing more than pretty legs and feet and Margot Fonteyn look-alike oval heads, smiling vacuously because they had been *told* to smile, was definitely not going to accommodate someone like me.

On the whole the people I admired tended to be condescending about classical ballet. They thought it pretty enough, but lacking in depth, and I had to admit that they had a point. If Harry and his friends were condescending about ballet as they had seen it at Her Majesty's Theatre, I sometimes also winced with embarrassment when I saw male dancers camp it up on stage, often making a travesty of the roles they were supposed to portray. All too often the ballerina would find herself emoting to a prince who had forgotten she even existed and was already flapping his eyelids at some other male on stage, or at the double-bass player in the orchestra pit. Or the prince would mince coquettishly around the stage, using his skilful body language to dare all those in the audience with similar inclinations and adventurous intentions to come back after the show.

In Australia ballet was considered a profoundly unmasculine pastime. Ockerism still ruled the roost, and any overt display of masculine aesthetic sensibility was ridiculed. In the early 1960s, however, change was in the air. This was largely due to the Bolshoi Ballet's Australian tour, and later to the exciting new wave of American modern dance, particularly the black Alvin Ailey dancers, who graced the Melbourne stage with spectacular displays of strength and beauty.

The Bolshoi dancers who visited Australia in 1959 were a revelation. Never before had I seen such excellent dancers. They were the embodiment of everything I could hope for in dance. Russian films had given Australians a preview of Russian dance; I had sat spellbound through the Bolshoi's *Romeo and Juliet*, danced by the great Ulanova, and her exquisite rendering of *Giselle*. But nothing could beat the experience of seeing these amazing dancers live on the Melbourne stage. The ballet world was agog with excitement. It seemed every balletomane, dance student, professional and director was waiting to worship these living legends.

I was invited to go backstage and meet the dancers at a reception after the first performance. When I was pushed gently forward for a special introduction, I was speechless. But there were to be many more opportunities to get to know the dancers, as I was allowed to watch rehearsals and classes, and then later to participate in some of the classes myself. Inevitably, I fell in love with the leading man, Gennady Lediakh. Whenever we passed in the draughty theatre corridors I was quite sure he could see the chills running up and down my spine, and sense the innocent sexuality I was fighting to contain. It was both magical and disturbing. I hadn't expected love to bring about strange, queasy feelings in the pit of my stomach. I even began to suspect that I was suffering from some new malaise, a sort of sinfulness.

Lediakh was a spectacular dancer, a charmer offstage, and had the physical countenance of Adonis. Nothing that I saw later would ever match his brilliance in *Ocean and Pearls*. The Russian dancers performed technical feats that we never believed possible. They gave our Australian male dancers new goals to work towards. The women were like celestial spirits; their feet seemed to skim the stage surface as they breezed through their dances, afloat on the swirls of their chiffon tunics. We didn't see the mechanics of the dance; their movements flowed into one another as if these dragonfly-like creatures had been born to live out their lives in this nocturnal, floodlit sanctuary. But for all that they could also exude earthly emotions when the role required. The sylphs could become passionate, tempestuous Spaniards on the roll of a castanet, or fiery, sensual gypsies, baring their anguished souls to the plaintive tone of the violin.

Much to my delight, offstage the dancers were very real people. The men looked like men, and the women looked like women. By Western standards, the female dancers were quite fleshy. I found their femininity aesthetically pleasing; the dancers' movements were soft, curvilinear, and their pleasantly rounded physical contours did not detract from that proverbial 'good line' most Western dancers strive for.

For the first time too I saw people who exemplified their art and yet appeared to live normal lives. The majority of the company members were married, many with children. Their humanness was quite apparent in their performances. Like Monsieur's company, the Bolshoi consisted of different shapes and sizes; we were spared the sight of row upon row of doe-eyed, oval-faced china dolls.

The Bolshoi's visit was just the impetus I needed, a shot in the arm. With new determination I was ready to work myself into the ground if I could become even a quarter as good as Bogomolova, Struchkova and Karelskaya. By hook or by crook, I was going to get behind that Iron Curtain to study with these masters of dance. I was certain that if I could have the opportunity to study in one of their magnificent institutions I would do more than justice to the privilege. At the Bolshoi or Kirov I would have a balance of academic studies and the arts; if all else failed, at least I would have a comprehensive knowledge of the theatre and associated arts, and would be equipped to do something other than dance. My mind was made up—only Russia would do.

Big Brother Harry was somewhat sceptical about my ambitious plans. Though a committed socialist, he did not hold any brief for the Russian Communist regime. I urged him to go and see the Bolshoi miracle for himself. To my immense satisfaction, he came home almost as much of a fan as I was.

On the second-last day of the Melbourne season, weighed down with self-pity, I was moping around at the back of the Bolshoi class when Mr Gusev, the famous ballet master, called me to the front of the class and told me that he was very impressed with my dancing, and believed that I should have the opportunity to study in Russia.

Alida (centre) with Rimma Karelskaya and Gennady Lediakh outside Melbourne's Palais Theatre during the Bolshoi Ballet Company's tour of Australia, 1959

From there on in, the complications of obtaining a visa to enter a Communist country at the height of the Cold War seemed quite irrelevant. My determination would overcome such paltry obstacles. As Australia and Russia had no formal cultural exchange, an official scholarship was an impossibility. But Mr Gusev suggested that if I managed to get to Moscow, I would be offered a two-year scholarship at the Bolshoi school. I could not believe my ears, but this vote of confidence in my abilities was the catalyst I required to fight the odds and get to Russia.

After the Bolshoi departed, I became an avowed Russophile. With all the intolerance of the converted, I dismissed all criticisms of anything Russian. Meanwhile there were other more pragmatic matters to attend to, such as passing my school exams here in Melbourne.

The pressures at MacRob were mounting. As 1960 went on the teachers seemed to be close to panic, and the lessons began to take on an almost feverish urgency. I took all their warnings quite literally, and worked as if my life depended on those final results. Whenever I had a spare moment, my head was buried in a school book. No moment could be wasted. My school books were my constant companions in trams, trains, in the dressing room, on the loo, and right through most of the night. I crammed my head full of facts and figures, only to have them vaporize as soon as I completed the examination.

I was also finding it difficult to live with the guilt of betraying Madame, and hated the furtiveness of attending outside ballet classes without her approval. I had no wish to hurt her. I would have been delighted if she had given me her blessing to further my dancing education, but she had not, and her selfishness greatly distressed me. I knew that my actions would inevitably destroy our relationship. There never could have been a gentle moving away from that kind of despotic attitude. It was a case of total affiliation or nothing.

About a week before the examinations Uncle Nico died of leukaemia. I was sitting by the phone when it rang, and it was I who took the message from a sobbing Auntie Maria to pass on to the rest of the family at Grant Street. Until then such dreadful illnesses were things that happened to other people in other families. As we had no old people in the family, this was my first direct experience of loss. My mother flew to Sydney immediately, to be with my Auntie Maria and attend the funeral, while I tried as best I could to get my act together for that all-important examination.

On the eve of the examination I received a phone call from Madame, summoning me to her residence. Her voice seemed warm and friendly enough, although the timing of the impromptu meeting, at 7 p.m. on the eve of my exams, implied that I was not going for a friendly chit-chat over tea and cakes. There had to be a more urgent purpose. Madame still had great power over me. My skin tingled with anticipation as I tried to imagine what surprise lay in store for me, and the anticipation allayed my anxiety over the following morning. I threw down my school books and asked Dad to take me to Madame Borovansky's house by cab. As Madame had assured me that the meeting would not take long, I asked my father to wait in the cab outside her house. I am ashamed to admit that it never even occurred to me to ask my father to accompany me inside the royal residence.

My father settled into the cab for an indefinite wait. Madame greeted me cordially and ushered me into the living room, where I discovered to my horror that I was not the only guest. There, seated in a semicircle, were members of the Borovansky Academy teaching staff. Madame's friendly telephone composure had belied her intentions. She had intended to lure me into this den, the stage of a B-grade movie set, where I was about to be subjected to a kind of people's court, a mock tribunal, before a jury who had no doubt already condemned me.

'You have just lost your Uncle Nico', Madame began, striding up and down like a Hollywood public prosecutor.

> I know how much you loved him. Now maybe you will begin to understand what it feels like to lose someone dear to you. I have also been hurt by the loss of Monsieur, and now I am especially saddened by the lack of loyalty from those very people for whom he had such grand dreams. Monsieur and I worked hard to make you who you are today, and now you have abandoned us by attending outside classes.

On and on she went, berating me for my disloyalty and selfish disregard, while everyone else in the room listened in respectful silence. Fifteen minutes or so of this soon had its desired effect. I was reduced to tears, and Madame was truly the mistress of the situation.

Scores of Borovansky students had been attending outside classes for years, and I knew that all the teachers present were aware of this. Presumably I had been made the scapegoat because Madame believed others would follow my lead. As if this wasn't enough, Madame could not resist having a go at my mother in her absence. 'Of course we don't blame you, darling', she said.

We blame your mother. She is the one who has put all these ideas into your head. She has been a troublemaker for years. We know that in families with your kind of background, mothers tend to be very ambitious for their children. But, darling, remember: I am the professional, not your mother. You should listen to me.

She levelled her Svengali eyes on me. I knew I should be protesting at this attack on my mother, but I gratefully accepted the tissues that Madame offered me, and mopped my eyes without managing a word in mother's defence. My throat felt constricted. Madame's performance was so manipulative and her timing so superb that I ended up feeling positively guilty and remorseful, believing that I had committed some heinous sin against her.

My audience was being drawn to a close. The other teachers rallied round to offer me best wishes for my exams in the morning, and to place insincere kisses on my wet cheeks.

'Mustn't keep you, darling', Madame finished. 'I am so pleased we've cleared everything up.' And with that, I was dismissed out into the darkness, where my father was still patiently waiting.

When he saw how agitated I was he became quite furious, and I literally had to wrestle with him to restrain him from bursting into Madame's house. By the time I reached home I had little heart for study. I felt utterly depleted, and hated Madame for what I now believed to be an inevitable failure in the exams. I cried and cried until I could cry no more. But then I calmed down enough to recapitulate. Removed from the aura of Madame's orchestrated coup, I slowly regained my composure, and then a cold anger began to rise in me until every last vestige of guilt had been extinguished.

I recognized the charade for what it was, a carefully planned manoeuvre to deny me my independence. From that moment on, Madame Borovansky lost her hold over me. I lost all affection for Madame and her henchmen. The way was now open for me to make my own decisions. The umbilical cord had been cut.

9

Ballerina in the Bush

I approached my exams in much the same way as I approached performing. I had walked the length of the diving board, and it was a matter of 'Oh well, it's now or never'. Having prepared for so long, I anticipated the trial ahead with a mixture of excitement, nausea, challenge and fear. And the joy of success had no equal. That wonderful feeling of knowing I had brought everything together—in the examination room or on the stage—was an exhilarating experience that made me lust for more.

In spite of my reservations, once again I found myself among the prizewinners, and once again on speech night I waited my turn in that line of young girls in pristine white to receive the inscribed book that would tell my children of my scholastic achievements. I felt proud to be up there among the achievers. Miss Barrett was quite horrified to find out that I was leaving school in order to pursue ballet training. I imagine that she found that excuse particularly hard to take, as she regarded a life in the theatre as frivolous, a waste of academic talents, and maybe even a little vulgar. 'Oh dear, I had expected you to go on to university', she moaned. 'We expect most of our girls to go through university, especially girls of your calibre.'

As she lectured me, I realized I had managed to shatter the illusions of two *grandes dames* in the space of a matter of weeks. I was becoming an expert at showing people I was someone other than they expected. I felt not the slightest sadness at leaving MacRob.

My friends and I promised to maintain our friendships, and for me that was all that mattered. I knew I would feel no nostalgia for my school days. As far as I was concerned I was now unshackled, free to pursue my own life in an adult world.

I had not, however, abandoned my studies entirely. After many heated arguments with Harry, more to please him than out of any real conviction that additional academic study was necessary, I enrolled in a matriculation course by correspondence at Taylor's College. Lynne promised to help me whenever she could, by lending me her notes and discussing the areas of emphasis in each subject, but I felt relaxed about the whole project. I had made up my mind that I would do it if I could, but I was certainly not going to get hot under the collar about it.

My new-found confidence made my life easier at the studio. I waltzed into classes with too much bounce to please my adversaries, and continued to do classes outside with Paul Hammond, Rex Reid and Margaret Scott, despite Madame's ban.

Madame had at least tried to provide me with some incentive and challenge. Despite all the news that Peggy van Praagh was forming a new company, Madame still hoped that a company bearing Monsieur's name might be formed in the future. Failing that, she hoped there would at least be a vehicle for some of the superb artists Peggy van Praagh seemed so eager to discard, and that the memory of Monsieur might live on through these talented Borovansky devotees.

In the summer Madame told me that the Belgian dancer Paul Grinwis wished to see me, and that he might be able to offer me a big chance to dance main roles. Paul, the former fiancé of my idol, Kathleen Gorham, was himself a brilliant character dancer and a fine choreographer. His cultured, aloof, sometimes unapproachable manner tended to set him apart from the more down-to-earth Aussie company members. Though I didn't know it in my *Nutcracker* days, when he was Prince to my Clara, Paul exemplified the intellectual approach to ballet so sadly lacking in many of the dancers I knew then.

Paul was planning to take a small group of former Borovansky dancers on an Arts Council tour of New South Wales and Queensland, and asked me to be his partner. I was delighted; it seemed incredible that an artist of his experience should ask a mere student to share a leading role with him. And I was pleased that I would not have to face another year of endless classes, despite my resolution to spend that year concentrating on my technique. I knew that I would learn more by performing with the professional dancers who would make up the rest of the company. Predictably, Madame tried to claim all credit for my good fortune, and made another attempt at emotional blackmail, trying to make me feel guilty that I had ever doubted her. This time she did no more than embarrass me and make me wonder at her insecurity.

The Arts Council tour involved two companies, the one led by Paul Grinwis, consisting of Estella Nova, Jeffrey Kovel, Jan Topham and me, and the other a Queensland company of five directed by Charles Lisner. We were billed as two distinct companies, which was just as well, as it became painfully obvious from the start that Lisner's company was quite inexperienced. There was no lack of effort and enthusiasm, but next to people like Grinwis, Nova and Kovel the discrepancies in standards were obvious.

On tour Paul used every means possible to distance himself from the Lisner company, and this led to a great deal of friction. At that time the gap between professional and amateur ballet was gigantic. Outside the main companies there was little that anyone with a modicum of talent could find tempting. But the established companies did not tour small country towns, so the task of pioneering fell to a hotchpotch of

Rehearsing in the heat: Alida and Paul Grinwis during the Arts Council tour, 1961

smaller groups thrown together specifically for that purpose. It was only now, with the demise of the Borovansky company, that there were a few professionals to whom the idea of travelling over the Australian countryside was appealing.

A tour of this nature demanded far more than mere talent of its artists. The dancers would be expected to learn to be Jacks of all trades, tolerate appalling living and performing conditions, and above all to have a well-developed sense of humour. The five-month tour covered huge distances north to Cairns and inland as far as Mount Isa, and it was not designed for ethereal, temperamental dancers.

My colleagues were a mixed lot. Estella Nova was a beautiful Spanish dancer who with her husband, Jeffrey Kovel, had danced with Borovansky for the short season before his death. Both had chosen to stay in Australia, and would join Peggy van Praagh in her new company at the end of our tour. Jan Topham, the fifth member of our small group, was also a beauty, tall and lithesome with a passable technique. There were some fiery exchanges between Jan and Paul, and some very strained periods, but the dramas that resulted from Paul's ardent pursuit of this recalcitrant damsel were often a welcome relief.

We all gathered at the Elizabethan Trust head office in Crown Street, Sydney, where we first encountered the forty-foot monster that was to be our travelling home. It was long and blue, and looked more like a furniture removal truck than a vehicle designed to carry human beings. We were all thrown in together—costumes, sets, lighting and our baggage. No concession was made to comfort. Eventually Paul Grinwis and Estella and Jeff used their own Volkswagens, as much to avoid the constant company of all the others, I suspect, as to have the freedom and comfort of a vehicle designed to carry people. Jan and I vied with each other to beg a lift with Paul as often as possible; Paul's Volkswagen felt like sheer luxury.

I greatly looked forward to being alone with Paul on these journeys, for I thought him fascinating. He was obviously having a wonderful time traipsing around Australia, and indeed he proved hardier than the rest of us. He seemed to thrive in those primitive conditions, and I got the impression that as long as Paul had a good book to read, his Volkswagen and his own company, he would have been quite content, even in the remotest spot of outback Australia. Although I was still inclined to look up to him with some awe, we soon established a close friendship.

Before very long the strain of coping with such erratic performing and living conditions had people jumping at each other's throats for the pettiest reasons. Yet we all took our task seriously; we were true theatrical pioneers, taking ballet to remote places that had never before seen live theatre, let alone ballet. No one ever performed in a condescending, half-hearted manner, even when the makeshift performing conditions were absurd. Each performance was a brand-new challenge.

Touring under such difficult conditions makes it difficult to maintain one's technique. If that eternal dancer's guilt had not played such a large part in all our lives, we might well have succumbed to flabbiness and apathy. The first obstacle was the tiredness; even the simplest movement seemed to require a Herculean effort. The tour consisted mainly of one-night stands, sometimes more than 350 miles apart. It is impossible to describe the strain of straightening out one's cramped body to climb out of 'the monster' for yet another set-up, performance and pack-up. Often it seemed that only a miracle could psych my body up to performance level, and make the spirit willing to receive the music, to paint on yet another smile and appear fresh and full of joyous enthusiasm. It was hard not to feel shirty about having to unload the truck and set up stage, when in just a couple of hours' time, having worked the grit and dust off your body but not out of your system, you would be required to look radiant and flit around the stage like an elusive nymph.

The roles I had been given to perform were challenging, the more so when the venues were less than adequate. Ironically, all those years after I had danced the role of Clara to Paul's Prince, I was dancing the role of the Sugar Plum Fairy with the prince of my childhood. The other role I performed on the tour was that of the Beloved in Lichine's ballet *Corrida.* This was a superbly dramatic ballet set to a haunting Scarlatti score for harpsichord. I thoroughly enjoyed every soul-searching moment.

But there were times when we had to admit defeat. Some of the country towns had never had visiting ballet companies before, and their expectations of our performing requirements were comically pathetic. Faced with a splintery, postage-stamp-sized stage, or a floor with a slope like Everest, we were reduced to having to mark out all our movements; for fear of injury and for the sake of some much-needed dramatic content, we sometimes exaggerated our mime to such an extent that our performance looked more like a mummery than a ballet.

In one town we arrived to find a spectacular new civic hall, which was obviously the municipality's pride and joy. The feeling of relief was unanimous. At last we would have a proper stage to dance on, and clean, airy dressing rooms backstage. Our relief was short-lived. The Lord Mayor, who was proudly conducting us on a tour of the theatre, stopped short of the huge expanse of stage, and, with a conspiratorial grin, threw open his arms and announced that he had asked his staff to polish the floor to the highest possible gloss in honour of our visit. The stage shone like a mirror. To our horror, we realized that we wouldn't even be able to walk across it, let alone dance.

Though we attempted to perform, our efforts were farcical. We removed our shoes and then our tights, but we still slid and tumbled round the stage like demented ice-skaters. The tension gave way to hysterics as the company members went down one by one. The rest of us rocked with laughter to see so many tangled, splayed legs and arms waving around in mid-air, and the surprised expressions of the arse-over-head dancers as they tried to give their antics a semblance of balletic grace. Eventually we gave up. There was no way we could pass off this circus as a ballet performance.

In one town I feared for body and limb as I hopped around on a temporary stage constructed out of a table-top-like sheet of hardboard balanced precariously on trestles. I suppose the country folk were testing the myth that we dancers were lighter than thistledown. Perhaps the fact that our stage tipped and wobbled as we tried to keep our balance increased their enjoyment of our performance. We were, after all, just ordinary mortals like them, mortals who had done a fine job, fully deserving of the hot tea and asparagus sandwiches that awaited us after we had finished.

A couple of stages looked like ski slopes, with grades so steep that you had to go with the impetus and run downstage. I was constantly terrified that I would fall over the edge, which sometimes had a sheer drop of eight feet with no footlights. Paul would hiss at me to lean back to counteract the gradient, but I couldn't see that looking as if I had been caught in a howling gale would be much better than lurching forward. I loathed presenting less than my best for people who had, after all, paid to see a professional company.

No doubt the conditions in which we were required to perform would seem unbelievable to dancers today. Certainly the theatrical unions would not permit their members to hazard their lives under such primitive conditions, and justifiably so. Even leaving aside the element of danger, it is impossible to look professional balancing *sur les pointes* on a stage that seems about to collapse, or to appear serenely sylphlike when the burrs in your costume are sticking into your skin.

On the positive side, such experiences did inure me to all sorts of conditions. We had to use our ingenuity to adapt to all kinds of stages. Humping the heavy lights and weights and backdrops in and out of the monster each night certainly made me appreciate the work of the stage hands in later years (though I did not volunteer to help them).

One performance stands out in my mind quite vividly. The barn that was to be our theatre was in the middle of an overgrown paddock. Its rusty, sagging corrugated-iron roof looked as if it had been flung carelessly over the timber frame, which had clearly not seen a coat of paint since the 1860s. The building had been derelict for years. Several sheep grazed blissfully in the paddock, and there were mouse droppings on the stage and in the dressing room. The dressing room, in fact, was a nightmare. The roughly hewn beams were full of cobwebs and speckled with pigeon droppings. As I cleared a small space to lay out my make-up, I prayed to God that there weren't any snakes in the corners.

It was clear that we were intruders, cultural do-gooders who were upsetting a balance of nature far more creative and theatrical than any of our own making. Who the hell were we setting up the stage for—the sheep? We had driven for hundreds of miles without seeing any sign of humanity before coming across the town, which consisted of a small post office-cum-general store and the proverbial pub. We dragged the lights, props and sets through the long grass to create a surreal theatre extraordinaire in the middle of nowhere, then wandered across to the pub. To our amazement it was abuzz, jam-packed with men. Where they had all materialized from was a mystery, but they didn't appear to be in a hurry to return to anything in particular. The bar remained packed all afternoon.

We set up kitchen in the field behind the theatre. As we sat in the sun, munching our steaks and sipping our Beaujolais, I couldn't help pondering on the incongruity of it all. It was definitely not the stuff of Covent Garden, but there couldn't be too many artists in the world who could eat their meal sunning themselves in the open air, throw the paper plates in the fire, and step into the theatre to prepare for the evening performance.

About thirty minutes before the performance, our paddock was suddenly transformed. Scores of people arrived in jeeps, in sleek up-to-date limousines, by horse and buggy, and even by helicopter. It was a full-dress occasion. Women strode across the paddock in long dresses and high heels, and the men in patent leather shoes and tuxedos, all of them looking as if they did this sort of thing every evening.

Though the stage was rough, the first scene went well enough, but I was jolted back to reality abruptly when I realized that there was no passage backstage. To get from one corner to another, I had to go out through the girls' dressing room, down some rickety wooden steps, wade through that long grass past the munching sheep, climb some more wooden steps, race through the boys' dressing room, then gasp and pant on to the stage, blue in the face, my face covered in painful scratches, my shoes and the netting layers of my costume full of burrs and anything else that I had stepped on in that turd-covered paddock. It was hard to switch back into nymphlike serenity after that, but I had to exit and enter several times in this eccentric manner, each time enduring jokes and sarcasm from the males, who were clearly enjoying my pained expression as I whizzed past like a frenzied cat. Every time I burst through their door, accompanied by a gale of wind, they would ask with exaggerated pomposity, 'Good grief, Madam, why can't you knock?'

The audience's response was warm, and the reception after the performance was an eye-opener. Far from being uncultured country yokels, these people were on the whole very cultured people, wealthy graziers who had flown or driven in from properties hundreds of miles away. I was even more surprised to find that many of them spent part of each year in Europe, where they tried to see as much theatre, opera and ballet as they could.

Almost everywhere we went we were made very welcome. Our billets were as varied as our performing venues. In Mareeba, a town in the tobacco-growing district of Queensland, three of us were billeted with a family who belonged to the local Arts Council. I am ashamed to say I had misgivings when Mr and Mrs Titlow arrived to pick us up. When Mr Titlow cocked his head in the direction of a very shabby utility truck, and said 'Sorry about the rough transport, but it'll get us there', I nearly ran back into the theatre. I sat in the front with Jan, wedged between Mr and Mrs Titlow, while the other girl hopped on to the back to sit among a rather strange conglomeration of tools, rubbish and miscellaneous debris. When we arrived at the house seven little Titlow boys were lined up to greet us. They exuded an aura of spectacular unintelligence.

Washing was most definitely not one of the family's favourite pastimes. After lunch, still hot and dirty from my long journey, I asked if I might have a bath. 'Sure thing, Tiny. Paul, get Tiny some water', bellowed Mr Titlow. Had I known what such a simple request entailed, I might have settled for a cold-water body wash instead, for the house had no running hot water. Neanderthal, sweet-natured Paul had to collect the water bucketful by bucketful from a tank some distance up the hill. After he had laboured back and forth for about twenty minutes, the bath was ready. I locked the bathroom door, threw off my filthy clothes and put one leg into the bath. This is where I stopped short. My bath consisted of about six inches of murky green water. On closer scrutiny I noticed quite an abundance of insect life, grass and weeds floating or swimming near the surface. But I climbed in and let the warm slime relax my aching limbs. I soaked for quite some time in a trance-like state, until Mr Titlow became concerned. 'Hey, Tiny', he yelled through the keyhole, 'what's up? Haven't fallen through the grease trap, have ya?' Our stay turned out to be a laugh a minute, and the Titlows showed a genuine warmth and kindness that I shall never forget.

The highlight of the Queensland tour, however, was our visits to Mount Isa and Mary Kathleen. We had all heard rumours about the hard-drinking roughnecks who gave these mining towns their macho reputations. We had also heard that these places tended to attract more than their fair share of criminals, who could work for high wages in comparative anonymity. We all felt apprehensive about the reception we would receive. Some of our costumes were quite revealing and, I suppose, provocative, although until this time we had not thought twice about it; the women in our company were feeling nervous, and the men were almost ready to leave the tour there and then. Every male in both our groups was heterosexual, but they knew that they could expect some poofter-baiting.

Fortunately I was asked to drive to Mount Isa with Paul. It was a tough trip, and no one would have hazarded it without extensive preparation. It was the route used for the Redex car rallies. There were no made roads. We had to cross dried-up river beds, plough through rocky tracks and traverse countryside where a breakdown would have been a major drama. The country was drought-stricken, and the carcasses of hundreds of kangaroos lay strewn around the barren countryside. In this stark, cruel setting I found a little incongruous comfort at the sight of the beer cans that littered the roadsides. In some places the cans were piled up like colourful termite hills.

The terrain looked very much as the world might look in the aftermath of a nuclear holocaust. Then, after miles and miles of boring, flat, hard-baked expanses, the topography suddenly changed into the dramatic hues of Albert Namatjira country. Subtle reds, purples and

The touring company at Mount Isa, 1961 (Alida third from left, in checked shirt)

rust colours offset by a flawless blue sky created a most spectacular backdrop for the stark white ghost gums. For the first time I felt a definite empathy, not only for my adopted country but also for the Aboriginal people who had once roamed this land in total harmony with their environment. The majestic countryside just seemed to stretch on forever. I felt that all dictators of the world, past, present or future, could do with a period of solitary confinement right here, if only to be brought down to size. The Aborigines had it right all the time. This land was worthy of respect.

We drove and we drove and we drove. Then suddenly we saw a foreboding finger pointing up to the sky, belching forth an ominous cloud of black smoke which hovered over the beautiful purple hills. A cluster of homes seemed to spring up out of nowhere. We had come to our oasis.

We were met by the manager of the Mount Isa Mining Company and taken to our living quarters, which were surprisingly comfortable. Later we were taken on a tour of the mines and residential areas, and I was amazed to see that it was not the ugly shanty town I had imagined. It was carefully planned and well laid out, with clean, modern homes surrounded by well-tended gardens in wide, tree-lined streets. The *pièce de résistance* was the huge man-made lake, where the workers could swim, boat, water-ski and even fish. I couldn't believe that such a town could occur in the middle of such a barren wasteland. And, contrary to our expectations, the performances went very well. There were no hecklers, no hurled rotten tomatoes, nor even any obscenities or improper suggestions.

Our trip along the Barrier Reef was like a working holiday. We picnicked or barbecued wherever a pretty spot took our fancy, swam in the clear water and sunbaked on those amazing white beaches. From Townsville we took the glass-bottomed boats on a tour of the coral reef, and visited paradisiacal tropical islands. The sun and sea filled me with new energy, and my muscles felt pliant and relaxed. Even my homesickness abated.

Continuing our southward journey, we found a little bit of Europe where we least expected it, at Cooma in the Snowy Mountains of New South Wales. Most of the advisers and skilled workers involved in the Snowy Mountains Scheme were European, and Cooma had become a cosmopolitan community. There were delicatessens with an exciting array of continental food and cheeses, boutiques displaying European designer clothes, and entertainment venues featuring films and shows from a variety of different countries. I was in seventh heaven. It seemed years since I had eaten yoghurt, roquefort or herrings.

After the luxury of urbane, sophisticated Cooma we were faced with the rural tragedy of Moree, where I had my first encounter with racial prejudice. I was not prepared for the squalid conditions on the outskirts, where the Aborigines were expected to live. The bigotry in the town was terrifying, but I was even more dismayed by the attitude of the people in our own company. Most of the dancers just seemed to ignore the Aborigines, while others made embarrassing jokes about the colour of their skin or hair. These missionaries of artistic endeavour turned out to be as narrow-minded and bigoted as the locals. Poverty and alienation had transformed the Aborigines into downtrodden, obese, shabbily dressed people who lounged round the steps of the saloon bar, or ambled drunkenly through the streets, easy targets for police aggression and the pick-up paddy wagons.

Their humpies looked like ill-fitting jigsaw puzzles of rusty corrugated iron, cardboard, slabs of old wood, and to keep out the wind and dust, strategically draped hessian bags. The people of Moree objected to this blot on the town's landscape, and would have done their damnedest to get rid of it. 'We can't give them better housing', one lady winced. 'Look at them, they are just pigs.' A man told me that Aborigines were not allowed into the town swimming pool because they were dirty and would spread disease.

Even more depressing was the fact that Aborigines would not be allowed into the theatre to see a performance. I had become an unwitting accomplice of segregationist policies. I was ashamed to think that, in spite of all my years at school, I had been ignorant of this terrible injustice right here in Australia.

Towards the end of the tour, the nearest thing to bliss I could think of was to be allowed to sink into a cool, clean bed and sleep and sleep without the noise of the carousing Ockers drifting up from the hotel saloon bar, and without the lowing and bleating of the ubiquitous cows and sheep—just to be allowed to sleep without any thought of having to survive another endless trek to another one-horse town for a single performance under a hot tin roof. I don't know how I managed to get the adrenalin pumping every night, but somehow or other my poor, startled body always responded just enough. Then, at the end of the performance, after the inevitable reception with its tea, buns and old ladies, I would return to the solitude of my room and spend hours pacing up and down, simply to try to coax my body back to quietude. Each morning I would turn up for bus call looking like something the cat dragged in.

I had more than my share of ups and downs to contend with. Young as I was, I tended to see things in black and white. I was either ecstatic or depressed, lonely or in love. But part of the growing-up process is to run the gauntlet of extreme emotions, and in this way the tour benefited me greatly. There was no one with me to cushion the blows, no one to protect me, no one to pander to my whims. I also learned to conquer a fair degree of physical pain, for there was no one else to go on for me when I was sick or injured.

Some of us could scarcely believe it when the tour came to an end and our battered little group parted company. Melbourne seemed like a concrete jungle at first, but it didn't take me long to get back into the swing of things and discover that urbanity was my preferred lifestyle. I had a wealth of anecdotes, which I used to great effect on all who would care to listen. In hindsight even the most harrowing times sounded like exciting adventure stories. But the only thing that impressed Harry was that up in Mount Isa his little sister had learnt to crush beer cans with one hand. And those were the days before aluminium cans.

10

A Student Again

It was October, and my friends at MacRob were just entering the panic swotting stage, with the matriculation exams looming dangerously near. I was looking forward to a period of luxurious inactivity, but I had underestimated my brother's concern about my education. Harry fervently believed that I should sit for matriculation so that I could at least enter university later if I wished to. I still had my sights set on a study period in Russia, but I decided it would be just as well to have a bash at the final exam. I had nothing more to lose than a suntan.

I chose four subjects, the minimum needed to obtain the certificate: British History, Modern History, Dutch and English Expression. In Dutch I did have an advantage in that I spoke the language, more or less. At home we still communicated in a hotchpotch of Dutch and English; though I spoke Dutch, I spoke a rather bastardized version, not the pure high Dutch required by my examiners. I had never been taught grammar, or how to read the language. I was rather excited about studying my native language and having an opportunity to read some Dutch literature.

My study period was far more fun than I anticipated, for Harry took me under his wing. I had a delicious introduction to university life. As far as I could make out, not much frenzied study went on in the law library where I now came to work with Harry. The library seemed to be a centre for passionate discourse on his favourite subject, Australian Rules football, rather than a solemn place for legal study. Harry would take the floor to start a post-mortem on a previous match or an analysis of the state of health of the various teams scheduled to play the next weekend, and, with the green sports pages spread out on the lectern in front of him, he would pontificate for hours with an oratory that held his audience spellbound. The other law students sat around his feet like ardent disciples. At least that is how I interpreted it. Maybe no one else could get a word in edgeways.

We pooled our pennies on arriving at the university, and, funds permitting, we went off to Genevieve's for morning coffee. Mostly after morning coffee we paid the obligatory but brief visit to the law library, and then, following university protocol, took a lunch break after about an hour and a half. When our finances were low we were forced to suffer the university café, where the coffee was quite odious and the food almost inedible.

I loved every minute of it, as the company was guaranteed to be witty, stimulating, and never too painfully earnest. Somehow I managed to do a lot of work without appearing unduly studious. I crammed an enormous amount of study into that short period. At 3.30 every day I had to leave the library and dash off to my ballet classes, and then resume my studies at night, when my insomnia worked to my advantage.

Madame Borovansky and I had parted company. The break was not an amicable one, and, though I would never have admitted it to her, I think I was the one who initially suffered most. Away from the protective umbrella of the Borovansky Academy, I felt extremely vulnerable. I was back at first base, but this time I didn't have my cuteness or my precocity to depend on. Other people's objectivity is never a pleasant experience. These teachers had no ties with my past to stop them from passing judgement on my dancing now. I hoped they might see past the flaws to the positive aspects of my dancing, which I thought, with ever-increasing nostalgia, had so pleased Monsieur and Madame.

My ego took a terrible beating. Each day I felt I was being appraised, gawped at by an audience of competitors who wished me no good. Without my performing bubble I stood naked. It wasn't very long, however, before I began to enjoy the thrill of making genuine progress. All the muscles that had remained a mystery to me suddenly revealed themselves. Not only did I find out where they were located, but I could control which muscle I would use for a specific exercise instead of relying on willpower, pot luck and a lot of unnecessary tension.

It was also a revelation to discover that perhaps I was not doomed to a life of misery trapped inside my inherited body after all. Before my very eyes I saw my limbs becoming more and more streamlined, and this transformation was not occurring by chance. I was determining the line of contour my body should take by working on exercises chosen for my own particular requirements; not only was I getting stronger, but my appearance was enhanced as well.

I attended classes at Rex Reid's, Paul Hammond's and Margaret Scott's. Although Margaret's classes were the most demanding, and the classes in which I was least able to star, these were the ones I attended most regularly. Maggie approached classroom work primarily from a scientific point of view. Every exercise was meticulously analysed, every single movement scrutinized, and every muscle identified before it was carefully brought into use. As a result I began to acquire a new physical confidence without that perpetual cloud of fatalistic doom hanging over me.

My anorexia nervosa was still with me. All I had done, devious creature that I was, was to make the symptoms less obvious and the modifications less drastic. Laxatives were still the most important supplements to my daily diet, and though I feigned a healthy appetite I was fanatically cautious. Now that I had arrived at what I considered to be a suitable body image, all my defence mechanisms came to the fore. I was prone to bleak moods in which I felt completely out of control, and these bouts of depression always seemed to be followed by physical self-destruction. In those times of mental anarchy, I consoled myself with the thought that I would be the sole arbiter of how fat or thin I would become. Perhaps this was one way of deluding myself that I was creating order out of chaos.

My body had made some external concessions to feminine maturity. I had acquired a rather nice bustline, and my tiny waist was the envy of many of my friends. But biologically I remained the girl-child, and I was beginning to worry that I might not menstruate at all. Clearly my severe dieting had inhibited the development of my reproductive system. My whole family shared my concern. When our worries were finally dispelled, I was infuriated by their lack of sympathy. I was doubled up with pain, but those inconsiderate wretches celebrated my agony with cakes and back-slapping felicitation. I was embarrassed and furious. Secretly, though, I was as relieved as they were. At last nature had taken pity on me.

I was aware of my own sexuality, but boy talk did not rate highly on my list of priorities. My disciplined schedule could not allow for such 'trite' pastimes; I was more interested in intellectual callings. I was a very disciplined seventeen-year-old. I danced and studied. Apart from

Peanuts comics, which I read for light relief, my staple diet in literature was writers such as Koestler and Camus.

At the end of my ten-week swotting period, D-day finally arrived. The grounds of the Exhibition Building were milling with ashen-faced teenagers, some conferring in nervous groups, desperately picking each other's brains for last-minute information, while others like myself hung around, fearful of losing even one shred of information lest it unravel the whole fragile fabric of our temporary knowledge.

The cold, imposing Exhibition Building, better known then as the Flea Palace, did nothing to allay our fears. I felt sick. How in God's name had I allowed myself to be roped into this? I regretted the day on which I had so stupidly assented to Harry's preposterous demands.

My legs had turned to jelly, but somehow they carried me into the vast shell-like building where I took my seat with hundreds of other students. There was an outbreak of nervous coughing, which only stopped when the assistants had finished handing around the examination papers. Then one could feel the tension cut the freezing air, as we all scanned the questions, hoping against hope that we had concentrated on the right areas. The supervisor gave us a quick run-through of rules and outlined the regulations concerning the conduct of this hard exam. We were told to pick up our pens, and the test began.

Much to my surprise, I did very well, and was offered a Commonwealth scholarship to the University of Melbourne. I now faced another debate with Harry, who insisted that a university course would not go amiss, despite my protestations that ballet dancers never attempted such things. 'Come on, set a precedent. Why don't you become the first one?' Harry urged calmly. 'What's the harm in enrolling? You can always defer your course if you change your mind.' And so I went with Harry to enrol in an Arts course for 1962.

As it turned out I needn't have worried, as an opportunity finally arose to do something about my proposed trip to Russia, and I deferred my studies. The Eighth World Youth Festival was to be held in Helsinki in July. In theory the philosophy behind these festivals was to promote world peace via the arts. Every four years a city was chosen to host this gathering of young people, who would perform music, dance and literary readings representing their countries, and it was also hoped that the atmosphere would encourage a friendly interchange of different ideas and viewpoints, promoting a better understanding of the world. It was an enormously appealing concept. It was suggested that if I went to Helsinki with the Australian delegation, I might just manage to get to Moscow. I leapt at the chance, feet first.

If my parents felt apprehensive at the thought of my travelling all that way on my own, they were remarkably self-controlled. Most people thought them quite mad to agree, and warned of the dangers of my disappearing behind the Iron Curtain. It seemed incredible to everyone, even to me, that I, their clingy little daughter, was now seeking to leave home, and planning to fly right across to the other side of the world.

My mother and I sent off umpteen letters to Canberra to ask for a visa to Russia, but to no avail. The officials replied in cold officialese, asking why the Royal Ballet in London would not do. I believe they suspected my motives for wanting to go to the USSR to study. My only commitment lay to ballet, and in my book Communist feet were as good as any others. I ignored the nuances in their letters and persisted, stating as clearly as I could that my only reason for choosing Russia was that I was already trained in the Russian style of ballet. The Canberra bureaucracy was not persuaded. There was no official cultural exchange between the two countries, so I could not hope to enter the USSR with the agreement of the Australian government.

Apart from the legality of travelling to Russia, there was another major obstacle—money. My parents had nowhere near enough to finance such a trip. With a little help from my friends, a plan of action was put together. A circular was compiled consisting of a short biography, a statement to the effect that I was a very talented student and that the Bolshoi Company had already offered me a scholarship and free tuition, if and when I could manage to travel to Moscow. Ballet teachers, balletomanes and the Jewish community were canvassed to help me raise money for travel and living expenses. The donations soon started to roll in.

My departure was fast becoming a *fait accompli*, and as the date drew closer I began to experience a gamut of jumbled emotions, ranging from fear of the unknown to a mad exhilaration. But my strongest desire was to get the show on the road as quickly as possible.

I was excited for another reason as well. In a sense I was going back to my roots. My parents remained Europeans in Australia. Their personalities and life patterns had been shaped by European culture, and though I had only experienced it vicariously it had had a profound effect on my psyche. Now I was being given the opportunity to discover the sources of my being. I cherished a fervent desire to bring some form of cognitive substance to those hazy reminiscences culminating at

Fremantle on the rails of the *Toscana* in 1949. I took heart from the knowledge that, while I was distancing myself from my parents in a physical sense, I would also be moving closer to them spiritually. I would be the first member of my family to return to the scene where they had grown up so happily and suffered so much pain. I was going to cross the bridge to the past.

A farewell benefit performance was organized at the Malvern Town Hall. As the concert was primarily for my benefit, it was only fitting that I should be the star of the show, but the programme had quite an illustrious billing, as several friends had kindly volunteered to perform without payment. Ron Paul consented to partner me, and Gail Stock, Walter Burke and Helen Magner, all future artists of the Australian Ballet, danced solos and *pas de deux*, and Sol Segal played the violin, accompanied by Karl Ogden on the piano. I danced a beautiful solo Margaret Scott had choreographed to a Schumann Valse, and a dance called *Jedda*, choreographed by Jeanette Liddell.

I included *Jedda* with the intention of presenting it at the Helsinki Festival as a sample of our indigenous culture. After all, I was supposed to be representing Australia, and therefore had an obligation to share something which was exclusively Australian and not a European import. In hindsight I wished I hadn't. It was audacious to presume that I could plagiarize a bit of Aboriginal culture, or should I say put together a pastiche of primitive-looking steps, and lay claim to a knowledge of Aboriginal culture. I had never so much as seen a corroboree, let alone studied it.

The story was even more embarrassing. In it I portrayed an Aboriginal girl reared by white people who discovers she is black when she sees her reflection in a billabong. The trauma of this revelation unleashes her inherent 'primitiveness', and in the last part of the dance, armed with an imaginary spear, she evokes the spirit of an ancestral hunter and launches into a frenzied hunter's dance. But pride in her newly discovered origins is short-lived, for at the end she breaks down, and the curtain closes on this tragic figure who will eternally suffer the burden of the universal Black. I performed this dance with all the Jewish schmaltz and pathos that I could muster; having come from a background of suffering and persecution, I believed that I could understand what it felt like to be an outsider.

The rift between Madame Borovansky and myself made me feel sad. There remained a small possibility that Madame might realize that she had behaved unreasonably, and on this naïve assumption I determined to make another effort to make amends. I sent her an invitation to my farewell concert, accompanied by a carefully considered letter in which I expressed conciliatory sentiments and explained my plans.

Much to my amazement I received a reply, but when I read it I stumbled over the cheap, self-pitying rantings it contained. The author bore no resemblance to the Madame Borovansky I had once revered. Madame wrote that she remembered a sweet little girl with a rosebud mouth and large loving eyes, for whom Monsieur and she had so many hopes and aspirations. Now, she went on, that little girl would have to learn from the greatest teacher of all, life, because for her that little girl no longer existed. It was a chilling experience: I had been pronounced dead at the age of eighteen.

11

Departure

Many months earlier I had made a preposterous wish. Now the money had been raised, I had been accepted as the dance representative of the Australian delegation to Helsinki, my ticket had been booked, and I knew I couldn't change my mind. I had no confirmation that I would be able to study in Moscow or how I would get there, I didn't have a lot of money, and I had no idea whether I would stay away from home for two months or two years. But all I cared about was that the plane would be travelling in the right direction.

My mother and I went shopping, paying particular attention to necessities that were unobtainable in Russia: bath-plugs, Kleenex tissues, Nescafé, biros, mascara, a mohair rug and, of course, plenty of Duralax. The day before I was to leave Melbourne, sitting in the middle of a clutter of boxes and suitcases, I choked at the realization that my mother was packing me up and sending me away. The next morning I felt an overwhelming urge to jump back into bed, pull the bedclothes over my head, and stay there until 16 July 1962 had run its course. My self-assuredness simply evaporated.

Then the guests started to pour in to wish me a good journey, and I found myself confirming the facts: 'Goodbye, thank you, yes I shall write'. They have called my bluff, I thought; they think I'm grown up, but I'm not. But there was the plane ticket, propped up against the vase on the hall table. My mother was beginning to panic as she bustled between suitcases and well-wishers. She was being over-courteous, as if to compensate for my father's silence.

As the day progressed my father's countenance became more and more rigid. My father always internalized his emotions, but on this occasion his apparent indifference offended me greatly. I can't remember what I said, but without warning my father's suppressed emotions burst forth. I was shocked at the outburst; in all our years together we had never fought and now, on my last day at home, we were yelling at each other. I retreated to my room, wallowing in self-pity and outrage. How could my father behave so insensitively? The door burst open and my mother scuttled in, not to sympathize with me, as I had expected, but to reprimand me. 'Can't you see how nervous your father is?' she scolded. 'You should know him by now!' She was right, I realized. My father only exploded when he was deeply anxious. He was screaming because he wanted to protect me, and was worried that my ambitions might bring me unstuck. How could I have ever doubted my father's love? Humiliated and guilty, I wandered out to find my ashen-faced father stubbornly dusting the lounge-room bookshelves. Reaching up to him, for my father would never have brought himself to bend down to me, I pecked him on the cheek and muttered, 'Sorry, Dad'. He sniffed, as he always did when he was embarrassed by a show of emotion, and said, 'I've already forgotten about it'. He went on dusting, but I noticed that the colour had flowed back into his cheeks.

The moment for our final goodbyes arrived all too quickly. I managed to get through my relatives' hugs and kisses with comparative composure, and bid some ostentatious adieus to various ballet friends who had gathered at the airport to wish me well. But when it came to my immediate family, all sense of theatricality left me and I started to dissolve. I clung to my mother and my brother, choking back the tears, and when it was my father's turn to say goodbye I was simply overcome with grief. Dad had stood in the background, quietly waiting until the very end. He was dignified and calm, but when we embraced I felt this tall, dignified man snap in my arms. He sobbed, though it was hardly audible. 'Don't forget to eat, schatje. Look after yourself, and you know if you need something, you have only to ask. We will always be here for you.'

My legs shook as I made my way across the tarmac and up the aeroplane stairs. I turned to give my last little Hollywood wave, but my stomach was heaving. 'What am I doing this for?' I gulped, looking through the window at the diminishing figures of my family. But I knew I could not go back. I had to move on, for their sakes as well as mine.

I determined then and there that I would not return home until I had reached my goal.

My travelling companions seemed affable, although I was dismayed to learn that I was the only cultural representative in the group. The other members belonged to church organizations, trade unions, and the Eureka Youth League. I had persuaded myself that the Helsinki Festival was mainly a cultural festival, but not one member of our group had the slightest artistic pretensions.

There were four boys and three other girls in our group, all friendly, down-to-earth Aussies who made me feel instantly at ease. We touched down briefly at Darwin, then flew to Jakarta. We had been invited to spend a few days as guests of the Indonesian trade unions, and I was told on the plane that I would be expected to perform. We arrived at 1.45 a.m., but even at that late hour the atmosphere was steamy as we walked across the tarmac. I was terrified to find the airport crawling with soldiers, young boys barely in their teens carelessly swinging huge rifles as they strutted around. They all looked as if they were taking part in an absurd juvenile game, but they were not. The night resounded with the beating of drums, accompanied by people yelling out a slogan that I could not understand. Later I was told that the soldiers were chanting 'Free West Irian, Free West Irian'.

My one concert in Jakarta was an instant success, though it never should have been. Having been allotted only about six square feet of glassy surface to dance on, I quickly dismissed any notion of making myself a martyr for my art. Instead, I improvised a rather static, stylized display of *porte de bras*, mostly from a kneeling position, and hoped that my audience might think my performance was some kind of traditional ethnic dance, a reflection perhaps of the enervating Australian landscape. At the end I was almost bowled over and smothered by the crowd. Fingers poked at me, and I was kissed, lynched by embraces, and bombarded with flowers from all directions. I felt in mortal danger of being asphyxiated by the floral deluge or trampled to death.

I was extricated by the most beautiful woman I had ever seen. She obviously commanded the respect of the other onlookers, for she had only to utter a few softly spoken words and the crowd parted to let her through. Her name was Lely, and she was a dancer in Soekarno's royal palace. She told me she was interested in classical ballet, and asked me if I would mind giving her a few lessons on some of the basics. I couldn't imagine what I could possibly impart to her. As she spoke I couldn't

The beautiful Lely (second from left) with Soekarno

take my eyes off her long, eloquent fingers and her perfectly proportioned face. Indeed, most of the Indonesian ladies made me feel that God had played a terrible joke on Western women. Suddenly my skin seemed insipid, my bones far too large, and my movements embarrassingly ungainly.

Now that I was travelling, I could not control my diet. Naturally this was worrying. How was I going to maintain my condition and stay a reasonable size? Those sedentary hours in the plane were bad enough, but then we were expected to attend numerous receptions, each a veritable banquet, and to refuse was to offend. I attempted to do my exercises each morning before breakfast to escape the heat. I found my perfect barre on the patio of our hotel room. Not only was the railing just the correct height for body support, but the view was so splendid that it made the work quite pleasurable. It was hard, however, not to be self-conscious about all the eyes surveying me from behind the surrounding bushes. I did find some of the tittering and stifled laughter disconcerting, but I suppose my inelegant limbering-up movements must have seemed quite absurd, the very antithesis of their own serene and graceful temple dancers.

Most of the people we associated with were members of Young Communist Pioneer groups, and most of the officials who offered us such warm hospitality were prominent left-wing trade union members. I think we must have met every available local official, from the Mayor to the Secretary of the National Front. At the end of each meeting there was always the obligatory photograph. Everyone had to be in the photo: the official's wife, relations, cooks, servants and even the family dog, if it could be caught. Still, the cameras were a lot more benign than those equally ubiquitous rifles, which seemed to be flaunted almost as casually.

We left Indonesia by Czechoslovakian Air. The air hostesses were big-boned blondes, to be obeyed rather than argued with. Without a word of protest I submitted to a breakfast of frankfurters, dry rye bread and beer. I trembled to think how much weight I must be putting on, and felt in my bag for one of those reassuring little boxes of Duralax that my mother had packed for me.

We were an exhausted, motley lot when the plane finally disgorged us at Prague airport, our first port of call in a Communist country. After doing battle with the customs officials, we found that no one seemed to have bothered to come to meet us. I began to imagine all kinds of melodramatic scenarios. I had often heard that Westerners were apt to disappear without trace in these countries. I looked for tell-tale signs of repression engraved on the passing faces.

This dangerous train of thought was interrupted by a strident 'hello'. The person to whom the voice belonged was yet another big-boned blonde, who turned out to be our guide. She was obviously hell-bent on dispelling all our fears, and constantly babbled in a very guttural English about the virtues of this socialist Utopia.

Prague was a major departure point for most of the delegations. The noise and confusion that confronted us at the Central Station were quite overwhelming. There were so many excited people milling on the platforms that I wondered how everyone was going to fit into the waiting trains. Occasionally one voice would rise above the cacophony, screaming in an incomprehensible language. Following our leader's advice to hold hands, we somehow managed to snake our way through the crowd to our compartment. I stood on the top step of the train to peruse the crowd, and saw a range of faces of every hue imaginable, and with as many different national costumes.

Judging by the rate with which our compartment was filling up, it seemed that we might have our own little microcosm right there. We were joined by a contingent of Africans and some Algerians. The Africans, from Sierra Leone, began the night's entertainment by singing songs accompanied by clapping and bongo drums. Before very long everyone joined in, and we had a great deal of fun.

In each town we passed through the station was crowded with people who had come out to greet us with flowers and postcards bearing messages of peace and friendship. Some towns even provided a small band. Each time the train stopped we all gathered on the platforms to mingle with other delegations, and as the train continued its slow progress I learnt about a multitude of ethnic dance forms. It was impossible to sleep as we careered through the Polish and Russian countryside, so we lived it up instead. As the hours progressed our antics went a little out of control, and even became hysterical. We could hear just as much noise coming from the other compartments. The train had become a mobile bedlam.

We were brought to our senses when we stopped at Warsaw. Warsaw in 1962 was still a sad, war-ravaged city wearing all its scars as if Hitler's onslaught had happened only yesterday. I wasn't prepared for the extent of the devastation. Almost everywhere we looked there were huge areas of rubble, bomb sites and bullet-riddled walls. The people seemed weary and dispirited. Our interpreter explained that much of the city had already been rebuilt to the exact specifications of pre-war Warsaw. With the help of photographs the Polish people had painstakingly reconstructed their beloved buildings brick by brick, but, the interpreter reminded us, it had only been seventeen years since the end of the war, and there was still a great deal to be done. Seventeen years; such a long, short time ago.

I felt as if my insides were being ripped apart. All those shadowy wartime images that had haunted me were brought to life. Here it all was, projected in the sepia colours of my dreams. The city seemed almost devoid of colour and had a most dreadful, eerie sombreness about it. In my mind I heard thousands of jackboots resounding on these cobblestones, and before my eyes flashed the image of a photograph that had tormented me for years, of a small, terrified boy with his arms held over his head in surrender, a big yellow star of David on his overcoat, his eyes full of the anguish that was his blood inheritance. In this city, on these very cobblestones, this photograph had been taken to immortalize him and us.

It was here that the Warsaw Ghetto uprising had taken place. Under my feet, in the network of sewers, a handful of Jews had put the world to shame, knowing that their act of defiance could only ever be symbolic.

I couldn't hold back the tears. I cried for my parents and their families. I cried because I knew that this dreadful sadness would refuse to be expunged, and it would always remind me of my origins.

We arrived in Helsinki at 10 a.m. on a Sunday. The basement of a college had been transformed into sleeping quarters for 450 Americans and our tiny group. I eyed the beds longingly, but I was whisked off to a meeting to plan my participation in the festival.

The next day about 100 000 young people filled the Helsinki stadium for the grand opening ceremony. It was a fantastic sight. I glanced around at the bright *mélange* of colour jiggling around the stands, the array of international flags flapping lovingly at each other in the wind, and it seemed to me that the whole world was *here*, locked into a circumference of good will.

Following the tradition of previous festivals, the country that hosted the last festival performed the first spectacle. In this case it was the Russians, who put on a dazzling display of singing, dancing and gymnastics. Then came the grand march around the arena, with the crowd roaring its approval as each country passed, holding its flag proudly aloft. The Cubans in particular received an overwhelming ovation. This was not a time for analysing the pros and cons. I found myself yelling as loudly as the man next to me: 'Peace and friendship! Peace and friendship!' And if it was the success of the Cuban struggle against imperialism we were celebrating, well, why not? Not even an unexpected deluge of rain could dampen the enthusiasm of that afternoon's crowd. The climax was a spectacular fireworks display, after which thousands of white doves were released to soar to the heavens. If all this was emotionally manipulative, then it was masterfully done.

My festive spirit was curtailed abruptly when I was told that I was to dance the following day. In all the excitement I had put dance disciplines right to the back of my mind. How irksome to be reminded that I was here in Helsinki to represent Australia as a dancer, not as a peace advocate. I was so unfit, and almost certainly terribly overweight. Panic-stricken, I ran my hands over my waist and hipbones with disgust. Those reassuring protruding bones had all but disappeared. Over the past few days I had almost forgotten about the threatening catastrophe cleverly concealed beneath my street clothes. But now my rounded nakedness confronted me. I would certainly make a fool of myself. I had heard that top dancers from countries like Russia and Hungary and France were dancing in the same performance. These dancers were not students, but fully fledged artists, trained in the best institutions in the world. They would make mincemeat of me.

I didn't have much time to prepare for my first performance, so I decided to take the easy way out. I would dance *Jedda*. It was not technically demanding, and, though it had dramatic pizazz, it was obscure enough to pass as an authentic piece of Australiana. All I wanted was to get my act over and done with. I don't think my performance was a memorable one, though the audience was gracious. Fortunately I had a chance to make amends a few days later, when I danced *Valse Tendre* with considerably more confidence and conviction. The feast of theatrical activities, concerts, operas and ballets left me with a dilemma; there was too much choice. I attended as many performances as I could fit into any one day, and the more I saw, the more inadequate I felt.

Obviously any left-wing festival such as this was bound to cause some unpleasant reactions, particularly from the more conservative members of Finnish society. What we hadn't bargained for, however, was the Australian reactionaries who had travelled all the way to Helsinki to let their opposition be known. We had occasional smoke bombs thrown into our midst as we marched down the streets, and Fascist slogans could sometimes be heard above the supportive cheering of most of the crowd, but we never took these detractors seriously.

I was therefore quite shocked to receive a panic-stricken letter from my mother, who had read some sensationalist rubbish in the Australian press. The papers had claimed that our little group had been caught in a nasty exchange between the Communists and the Fascists, and that there had been dramatic scenes of violence. As far as my mother could gather, my life was being endangered by a great deal of indiscriminate bomb-throwing and a resurgence of unrepentant Fascism. I immediately let my parents know that all was well.

At the end of the festival all the other members of our delegation were travelling on to various destinations before returning to Australia. I alone planned to go to London. The moment of reckoning had come; for the first time I would be on my own. My friends wished me good luck, and bid me adieu.

For several days I had agonized over some important decisions. My parents had not received any news from the Bolshoi, so I had no definite plans for travelling to Moscow. Who was going to advise me what to do? I felt smaller and smaller, and less confident by the minute. I had been left to play grown-ups on my own.

I knew that the Kinmonts had recently spent time in London, though they were eventually returning to Australia to live. I took a punt and wrote to them at their London address, hoping that Jenny or Felicity might still be there, but I received no reply. I felt even more terrified at the thought of arriving in London with no accommodation, very little money, and only a handful of contact addresses. Still, I booked my ticket, and spent a couple of days in a much more subdued Helsinki, waiting for the arrival of the *Kalinin*, the Russian boat that would take me to London via Copenhagen and Stockholm.

Four days later the shores of England appeared on the horizon. We all rushed on deck to catch our first glimpse of those famous white cliffs, but as the *Kalinin* sailed closer to shore my heart sank. I could only see some bleak, fog-enshrouded grey rocks that seemed to rise ominously from an angry grey sea. No warmth or friendliness could possibly emanate from such a place. This time I felt ready to call it quits; all I wanted to do was go home.

Gloomily I shuffled to the end of a long line of disembarking passengers, where I submitted to the whims of a stern customs official. When finally I had been processed, stamped and approved, I was released into the crowds at Tilbury to find a train to London. Everyone else seemed to have someone waiting to greet them, and the arrival lounge was full of people shrieking with joyous recognition. What could I do? Obviously there was no point indulging in panic or histrionics, as no one would take the slightest bit of notice. I had to remain calm, and try to work things out slowly and methodically.

Suddenly I thought I heard my name being called. 'Now you're hallucinating, Alida', I told myself. But then a figure burst through the crowd and hurled itself upon me. I don't think I had ever been more pleased to hear anyone's voice than I was to hear Felicity Kinmont's that day. Felicity explained that Jenny had been unable to come to Tilbury because she was at work, but I would see her later at the flat, 'where, by the way', Felicity added, 'you are most welcome to stay for a few weeks'. One of their flatmates was away on tour, so there was a spare bed. Life was looking up.

From the train window I stared in disbelief at the rows upon rows of identical soot-covered houses that were the Dickensian reality of the London slums. It was only when we arrived at Tower Hill that the London of my mind's eye materialized, and I could see that London was a complex jigsaw of the old and the new, the positive and the negative, full of the necessary contrasts that make a city vibrant.

While we queued for a cab, I embarrassed poor Flicky by pointing and yelling at the sight of a bona fide English bobby, and I was delighted when the bobby crossed the street to talk to me in a perfect Cockney accent. The cab took us down the Mall, past St Paul's Cathedral, Buckingham Palace and London Bridge. This was the fantasy world of Monopoly games and J. Arthur Rank movies. I was impressed by the majesty and history of the place, but at the same time its immensity highlighted my own insignificance. This was the land of the big fry, and the first part of my training would be simply a matter of learning how to survive as one small, unnecessary fish in a very large, crowded pond.

12

Exploring London

I was given a lovely bedroom with a balcony overlooking Cromwell Road. The Earls Court flat had six rooms, and had been beautifully furnished by Mr Kinmont, who had obviously been intent on seeing his daughters comfortably settled before he returned to Australia. The Kinmonts were only staying in London for three more weeks, and then I would be on my own, but at least I was being eased into the rigors of the big city with the help and support of two dear friends.

When I woke the next morning the sun was pouring into my bedroom. I had slept my first really restful sleep in weeks. I padded across the thick carpet to the French windows and stood on the balcony feeling deliciously lazy. Sunny London was a London transformed. I had a 180-degree view right across the rooftops, and suddenly the city that only yesterday had seemed so grey and depressing was filled with colour, noise and life. I felt anxious to get out there and explore as much as I could.

The chic, expensive nucleus of London captured me immediately. Here, before my eyes, was the extravagant London depicted in all the glossy magazines. The chauffeur-driven Rolls-Royces parked defiantly and illegally in Knightsbridge while their owners popped into Harrods to do a little shopping. The pinstripe suits and bowler hats, complete with rolled-up copy of *The Times*, brolly and briefcase. The elegant, stolid buildings, monuments to the wealth and power of England's days of empire, the theatres of the West End, the glorious grot of Covent Garden. This was the centre of the world, a world of influence, affluence and culture, and I wanted to be part of it. The size and density of the city did not faze me at all. I took to it like a town mouse. Above all I loved the constant activity; unlike Melbourne, London never went to sleep, and the city seemed to affect even its most transient visitors with its vitality.

The Kinmonts' flat was rather like a transit station. At any time of day or night the floor would be strewn with the prostrate bodies of drop-in lodgers, almost invariably other Australians passing through London while working their way around the continent. I found this casual lifestyle appealing, and I quickly learnt that the conservative mores of Australian society were out of place in the swinging London of the 1960s.

I could scarcely believe my eyes when I saw the number and variety of theatrical entertainments listed in the daily newspapers. Jenny had booked tickets for several performances, and in a few nights' entertainment I saw Noël Coward's *Sail Away* at the Savoy, Marcel Marceau at the Piccadilly, and the Festival Ballet at the Festival Hall, where the disproportionate number of Australians in the cast made me feel I was attending a reunion of ex-Borovansky dancers. My fellow Aussies had done extremely well for themselves over here, but I was disappointed by the standard of the Festival Ballet, which I found quite mediocre at times. This was not entirely depressing. I had been terrified that the standard of British ballet would be so exemplary that it would discourage me forever, but now I felt that perhaps I would not disgrace myself in the classroom.

London was also, however, the home of the formidable Royal Ballet, which stood for everything that I was not. Didn't the girls from the Royal have perfect, streamlined bodies with plasticine limbs that stretched on forever? I had already seen them spilling out of the trains on to the platform at Barons Court station and waddling superciliously across the platform. I felt envious, but at the same time I didn't want to be part of this mindless mass of production-line perfection. 'You poor things', I mused bitchily, 'what a price you have had to pay!' Although part of me envied their privileged, primed physiques, and I could appreciate the aesthetic pleasure of watching those perfectly sculptured humanoids in harmonious motion, I didn't wish to be a cog in any such machine. Striking poses as a part of a bland backdrop for some other lead dancer had nothing to do with my dance aspirations. To move with the regimented line-up with not even an individualistic eye-flutter, not one give-away trace of personalized expression, was an inanity that I could not and would not give my sweat and blood for.

I longed for some news from home about my Bolshoi scholarship, but the weeks flew past and there was still no word. I was advised to ring the Royal Ballet. Apparently Peggy van Praagh had already spoken to the director of the school, Arnold Haskell, requesting that I be allowed to study for a term at reduced rates. But this had been intended to come *after* my return from Moscow. Now, as I hadn't had any concrete information from the Bolshoi, Miss van Praagh advised me to try to enter the Royal Ballet School immediately.

This plan threw me into an apoplexy of fear. I could already imagine all those almond eyes scanning my lumpy colonial body. Could I bear to be the victim of all the derision and criticism that would be heaped on me? The whole plan was absurd. I simply was not a Royal Ballet 'lovely'. I would stick out like a sore thumb. As far as I was concerned, to study there would be a painful waste of time.

Still, at eighteen I wasn't supposed to presume that I knew best. My orders stood. Half-heartedly I went through the motions of contacting the school. I realized that everyone would consider it folly to let such an opportunity go. How many boys and girls were champing at the bit to enter the Royal Ballet? I told myself that I should swallow my pride. If I valued my art above my ego, I should endeavour to learn as much as I could and from as many sources as possible.

I made an appointment to see a Miss Wilkinson in a couple of weeks' time. But could I possibly bash my poor body into shape in such a short period? The time had definitely come to venture out of my protective shell, and get back into practice at my first open classes in London.

I was quite certain that the bottom would drop out of my world when I saw the excellence of the other students. I packed my ballet bag with dread, but by the time Flicky had walked me to the tube I had managed to talk myself out of my self-pity. I became almost cavalier. I told myself that I could only feel humiliated if other people cared enough about my existence to want to set themselves up in competition with me. Why should anyone else waste a minute worrying about my lack of condition? I am just another anonymous gate-crasher, hoping to have a bash at the big time. So, OK, I would give it a bash. Time enough to throw myself into the Thames after class, and with equal anonymity.

Felicity took me to Andrew Hardie's studio for a class with another well-known teacher, Valerie Swinard. I felt all eyes upon me as I made my ungainly entrance into the classroom. Conscious of my unexercised flab, I felt about as graceful as a baby hippo thrown in among a flock of elegant egrets. With a nervous little half-smile, I fled to a place at the barre, trying to avoid my mirrored image. 'Think thin, Alida', I reprimanded myself. 'This is a workout, not a performance.' But, try as I might, I couldn't help noticing those beautiful, bony creatures preening themselves in front of my eyes, lovingly stretching and caressing their precious limbs, turning their bodies this way and that in order to find the most advantageous angles. I bet they are just poseurs, I thought bitchily.

I was just beginning to relish this flow of bitchiness when the teacher and pianist walked in. Much to my delight, the pianist was Dudley Simpson, whom I had known since I was a little girl dancing to his piano accompaniment for classes at the Borovansky Ballet. It was wonderful to see a friendly face, and our reunion seemed to take the chill out of the air just a little. Yet as I stood at the barre I could still feel all those eyes scrutinizing me from head to toe.

The chords for the introductory *porte de bras* before our first exercise sent a shock wave coursing through my body. Not having done a proper class for months, I had almost forgotten the thrill such concentrated intensity could produce. My body clicked back into action, and at once I was lost in my deep inner sanctum, a familiar love-hate world of muscular skills and cerebral tautness, a world where the only competition that really mattered was the one between my body and me.

I was so excited to be back in class that my body almost forgot to be unfit. In spite of weeks of negligence, it seemed surprisingly eager to respond to even my most demanding instructions. My pirouettes worked like magic, my elevation felt strong and effortless, my spirits rose ebulliently. Succeed or fail, it didn't really matter. I had arrived back home, in a cold, draughty classroom in London.

Anna Northcote's studio could hardly have been less appealing. It was in a dark, dingy basement. As if trying to cope with her technically demanding class was not punishment enough, the floor was hazardous in the extreme, full of bumps and crevices, and right in the path of one's running *grands jetés* there was a black pot-belly stove. With her penchant for classical purity and artistic honesty, Anna was just the benevolent tyrant I needed. She refused to allow me my usual classroom indulgences, and demanded clean, honest work with no frills or cosmetic touch-ups. Her stern countenance called for respect. Clearly she would not tolerate any bluff, even from an artful dodger like myself.

And gradually I found myself reaping the benefits of disciplined hard work.

Then an emissary from the Royal Ballet rang to summon me to Barons Court for my interview. Though I prayed for word from the Bolshoi so that I could cancel this dreaded appointment, the day inevitably rolled up. I squeezed myself into the most figure-flattering clothes I could find, dragged my hair back into the required balletic topknot, and sucked my cheeks in to acquire that hungry, hollow look. But my reflection did not pass scrutiny. I looked revoltingly healthy; even my complexion, which had always seemed so pallid in Australia, now looked ruddy beside those English roses.

When I arrived at Barons Court I was ushered into the corridor to wait outside the secretary's door. This was obviously Intimidation Programme Number One, for I had no choice but to watch the passing parade of peacocks, who seemed to be strutting entirely for my benefit. They stared at me with that 'Who are you, little fat girl?' look. I was prepared to hate them all. I loathed the way they looked, the way they spoke and the way they ate their silly little Ryvitas spread with fat-free cottage cheese.

By the time Miss Wilkinson invited me into her office, I was determined to be as different as possible. Miss Wilkinson explained to me that she was substituting for the permanent secretary, Miss Moreton, who was away on holiday, and then proceeded to tell me what a big favour they were doing me. When the subject of fees was raised, I was quite shocked to hear that Peggy van Praagh had not discussed the matter. The last thing I wanted now was an act of charity, but there was no way that I could raise the full fees, and so I was forced to explain my financial predicament. Surprisingly enough, although Miss Moreton was supposed to be holidaying in foreign parts, Miss Wilkinson had no difficulty in contacting her by phone. They discussed my plight matter-of-factly, and arranged a further appointment, this time with Miss Moreton herself.

Were it not for that Bolshoi tag, I am certain I would not have reached first base at the Royal Ballet. At the time there was a lot of excitement about Soviet ballet. The Bolshoi and Kirov companies could only make a few tours of the West, and Nureyev had just made his famous 'leap to freedom'. Any chance to venture into the inner sanctums of the Bolshoi or the Kirov was like gaining an audience with the Pope. The West was aghast at the technical superiority of the Russian-trained dancers, particularly the male dancers, who had taken London and New York by storm. Even that most imperialistic bastion, the Royal Ballet, was eager to obtain as much inside information as it could. Only two English students had managed to obtain permission to study ballet in the USSR, and I would be the first Australian. The English school of dance's last contact with Russian training had been in the Diaghilev period, when quite a few Westerners had joined the famed Ballet Russe in Paris.

Alida in London, 1962

On the second interview, to prove that I had indeed been accorded VIP status, I was honoured by the presence of both Miss Moreton and the school's director, Arnold Haskell. Mr Haskell was enthusiastic about my invitation to the Bolshoi, and assured me that I would have no problem in getting a grant to study at the Royal with such credentials. After giving me some addresses of friends in Russia, he asked that I keep in touch with him and inform him of my progress. We chatted on in a warm and friendly vein for quite some time. But the crunch came when Arnold Haskell said 'Naturally we would love you to attend some Company classes before you leave for Russia'. A date was set several weeks away. I felt instantly doomed. Out there in the classroom all my balletic flaws would be laid bare. The ring of exclusivity no longer seemed so illustrious. Much as I disliked, or thought I disliked, all those Royal Ballet lovelies, I had to admit that they were beautifully trained. I said my goodbyes to the congenial couple feeling quite petrified.

In the next couple of weeks I managed to pull myself out of the doldrums and attend a great deal of theatre, including a number of performances by the Royal and Festival Ballets. Each time I became more determined to put up with anything to share in the performer's glory. But still I received no word from Moscow. My journeys to the Commonwealth Bank in the Strand became more and more frequent. I watched my meagre bank balance dwindle away. Even if I had wanted to, I didn't have enough money to return home. It was too late to retreat.

The Kinmonts' departure meant that I would now have to search for affordable accommodation elsewhere. Just when I was beginning to believe that I might find myself destitute and on the streets, I remembered that a friend back home had given me a number to call if I should find myself in this kind of predicament. Normally I felt reluctant to call friends of friends, but this was no time for embarrassment.

The Fealdmans turned out to be a delightful couple. They agreed to accommodate me until I found something more permanent. Mr Fealdman was the director of the Ben-Uri gallery, and lived with his wife and two children in a small flat in Maida Vale. Until now London had seemed strangely bereft of family life. I couldn't recall having seen a child in London until I moved in with the Fealdmans. It was immensely reassuring to be living in the midst of a family once more.

Christmas was only a few months away, so there was a possibility of working in one of the many pantomimes that proliferated in and around London in the holiday season. Royal Ballet students were usually given first preference, but Peggy van Praagh told me to contact Betty Astell, an ex-dancer friend who was married to the comedian Cyril Fletcher. Every Christmas they produced and directed a traditional pantomime, with Cyril playing the Panto Dame, and Betty and her daughter taking on the other leading female roles. This year's venue was the newly built Ashcroft theatre in Croydon, about an hour and a half from London by train.

I didn't want to perform at this stage of my training, but my economic situation gave me no choice. I was asked to go for an audition at Eastbourne, where the Fletchers were currently performing. Although Eastbourne was not Covent Garden, I was still extremely nervous. Most of the country's top students and unemployed professional dancers coveted these panto positions, so I expected to come up against some stiff competition. The closer the train hurtled towards Eastbourne, the more I realized the importance of this audition. As well as being a ticket to survival, it would give me a chance to assess my standard against the top echelon of English students and graduates.

When I arrived at the Hippodrome a rehearsal was in progress, so I slipped quietly into the stalls to watch. The entire Fletcher family was on stage. The slapstick humour and song-and-dance routines were a far cry from the rarefied atmosphere of classical ballet. I wouldn't even buy a ticket to see this tripe, I thought. But there I was, preparing to do battle with scores of other dancers for a role in the show. A horrible thought struck me. Perhaps this was some sort of divine retribution for all my lofty ambition. Maybe now I would simply have to come to terms with my ineptitude.

By the time Betty Astell had broken through my self-indulgent reverie and called me on to the stage, I had begun to search for an excuse that would let me off the hook. But when I walked out on to the bright stage, I felt that other Alida stir within me. Besides, I could never live with the uncertainty of my current status. I was not sure that I was all that good, but I was not certain that I was all that bad, either. I was not asked to do much at all, just a few pirouettes and jumps, and much to my amazement the Fletchers offered me the position of principal dancer.

With the promise of a future salary packet tucked up my sleeve, I returned to London to organize a weekend in Amsterdam with my relations. The idea of this pilgrimage back to my father's birthplace had been in my mind ever since I landed in England. I hoped the trip would help me come to terms with a past that seemed only a figment of my imagination. If I could make those sepia images a little more tangible, then maybe I might also overcome my nightmares and bouts of war-related anxiety. At last I would have an opportunity to see my relations as three-dimensional people instead of those weak, composite identikits that I had tried to piece together from my parents' reminiscences.

I had not seen these particular relations since I was five, so I anticipated some difficulty in recognizing them when I arrived at the Central Station. But as soon as I stepped off the train I heard my name being called by a man running towards me, who I presumed must be my Uncle Sam. He smothered me with a bear hug, declaring in between kisses that he could not have failed to recognize me, because I was the image of my mother. 'Imagine how it felt', he told the others, 'to see the visage of Celien step off that train, looking just the same as she did twelve years ago'.

After only a few hours with Uncle Sam, Auntie Esther and their daughter Sonja, I felt as if I had known them all my life. Considering just how much they had suffered, this caring, loving family had shown remarkable resilience. Uncle Sam had survived Auschwitz to learn that he had lost his wife and children. Esther, his second wife, was the widow of one of my father's brothers, who had been killed in the war. Sonja, my father's niece, looked a Glasbeek to the core, her dark Sephardic features declaring her Portuguese Moorish ancestry.

Later, as I was driven through the streets of Marken, I felt as if I had once known the place quite intimately, and that in no time at all I would be finding my way around the town like a local. Yet the ghetto had effectively been erased. The narrow, cobbled streets had been widened into broad thoroughfares, and the tall terrace houses had been pulled down to make way for 'better housing'. I wandered along the modern boulevards and superimposed the image of those impossibly narrow, dirty streets, alive with the hustle and bustle of Jewish traders vending their wares from carts or barrows, haggling Jewish matriarchs, and mischievous street urchins playfully learning the art of survival from their elders. It wasn't hard to imagine the blend of aromas wafting through the doorways of the bakeries and delicatessens that once proliferated in this densely populated area. In the sidewalk cafés the notoriously gossip-hungry '*Amsterdamse Joden*' would gather to drink Bols or coffee, while the more energetic of them danced to the strains of the street organ.

Later that afternoon I stopped to linger in front of the Portuguese Synagogue where one of my uncles had been shot, along with hundreds of other Jewish men. Then, almost by gravitation, I found myself standing in front of the house where my father had lived as a boy, sharing a single room with ten other members of his family. The tall, narrow, three-storey house was the only terrace that had survived the town planners' passion for urban progress. There it was, defiant, triumphant. The failing light of the afternoon seemed only to accentuate the symbolism of this solitary building. *They* had tried to blot it all out, but in one sense my father had had the last word. The silhouetted outline thrilled me, but also sharpened my sense of bereavement. I burst into tears, while my uncle took photos of the house, which meant more to me than all the museums and galleries in the world.

Everyone I spoke to who had known my father and his family reminisced in glowing terms about the family's generosity, and also about all the boys' roguish exploits, which it seemed had become quite legendary. I was delighted to hear that my father had been quite a wild young lad in his day. I must say I had always suspected the twinkle in his eye when he had recounted tales about his life in Marken, but he had obviously censored his stories to ensure that his daughter's innocence remained untainted. This city and the stories of Dad's youthful exploits made me feel closer to him.

I would have loved to stay on and be pampered, but I was committed to another interview with Arnold Haskell at the Royal Ballet School, so it was back to the cold, impersonal ballet scene. The effects of the good life were, as always, far too evident. There was nothing else for it but an all-out war against all that upholstery that padded over my balletic line. Perversely, I felt quite relieved to be back within the rigidly structured lifestyle. I had long ago accepted that abjuring indulgence was a basic tenet of the ballet dancer's existence, and any lapse of self-control left me feeling so overcome with guilt that my pleasure was totally destroyed.

My weight increase was not due to careless gluttony, and so could not be rectified by a change of diet. Like so many other Australian dancers, I had found that my metabolism had been affected by the change of climate. I could not afford to wait for my body to adjust and settle down, so I panicked. Although I had reduced my food intake to little more than cottage cheese, yoghurt and liverwurst, I felt as if I was blowing up like a hot-air balloon. I sent urgent missives to my mother, requesting further supplies of laxatives, but my punitive measures served only to wreak a devastating effect on my morale and physical well-being. It was depressing to see other people gleefully tucking into apple tarts,

Mars bars, potatoes and even glorious white bread, yet remaining pencil thin, while I was soulfully starving, yet remaining a bloated colonial blob. How could I stretch my limbs out with confident, sensuous, feline grace when they were trapped in a cocoon of blubber? How could I look wistfully ethereal from within a doughnut-like countenance? I was earthbound, when all I wanted was to soar with the joyous abandon of the naturally thin.

Then the long-awaited telegram finally arrived from home, telling me to begin my travel arrangements for Moscow. The Bolshoi had written to my parents to say that I had been accepted for the following term. The good news threw me into a state of shock. My dreams were being realized, but why couldn't it all have happened when I was more prepared?

13

The Road to Moscow

After some investigation I discovered that the only way I could travel to Russia was on a tourist visa, though our correspondent in Russia assured me that I could easily change to a student's visa once I had made contact with the Russian Minister for Culture in Moscow. Then the tourist bureau informed me that I would have to stay in one of the registered tourist hotels, which were all de luxe and cost £12 a night. This information sent me into the depths of despair. Having got so far, I feared that Moscow would be out of the question after all. Then someone had a brainwave. Why didn't I join one of the cheap tours organized by Intourist, the official Russian agency? Once I had my foot in the door, I could renegotiate my visa and accommodation with the authorities. The Intourist package involved four to five days in Leningrad and Moscow. I knew it was risky, but I booked my fare.

As I had only a week to arrange my affairs, I was able to postpone those dreaded classes at the Royal. It was only a temporary reprieve, however; Mr Haskell insisted that I remain in contact with him while I was in Russia, and offered me a whole term of free tuition on my return.

The *Estonia* was a Russian ship with an all-Russian crew, and as soon as I boarded I knew that I had effectively left the sovereignty of Britain. The monotony of shipboard life soon saw me at my melancholic best. When I wasn't eating, sleeping or taking a brisk constitutional on deck, I wrote long-winded, sentimental letters to my mother. In my mind my mother had become almost superhuman, the protector of all frightened, over-ambitious adolescents like myself. All the stories of Communist brutality that I had conveniently ignored while dreaming

Packing to go to Russia, 1962

of the Bolshoi now sprang to mind with startling clarity, and I began to envisage coming to an untimely end in one of the salt mines of Siberia.

The food on board was sumptuous. It might have been easier to avoid the dining room if I had had more distractions, but I found myself spending rather too much time in the dining room, where I could at least strike up conversation with some of the passengers while I ate. I ate and talked, ate and talked, and in this unproductive fashion I managed somehow to while away the long daylight hours. Sascha, the ship's captain, appeared to take a fancy to me. I gave him some hilarious lessons in the current dance fad of the time, the Twist, after the more sedate passengers had retired to their beds.

On Thursday 18 August the ship docked at Riga, where we had the whole day to look around the city. Though I was told it had once been a very grand place, Riga in 1962 was dowdy and depressing. For the first time in my life I felt conspicuous in my well-cut clothing, though it was quite modest by Western standards. Everywhere we walked we were conscious of being observed at a distance, as if the people in the street were wary of making contact with foreigners. We wandered through the sludge along the potholed streets, doing our best to work up some enthusiasm about the formerly beautiful buildings, which were now in a dreadful state of disrepair.

The worst thing about Riga was its lack of colour and gaiety. The shop windows displayed the most utilitarian merchandise, and a range of fashions that would have looked out of date in the 1950s. Outside the food shops there were long, patient queues of sombre people, waiting to buy eggs or fruit and vegetables. The best produce was exported to the USSR, and eggs were considered luxury items. The sight of these people standing in the cold and rain filled me with pity and apprehension.

My experience of Riga left me in the depths of despair. Certain that I would never see my family again, I was overwhelmed by remorse. I wished that I had been a less demanding daughter, that I had shown my love for them more often, and that I hadn't been so self-centred. So strong was my sense of melodrama that I almost persuaded myself to jump overboard. But finally I succumbed to sleep. The next morning I found I had slept right through Sascha's farewell champagne breakfast.

At about 8 p.m. the lights of Leningrad loomed through a bleak, foggy night. Was every port of call going to give me such a dismal welcome? Our group was met by an Intourist guide, who took us to an opulent hotel. I was allocated a twin room with a pleasant Irish lady, and her delight at seeing this magnificent city for the first time quickly broke through my stubborn negativism. She had no forebodings whatsoever about this trip. With cameras slung over her shoulder, she dragged me out to see the unique beauty of Peter the Great's city, and much to my amazement it was a bright, crisp, sunlit morning.

This time I did have cause to gape in wonder. Peter the Great's window to the West was the epitome of eighteenth-century imperialistic splendour. The exquisitely proportioned Italianate buildings, the wide boulevards and canals, combined to create a spectacle of aesthetic perfection. Certainly the shops didn't display luxury goods, and we could see no sign of individual ostentation, but, by contrast with Riga, Leningrad was a model of hospitality.

Our group was taken in hand by an officious young lady who, as our guide and interpreter, warded off any provocative questions with skilful prevarication. I had to stifle my laughter when she explained why the young Stalin was depicted in a very large painting of the Revolution, on exhibition at the Hermitage. 'Yes, that is Stalin', she said, 'but shortly the painting will be removed to be repainted properly'.

I swallowed all the official diatribes with the enthusiasm and optimism of one still eager to acknowledge the existence of a socialist Utopia. The concept of altruistic self-sacrifice appealed to me enormously, and I readily accepted all the evidence of the sinful decadence of the Tsarist regime. The thought of 'gold plates for the few and starvation for the millions' was enough to make me condone the cramped living conditions, food queues and lack of luxury items. I sympathized with the ideal of an equal share of the wealth and an equal opportunity for all. Scrimping for the sake of the long-term future did not seem unreasonable to such a disciplined creature as myself.

The people of Leningrad had suffered enormously during the Second World War. As a result of the wartime losses there was a great shortage of male labour, and women had taken over many traditional male jobs. It was not uncommon to see chunky women dressed in overalls and head-scarves, wielding drills and jackhammers, or driving lorries and buses. As in Warsaw, the clouds of war still hung over the city. Numerous rebuilding projects were in progress, but there were still many untouched bomb sites and damaged buildings. The hatred of Germans was unanimous and unconditional. Here, as in Warsaw, it was not advisable to speak German.

I was completely taken in, and faithfully recorded all the propaganda that the Party machine dished out. But no amount of brainwashing could negate the artistic achievements of Tsarist Russia. No one could deny that the old regime had produced some of the world's greatest writers, composers, musicians, dancers, singers, painters and so on. How could a formerly aristocratic form of entertainment now be produced for a mass public? No one could feel proletarian passing through the doors of the magnificent Kirov Theatre. I really had to pinch myself to convince myself I was there.

As the curtain rose to reveal those elaborately costumed slim paragons of ballet refinement poised to dance amidst the most sumptuous sets I had ever laid eyes on, I could see that perhaps the blue-bloods had had the last laugh. Ballet in Russia was still a most aristocratic form of entertainment, and as I looked at the audience I realized that the proscenium arch separated two kinds of people in two very different kinds of worlds. Russians might spend their days preoccupied with earthy, pragmatic matters, but here in the theatre they could fulfil their desire for the exotic, and temporarily escape into a world of legitimate royalty. They had not lost their zest for lavish pageantry. And the performance quelled any doubts I might have had about studying in Russia. I just had to learn from the teachers who had produced the finest dancers in the world.

The next day I walked down the legendary 'Theatre Street' to the Kirov Ballet School, the school that had trained Pavlova, Nijinsky, Karsavina, Kesshinska, Ulanova and Balanchine, not forgetting choreographers such as Petipa, Fokine and Ivanov. Inside the Maryinsky School, the corridors were filled with romping boys and girls, dressed in the charming uniforms first designed for the old Imperial Ballet School. As I passed by with my interpreter the children stopped to curtsy, then continued their robust games. Clearly those children did not share my reverence for these hallowed halls. Everywhere there was healthy light-hearted noise and chatter. Everyone seemed surprisingly normal, in marked contrast to the prigs at Barons Court.

I watched a mixed fifth-year class, a class of boys in their final year, and finally a class of ten-year-olds commencing their first year of ballet. The seniors were so close to perfection that their flaws could only be described as endearing idiosyncrasies. Dressed in their pink chiffon tunics, the girls were like magical sprites, soaring and spinning as if being airborne were natural, while the boys exuded a sensual but powerful grace. In Australia we would be lucky to find two or three men in a class, but here there were at least fourteen handsome young men working at the barre with delicious virility and vigour.

The ten-year-old class absolutely floored me. Never before had I seen an entire class of juniors so gifted. Although this was their first year of training, they already manifested all the elegance and stature of the fully fledged principal dancer. The children in this class were the fortunate few, chosen from the thousands of young hopefuls who came to audition every year. It was not enough to arrive at the Kirov with aspirations to grace and greatness; one had to possess all the prerequisites before one could put a foot in the studio door.

Once students were chosen, however, conditions at the academy were surprisingly relaxed. I had expected to see a strongly disciplined class conducted by humourless teachers, each equipped with a rod to beat out the rhythm or rap the occasional lagging foot. But I found that the rapport between the teacher and pupils was one of gentle and respectful co-operation. There were no harsh directives or intimidatory measures. The teachers seemed to expect the students to understand the responsibility they owed to themselves. Clearly the Kirov did not wish to train martinets but thinking artists. The students responded enthusiastically, and appeared to enjoy the challenges presented throughout the class.

One of the girls in the senior class was obviously off-colour. After the traditional curtsy, she asked to be excused, explaining that she did not feel well enough to concentrate. The teacher agreed immediately, and warmly put her arm on the student's shoulder. 'Go home and relax', she said. 'Read a book, or have a bath. Come back when you are fresh and well. Classes are of no benefit if you cannot concentrate.' I was amazed by this humane approach, which contrasted so starkly with Madame Borovansky's code of moral and physical flagellation.

The journey to Moscow was long and uncomfortable. After seven hours in a cramped and dirty train it was a disgruntled group that trundled into the lobby of the Hotel Baltchuk. All we wanted was a shower, a hot drink and bed. But in Russia at that time performing one's ablutions was not a simple matter. The hotel plumbing had obviously not benefited one iota from the People's Revolution, and often did not work at all. There were no plugs in the baths or sinks, and soft toilet paper had yet to make its way on to the Russian market.

I had been warned, and had come prepared with a survival kit of my own, to the envy of many of my companions. If I had been more commercially minded I could have made a great deal of money by selling some of these commodities on the black market. Everywhere we went we were approached by Russians from all walks of life, offering us huge sums of money for items that we in the West took for granted. There was no denying the inadequacies of the Russian standard of living. Still, it annoyed me to hear some members of our tourist group constantly criticizing the lack of modern facilities and the dowdiness of the shops and streetscape. I preferred to believe that the Russians could see beyond the tinsel trappings of commercialism. Perhaps I also hoped that they had succeeded in vanquishing the evils of greed and war.

While the other women in my group were haggling with the bathroom attendant to get a piece of soap, I went and stood before my bedroom window, which overlooked Red Square. I could see the red star twinkling omnipotently from the highest turret of the Kremlin, and in the gloom of the night I could just make out the onion domes of St Basil's Cathedral. A warm feeling coursed through my body. So far, so good. I had arrived in one piece, ready to commence my studies at the greatest school in the world.

All the next day I listened attentively to the patter of our well-rehearsed guide. Although her country still had a great deal to work towards, she said, a great deal had already been achieved in the way of full employment, free health care and education, and proper care of the aged and infirm. As we walked around the University, which was built in the wedding-cake style that seemed to be the most popular architecture of post-war Russia, I scribbled down the trivia that our devoted interpreter fed us—world-shattering details such as the fact that this monstrous university took four years to build, and that a building was erected every minute in Moscow. I must have been a propagandist's delight.

Everywhere we went people seemed to be reading hard-cover books, and even the ice-cream vendor at the street corner had her head buried in a Tolstoy. Our interpreter was quick to explain that literature and musical recordings were cheap and readily available. Wasn't this better than making seven hundred brands of lipstick? It was hard to argue.

Whereas Leningrad was decidedly European in character, Moscow was a more multicultural city. People from Uzbekistan, Georgia and Turkestan added a spattering of colour to a rather sombre city. Apart from the marvellous onion-domed churches, the stolid architecture was in direct contrast to the deliberate aestheticism of Leningrad. As in Riga, vast areas of Moscow were run down, with potholed streets and footpaths, lacklustre shops and dilapidated apartment blocks. The gloominess was exacerbated by the sheer number of people who teemed through the streets. The greatest luxury in Moscow was privacy, for there seemed to be no respite from crowds, not even in the home, where two or three families often shared one apartment.

The underground stations were magnificent. As we travelled down the escalators we passed an array of mosaics, paintings, murals and sculptures, all exhibited in glorious marble surrounds. In spite of all the impressive statistics, however, the omnipresence of Lenin's impassive gaze was beginning to get on my nerves. Even in the underground station, poorly executed images of the founder of the Soviet Union were draped tastelessly all over the place. From time to time we noticed rectangles of clean paint along stretches of wall that had otherwise been mellowed by time. When our guide was asked about these pristine spaces, she blushed and hurriedly explained that Stalin's pictures had once hung there, but had been removed.

At last we came to Terpsichore's temple, the Bolshoi Theatre. The building was quite as imposing as I had hoped, though it had not escaped the current fad for kitsch iconography. This time Lenin and Gagarin were joined by the precursor of it all, Karl Marx, but even this boring trio could not deter me. I gazed in wonderment at the object of my pilgrimage.

14

At the Bolshoi

The next day I contacted Pyotr Spitalni and his wife Nina, who had met some Australian friends of mine during the Moscow Festival. Fortunately the Spitalnis spoke German, so I managed to communicate with them reasonably well. They invited me to have lunch at their home. The Spitalnis were no average family, for Mr Spitalni was a professor of conducting at the Conservatorium. But, seeing the cramped quarters in which he and his family lived, I wondered how poorer people were housed. The couple, with Nina's mother and their son Yuri, an engineer, occupied two rooms in a flat that was shared with another family of four. The bathroom and kitchen facilities were communal. Yuri and Grandma slept in one bedroom and Pyotr and Nina slept in the other room, which was the living room by day. It was a spacious room with a magnificent parquet floor, but that is where the luxury began and ended. The Spitalnis seemed to be a very warm family, and I was reassured when they offered to help me while I was in Moscow in any way they could.

The next day, as planned, I went to Friendship House to arrange a meeting with the Russian representative of the Soviet-Australian Friendship Society, Nellie Maslova, who was expected to take over from there. Pyotr Spitalni accompanied me, which was just as well. Nellie Maslova was on vacation, and no one in the place had any notion who I was, nor of any arrangements for me at the Bolshoi school. Though I could not understand a word of the conversation, I could tell that something was wrong. There were too many *nyets* and shrugs for my liking.

An austere-looking dowager explained that there was no possibility of my being accepted at the school. I was too old to begin training there, and I would require a personal interpreter, which was far too expensive for them to contemplate. This was the ultimate blow. Who could I turn to now? What a joke, I thought. I had gone away in order to study, and now I was stranded in this totalitarian state alone and almost out of money.

I dug my heels in. If I couldn't participate in classes, then I would sit and watch them; not even the Russian dowager at Friendship House could object to that. Though it would be a sad compromise, I could still learn a great deal by observing the teaching methods. I was loath to return home without something to show for my Russian experience. I decided to go to the Australian Embassy and seek an extension to my visa.

At the embassy my reception was even more frigid than at Friendship House. The Australian staff treated me as if I were a spy. They couldn't, or wouldn't, understand my reason for wanting to stay in this country. Again my motives for choosing the Bolshoi rather than the Royal Ballet were questioned. Finally they made it quite clear that they would not condone an extension of my visa. A Russo-English dictionary was thrust into my hand, and I was tersely shown to the door.

My mind was full of fear, defiance and confusion. Even if I did manage to stay, how in the world would I communicate with the Russians? The language posed no end of difficulties; in most European countries I had managed to detect quite a few familiar words, but here it was all gobbledegook. I also couldn't be sure that my hotel room would still be available after the rest of the Intourist group had departed. And whatever I did, I only had money for one more month, either in Moscow or in London.

Alone in my hotel room, I bemoaned my rotten luck. I don't think it would have been possible to feel more isolated than I did at that moment. Letters to Russia from Australia sometimes took weeks or even months to arrive, so I had to make the hardest decision of my life on my own. It would have been far more sensible to return to London with the other Intourist members, but I decided to stay put, and hang the consequences.

My fellow travellers thought I had gone mad, and begged me to return with them. Frankly I would have given my right arm to do just that. The prospect of staying behind, on what most people construed as enemy territory, was terrifying. While I had been touring with the group I felt reasonably secure, but once I cut myself adrift, who knew what might happen? Yet I could not go. With a heavy heart I watched the Intourist bus, my last link with the familiar, disappear over the horizon. After I had limply waved away the last exhaust fumes, I returned to my room and stared out at the cold, grey stone bastions surmounting Red Square. It all seemed a great deal less romantic now. In just a few days I would become an illegal immigrant.

I decided to find someone who spoke English, and glumly walked the hotel passageways muttering 'Bolshoi, Bolshoi', in the hope that some kind *mamushka* would find an official from the Bolshoi Theatre who would take pity on me. The kindly charladies raised their eyebrows and shrugged their shoulders. They did their utmost to extract more information out of me by plying me with a babble of quizzical Russian. They must have thought me quite demented, and they were obviously perplexed as to why I was still in the hotel when my bus had departed.

A couple of days later I learnt why the magic word had not opened any doors for me. 'Bolshoi' simply means 'big' or 'grand'. No wonder the charladies had been so confused!

Staring at four inanimate walls was not going to help me stay sane. I went out, partly in search of the reassurance of being among other members of the human race, and partly in search of food. Anyone who has been faced with the task of shopping in Moscow can be guaranteed never to take capitalism for granted again. Simply buying a jar of yoghurt was a preposterously complicated business. Each shop had long queues, and people sometimes spent hours in line waiting to purchase substandard products. First there was the queue to inspect the merchandise; then, once you had decided what you wished to purchase, you went to another queue to buy a ticket for the said article. You might think that would be the end of it, but there was a third stage, yet another queue, from which customers finally emerged with their paltry pockmarked apples or watered-down milk.

Later I learnt that bribery and corruption were an accepted part of daily life. If one wanted better than the standard government fare, it was necessary to slip a little money under the counter, or offer to exchange favours in kind, or exercise one's position of authority. Housewives were in a constant quandary as they tried to find ways of purchasing meat that wasn't all gristle and bones, undiluted milk and fruit that was fit for the dining table. It even required a bribe to obtain anything better than a pudding-bowl haircut. Wealthier Muscovites were prepared to pay huge sums of money for Western items, which quickly became status symbols.

I wandered around the congested streets for some time, but my expedition outdoors did nothing to cheer me up. Everything and everyone looked so depressing. A heartfelt weep would have been some consolation, but I had no shoulder to cry on, and the tears simply dripped out with monotonous regularity. In this mood I went back to the Baltchuk, flopped down on the bed in my little room, and looked gratefully over my familiar belongings, which I had already managed to strew right around the room. I must have lain there for twenty minutes before I noticed a small parcel lying on top of the pillow. When I opened it up and found a piece of cake, I burst into tears. The unexpected gesture of kindness was more than I could cope with. Someone cared. Indeed, it transpired, someone cared enough to leave a small piece of food for me every day. It seemed that one of the *mamushkas* had taken pity on this reckless little fool.

The next day, true to his word, Mr Spitalni arrived to take me to the Bolshoi School to watch a class. I was received most courteously by one of the Bolshoi teachers, who escorted me around the entire building, and then invited me to watch any classes I wished. The standard of the teachers and students was impeccable, but I could take little pleasure from such vicarious participation. My dejection was deepened by the knowledge that these teachers were the only people I trusted to give me the solid technical foundation I so longed for, and to assess me impartially, without exploiting me or pandering to my fluctuating ego. Now I would never know if I had been fooling myself all these years.

At the end of the day I thanked the teachers for their hospitality and returned to my hotel to prepare for another lonely, sleepless night. The last few nights had been absolute misery. My pain was not only emotional. The days of inactivity had made me feel conscious of my lack of physical condition. Certain that my silhouette must have expanded tenfold, I had put my body through the third degree. I increased my dosage of Duralax, and the consequent intestinal pain, which usually climaxed at night, was so agonizing that, had I not been so insanely obsessive, I think I should have passed out altogether. Sharp paralysing pains shot up from my coccyx through my spine like poisonous arrows, and my abdominal muscles contorted violently in their desperate bid to push that dreaded food out. The repeated trips from my room to the toilets, which were at the end of a long corridor, did not leave me much time for sleep. I felt totally at odds with myself; nothing seemed to be working.

And then, some hope! The next day the director of the Bolshoi School suggested that there might be a possibility of my doing classes with the company.

Accompanied by the kind Mr Spitalni, I walked through the stage door. I was in, backstage at the Bolshoi, with the familiar odour of greasepaint, resin and sweat drifting into my nostrils. Everything would be OK now. I was at home.

A tiny blonde lady tapped me on the shoulder and asked in perfect English if I had somewhere to change into my practice clothes. 'No', I said nervously. 'Well, please share my dressing room', she suggested sweetly, and before I could say anything she took my hand and led me through a maze of corridors, where a veritable army of *mamushkas* seemed to be sweeping and polishing. Breathlessly Mr Spitalni caught up with us and whispered: 'That lady is Olga Lepeshinskaya'. This information bowled me over. Olga Lepeshinskaya, the famous Russian *prima ballerina assoluta,* was concerning herself about me, an insignificant little student!

Olga Lepeshinskaya and virile attendants in the Bolshoi's *Walpurgisnacht*

We went up a few storeys in an elevator, and finally I was ushered into a large plush dressing room. 'You can use that dressing table', Lepeshinskaya said, pointing to one of two dressing tables, 'and if you are tired, have a little rest on the settee over there. You have half an hour before class commences'.

Later I was taken to an enormous studio that seemed to contain acres of full-blooded Russian men. Lepeshinskaya explained that I had arrived too late for the women's class, but I could do the men's class. After I had found the resolve to drag my eyes away from the array of masculinity, I noticed that some other females had come to attend the male class. To my joy I was able to recognize all of them: Raissa Struchkova, Ryabinkina and Karelskaya. There were a few familiar faces among the men, too. I recognized Tichonov and (the floor almost fell away from under my feet) Gennady Lediakh, the object of my adolescent passion. 'Miss Australi!' he yelled, with obvious delight. 'What are you doing here?' He ran over and enveloped me in a hug that sent my heart fluttering. 'Come along with me, you must stand here', he said, escorting me to the head of the barre, where I would be embarrassingly conspicuous. Then, seeing my discomfort, he whispered, 'Don't worry, just follow me'. Suddenly I lost all sensation in my body. I can't remember much about that class at all, save that I managed to stumble through to the end with, I suspect, more than a little help from my friends.

I had few problems following classroom instructions, as I could recognize the French names of the steps, and the rest was easy enough to pick up from the teacher's demonstrations. On several occasions I was corrected in German and smatterings of English. At the end of the class, Lepeshinskaya took me aside for ten minutes' extra work and a little pep talk about things she felt I needed to concentrate on. It wasn't until I returned to the dressing room that the penny finally dropped: for the last hour or so I had been auditioning for the chance of my lifetime. I was so numb with fear that I didn't have a clue whether I had succeeded or failed.

Later, back in civvies, I saw Pyotr Spitalni and Lepeshinskaya engaged in deep conversation. I hung back in the dressing-room doorway as discreetly as possible until Lepeshinskaya walked away. 'Well?' I asked, walking up to Pyotr. He planted a warm kiss on my cheek. 'You have won a great privilege, Alida', he said. 'You are in. You may do classes with the Bolshoi Company.' Apparently Lepeshinskaya had told Pyotr she thought I was extremely talented. She had noticed some faults, but she was prepared to work on them with me.

I was made an honorary member of the Bolshoi Company, and I was given my own pass card with my photo on it. This pass gave me the right to enter the Theatre whenever I wished, just like any other member of the Company, and it also gave me an entrée to any performance of opera or ballet I wished to attend. But my Jewish pessimism could not allow me to enjoy this happiness without reservation; after all, every silver lining has its black cloud.

Later in the day, Lepeshinskaya and the Director of the Bolshoi explained the details of my study period. I was offered free classes with the company, but I would have to pay for my own living expenses. I immediately sent a telegram to my family to announce the news. My parents cabled back telling me to stay at all costs, but it was my brother's two-word message—'Proud puss'—that made me the happiest person in the world.

That night I arrived at the stage door brandishing my Bolshoi pass, and stayed to watch the opera *War and Peace*. From my seat in the logue (a place usually reserved for directors) I savoured the experience of being able to look down at the common folk in the stalls. My arrogance may have been at odds with my support for the socialist cause, but I couldn't help feeling as proud as punch—the more so when I noticed the plebs star-spotting along the boxes reserved for VIPs and members of staff.

I can't say I enjoyed the opera, but I had to give the production full marks. The attention to realism was particularly impressive. I saw crowd scenes with old and young people, children, midgets, even

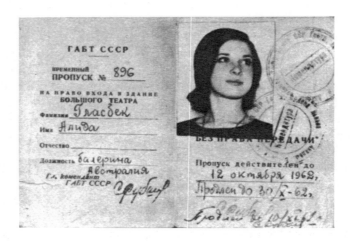

Alida's prized Bolshoi pass

animals, the whole spectrum of any city's inhabitants, rather than the usual farcical characterization attempts we were used to in the West.

The following morning I took my first class with Madame Gerdt, who was going to be my main teacher at the Bolshoi. The other dancers said I was extremely fortunate to have her, as she was one of Russia's foremost teachers. I was still nervous, but the aristocratic, elegant Madame Gerdt soon put me at ease. She paid me close attention, and spoke gently to me in German whenever she felt a correction was necessary. It was obvious that she was adored and respected by all. Everyone worked like a Trojan without any harsh reprimands or temperamental outbursts from Madame. All the classes were strictly one hour long, but it was one hour of concentrated slog. I couldn't believe how quickly the time passed. There was no need to watch the clock, as I had so often done back home.

Madame Gerdt gave me a short private lesson after the company had left the studio. She was extremely complimentary about my dancing, and told me that she would personally advise the Minister for Culture to extend my visa for as long as possible. So when I finally got to meet Nellie Maslova, the Soviet-Australian Friendship Society's representative, I was greeted with good news. Madame Gerdt had indeed pressed my case, and my passport was stamped accordingly. Henceforth my visa was extended from week to week, and every time I looked at that stamp my heart filled with gratitude.

The Spitalnis also suggested a financial arrangement that was mutually beneficial, and would enable me to stay on indefinitely. Given the unfavourable rate of exchange from sterling into roubles, they offered to pay for all my living costs, excluding my hotel room. In return, after I returned to the West I would buy various goods they wanted that were unobtainable in Russia. Money was obviously no problem to the Spitalnis. They had achieved status and a respectable standard of living, and now Nina, in particular, wanted the icing on the cake, which meant luxury imported goods. It seemed a neat little arrangement, but in the long run I began to suspect that Nina had not befriended me out of any altruistic desire to help, but rather to acquire a pawn in her elaborate scheme to acquire the material goods she coveted. Pyotr Spitalni, on the other hand, was a lovely man, and most enjoyable company. I suspect he went along with his wife's scheme to humour her, or perhaps to buy a little marital harmony.

Like most other Russians I met, the Spitalnis assumed that nearly all Australians were wealthy. Nina jumped to the conclusion that I would have no difficulty replacing the things I had packed into my suitcase. In the first week I felt quite happy to pass on my mascara, stockings and woollen jumpers. I was so grateful that I would have taken the clothes off my back to repay them. But, as time went by, I realized that Nina was out to get everything she could for her husband, her son and herself. Her callousness towards her aged mother shocked me. When I asked what I should send Grandma, Nina replied, 'Oh, don't bother about her, she is too old'. I was obliged to eat as many meals as possible at the Spitalnis' apartment, where Grandma was always excluded from the dinner table. I had to suppress my resentment towards Nina. We were fellow conspirators; our needs were interdependent. And, having been given a ticket to heaven, I was prepared to make compromises to keep it.

Within the walls of the Bolshoi the dancers lived incredibly privileged lives, much as the nobility might have done in the days of the Tsars. The Bolshoi theatre was like a small semi-autonomous city within a city, with its own restaurants, medical clinics, masseurs, hairdressers, costume and shoe factories. Even the quality of the food was vastly superior to that in the shops outside. The Party, however, was still the ultimate arbiter of status, progress and privilege, and to get on in the ballet it was necessary to toe the Party line and remain loyal to the Soviet state.

The Bolshoi company was one of the few Soviet artistic showcases on exhibit to the outside world, and the dancers were able to visit Western countries that remained out of bounds to the rest of the Russian population. The company members always travelled abroad under the watchful eyes of a manager or senior dancer, in case any of the dancers succumbed to the temptations of the West.

Other Russians seemed to accept that dancers and other members of the élite enjoyed perks and privileges not available to them. 'Ah, but she is an honoured artist of the USSR!' Nina would say, explaining away a prima ballerina's mink coat, Dior shoes and handbag. Indeed the fact that dancers wore the latest in European *haute couture*, smoked American cigarettes and brought back transistors from abroad only seemed to enhance their standing.

Nina Spitalni was not alone in her almost obsessive desire to acquire Western goods. Many young people would offer several weeks' salary for a pair of jeans or a copy of Nabokov's banned *Lolita*. Some of the university students I met told me about their clandestine jam sessions playing Western pop music in their rooms. Yuri Spitalni had a collection of tapes, pirated from Voice of America programmes featuring Frank Sinatra, Dean Martin and other crooners. I was being made increasingly aware that Russia had its own 'decadent', capitalist-inspired subculture, but I tried not to see the cracks in the social fabric of this place that had been my source of inspiration for so long.

Russian dancers were far more affluent than their Western counterparts, and they were looked after by the state for their entire lives, with handsome pensions and country *dachas* to retire to after their dancing days were over. Most of the principal dancers only danced a few times a month, so it was far easier for them to have a normal family life than for the nomads of the Western ballet companies. I was surprised by the large number of married couples in the Bolshoi. Whereas in the West constant touring, low salaries and the lack of heterosexual men made happy matrimony within the profession almost impossible, here in Moscow the dancers appeared eminently content and well-adjusted people.

I wrote home glowing reports of life at the Bolshoi, for as far as I was concerned the Bolshoi was the happiest place I had ever trained in. I had never felt such a complete sense of satisfaction from my work before. People like Madame Gerdt seemed to respect me without my having to resort to guile. I was at last able to discard my tired old bag of tricks and disguises, while I knuckled down to some real work. It was refreshing to work among unpretentious people, free of theatrical affectations or overt bitchy rivalry. I thrived in this atmosphere, and my head and body experienced a rare period of harmony.

One day Nellie Maslova called to tell me that, as Madame Gerdt was so happy with my work, I would be permitted to continue my studies at the Bolshoi for at least another month, and Madame hoped that my visa could be extended for as long as two years. I was elated. I was beginning to feel more at home in Moscow. Under its austere exterior, Moscow had a much softer and friendlier heart. Each day as I walked through the morning mist on my route past the Kremlin to the Bolshoi, I felt a little closer to understanding that enigmatic quality that the Russians identify as Russianness, or *Rodina*, an almost untranslatable word that encapsulates the primeval love and attachment that most Russians have for their motherland.

It was now October, and the stark grey outline of the Kremlin was softened by a rich autumnal glow. I was beginning to sketch in the human details of the vibrant society that lived in all the busy little sidestreets and laneways of the city, and some of the people I passed regularly began to greet me with smiles of recognition. When the snows finally started at the end of October, Moscow was transformed into a winter wonderland. Carefully swathed in numerous layers of warm clothing, I walked through the white streets, enthralled by my first glimpse of real snow.

The air was cold and dry, and I found the atmosphere invigorating. The onset of winter also introduced me to the ice-cream and hot-grog vendors who seemed to operate on most street corners, apparently quite oblivious to the seasons. I had not noticed them before, but now the sight of hundreds of Muscovites licking ice-cream in sub-zero temperatures appeared rather bizarre—as bizarre as the sale of the potent hot grog.

When one of my male friends from the Bolshoi persuaded me to taste this unique Russian concoction, the liquid hit my stomach like a fireball and I nearly passed out on the street. As my friend helped me to stagger along the rest of the way, I had to admit I felt considerably warmer. On another occasion I was taught how to drink vodka the Russian way, with disastrous results. 'Look, I show', Tichonov had laughed. 'It's—how you say?—down the hatch?' and he swallowed the contents of the glass in one gulp. 'Then you must eat a little of this black bread before you begin again. Hup, down the hatch.' I did exactly as I was bidden. After scoffing several glasses I passed out, and had to have my stomach pumped out at the Bolshoi clinic.

I also visited Moscow University, where I made friends with English and US exchange students. I had met one exchange student, an Oxford scholar named Tony, on the *Estonia*. In spite of the Spitalnis' disapproval, I kept up my friendship with him in Moscow. One night I was invited to a students' party at the university. As I didn't have a pass, I had to be smuggled in under Tony's huge tweed overcoat. The British students shared their living quarters with African, Algerian and Cuban students, and Tony told me that there was quite a lot of friction. It was quite a party. The English students had obviously come to Moscow prepared, and had also used their vacations as a chance to stock up on Marmite, Kleenex tissues, Nescafé, Scotch, and a host of other items that were unobtainable in Moscow. At about 4 a.m. I tiptoed past the concierge with a girl from the British Embassy, both of us looking the worse for wear. It was a dishevelled and sorry Alida who finally fell into bed.

On the whole, life in Moscow rolled on harmoniously. I visited numerous theatres, art galleries and folk-dancing exhibitions, and was also fortunate enough to see a wonderful production of *Esmeralda* at the Stanislavsky Theatre. After the performance I was taken backstage to meet Vladimir Bourmeister, the internationally respected choreographer and ballet director, who asked me along to watch some of their company classes. And naturally I attended as many Bolshoi performances as possible.

Madame Gerdt and Madame Lepeshinskaya couldn't have been more generous. Almost every day I would return to the dressing room to find that Lepeshinskaya had placed a bar of American chocolate, some first-class caviar or a pair of *pointe* shoes on my dressing table. By far the most valuable gift, however, was the hours of private attention bestowed upon me by my mentor, Madame Gerdt. Each day she would help me correct any flaws she had picked up in the preceding class, or teach me the Bolshoi version of Kitri's variations from *Don Quixote*.

The Bolshoi production of *Don Quixote* was gargantuan, with live horses strutting around among totally realistic crowd scenes. For the gipsy scenes the stage was filled with smouldering, sensual, full-bodied men and women, looking every bit the ribald bohemians they were supposed to be portraying. I was enthralled with the diamond brilliance of all the dancers, but it was Bogomolova who shone out as the most exotic jewel of all. Her technical impeccability was combined with a sparkling vivacity, making her a perfect Kitri.

Madame Gerdt thought the role would also suit me, and suggested that I learn Kitri's solo and *pas de deux* for my graduation performance on the Bolshoi stage. Nothing had been mentioned about a graduation performance before. To make all this even more implausible, Gennady Lediakh asked me if I would like to dance the *Nutcracker pas de deux* with him. What a question! I was being asked to dance with one of the greatest male dancers of the time. Lediakh and I rehearsed daily, with Struchkova, Lepeshinskaya and Ryabinkina helping me whenever they could. The date was set, but then Lediakh became ill and our performance was cancelled.

The Bolshoi women appeared disconcertingly relaxed about their diet. It seemed they ate like horses. They maintained that a dancer had to eat heartily to obtain enough energy for such a strenuous occupation. I was amazed to see them carrying around huge chunks of dark chocolate, which were part of their personal survival kits, transported from studio to studio. I knew that I could never support such recklessness. This was one lesson the Russians could keep entirely to themselves.

Instead I agonized about the stodgy fare I was served by Nina. Dinner time was like a scene out of Grimm's fairy tales, with Nina serving meaty soup bones to her family, while I had to make do with gristle. Eventually the scarcity of fresh fruit, fresh vegetables and lean meat did have an adverse effect on my health, and of course I became convinced that I was horrendously overweight. When I had my pink chiffon tunic made at the Bolshoi factory, however, the dressmaker told me that I had the smallest waist she had ever measured.

In the Bolshoi tunic

I was excited about acquiring a genuine Bolshoi tunic. When I put it on it seemed to give me inspiration. The chiffon drifted behind me like the wings of a butterfly in full flight. Swathed inside all that flowing chiffon, I felt that I had been invested with the spirit of the dance. The tunic definitely had far more feminine allure and artistic accountability than the stark, revealing leotard.

After about six weeks in Russia I finally received my first letters from home. They were delivered to me in a little bundle, neatly secured with an elastic band. No effort had been made to conceal the fact that they had been intercepted, opened and read. This invasion of my privacy left me feeling disturbed. My relationship with my parents had always been inviolate, and now some petty official was eavesdropping on my private confessions. Forewarned, my mother had written only of family matters or unpoliticizable banalities. Although my parents did not linger too much on just how much they were missing me, I could read between the lines.

I sensed that my mother would master her emotions somehow, but for my father it was all very difficult indeed. When I read his laboriously written letter, I blinked away my tears.

'We are here if you need anything at all', he wrote. 'To whom else should you turn for help but your parents? Popje, if the world does not treat you too kindly, be sure to come where you can relax and live a happy life, gekussed papa.'

15

On the Tightrope

My temporary visitor's visa continued to be extended from week to week. It looked as if these extensions might go on indefinitely, but then the Cuban missile crisis intervened. It seemed that if a third world war was about to break out. I shall never forget the gloom that descended on Moscow. People met in nervous little groups to debate the probability of a war. Ashen-faced men and women of all ages sat in the shabby cafés waiting for the latest broadcast. I could not think of the people around me as enemies. There was no doubt in my mind that the Russian people genuinely wanted peace. I could feel the fear building up in the streets.

Most of the Russians I met seemed just as sceptical about their government's policies as my friends back home, and most of my friends at the Bolshoi were not members of the Communist Party. A large section of the population seemed to accept the regime as a *fait accompli*, and learnt to be taciturn, cautious and passive in public, reserving their true feelings for their private lives.

I found myself absolutely incapable of taking sides. Had I read those dramatic headlines over breakfast at home in Australia, I might have found it easier to apportion blame, and might even have toyed with the hope that the goodies would quickly thrash the baddies. Now all that had changed. Living in Moscow, and having made many Russian friends, I could not possibly wish any of them ill.

But the fact remained that I was an alien in a country that was preparing itself for a possible war with America and her allies. I was gripped by panic. Reluctantly I contacted the Australian Embassy to ask them if they would keep me informed and advise me what to do if the worst happened, but the staff were no more inclined to help than before. In low spirits I walked out of the embassy to meet Mr Spitalni, who had refused to come right up to the gates of the building, preferring to wait inconspicuously on another street corner.

An English student from the university told the British Embassy about my predicament, and they were far more helpful. They rang daily, and when Kennedy ordered the US Navy to blockade the Russian ships the British Embassy advised me to contact my own embassy as soon as possible. The Aussies told me that Australian–Soviet relations had never been worse. Canberra had recently expelled Skripov, a Russian diplomat, and it now seemed likely that Australia's closest ally would go to war with Russia. I was advised to leave at once. The soundness of this advice was confirmed by the display of Soviet military might at the October Revolution celebrations. As a foreigner, I was placed with an array of foreign and Soviet dignitaries in a cordoned area right outside the Kremlin, where I had a superb view of the passing parade, and also of Khrushchev and his Politburo standing on the official dais to review their war machinery. The glinting grey tanks, artillery and missiles were followed by endless columns of khaki soldiers. I panicked. For the first time I realized that the military were on almost every street corner.

I was definitely no heroine, and had no desire to die for my art, which after all required me to be alive and kicking. I was terrified of being trapped in the USSR in the event of a war. I was also aware that I was doubly disadvantaged by being Jewish, as Russian governments past and present had a history of violations against Jews. My greatest fear was that I would simply disappear. All my hopes for a long period of study at the Bolshoi seemed to have been dashed. I had no alternative but to leave.

I was heartbroken at leaving the Bolshoi, but I expected my exile to be temporary, as I was determined to return as soon as things had calmed down. Madame Gerdt and Lepeshinskaya suggested that I try some other means of getting a visa next time, so that I would be assured of staying on for two years, culminating in a special graduation performance on the Bolshoi stage.

By now I only had enough money left to pay for my return fare to London, and I decided to stay there for a time. Although I would have loved to see my parents, they would have had to borrow the money to pay for my fare home, which would mean I was home for good. I felt my dance education had just begun, and I was desperate to keep the impetus going. Besides, London would be a better place to arrange my return to Russia, as it was geographically closer. I also had a contract with the Fletchers to do that dreaded pantomime, and the money I earned there would stave off pauperism over the Christmas period at least. My relations in Amsterdam generously agreed to take me under their wing until rehearsals started in late November.

Madame Gerdt was quite shocked when she heard I was going to London. She thought of England as a country full of workhouses and starving waifs, and, more realistically, she had also heard that there were thousands of unemployed dancers there. I too was nervous about having to leave the cosy sanctuary of the Bolshoi theatre for the world of free enterprise.

Both Gerdt and Lepeshinskaya wrote me beautiful letters of recommendation stating that, with correct tuition and careful guidance, I would become a great artist. Lepeshinskaya also wrote to Arnold Haskell to ask him to take good care of me. Armed with these credentials I felt a little more optimistic about being able to stand on my own feet. I bade Moscow and all my friends a warm goodbye, and refused even to think of not returning.

The train journey was tedious to say the least. The view passing through East Germany was decidedly bleak, so much so that when the train finally crossed into the Western bloc I nearly cried with relief at my first sight of a neon-lit Coca-Cola billboard. Ah, sweet decadence!

On my arrival in Amersfoort the Dutch customs officials demanded that I pay for my suitcases in guilder. When I tried to explain that I had no Dutch currency, one of the officials burst into a tirade of abuse. He was obviously adamantly anti-Communist, and raged on about my Russian trip with such ferocity that I burst into tears and almost missed my connection to Amsterdam.

The boredom of train travel had driven me to indulge in that most destructive pastime, eating. When I wasn't being frenetically worked by some unbending overlord, I seemed bent on my own destruction. I downed every one of Nina's thickly sliced, heavily buttered rye-bread sandwiches. When I disembarked in Amsterdam and my Auntie Esther and Uncle Sam said how well I looked, my heart sank into my boots.

My aunt and uncle showered me with near-lethal doses of familial affection. I'm sure they considered me a bit of an oddball, but they were chuffed to be able to exhibit this relation who had popped up out of the blue, this *Wunderkind* who could claim a fair degree of public recognition for her 'artistic' talent. But after a while the aimlessness of holidaying started to pall for me, and I became worried at my bonny appearance. I arranged to attend some classes at the Stadtsschouwberg, hoping that I might be spared the indignity of having to roll into the classroom like a tub. To my surprise Sonia Gaskell, the director of the National Ballet Company, offered me a position as a soloist. I was nearly persuaded to stay—Geneva and Monaco certainly sounded far more alluring than Croydon!—but I was under contract to Cyril Fletcher's pantomime, and I was optimistic about returning to Moscow early next year.

So it was back to London. Soon I was ferrying between Maida Vale, where the Fealdmans once again took me in, and the cave-like Ashcroft Theatre to rehearse my paces as the leading dancer in the Sleeping Beauty pantomime. Cyril Fletcher and his wife were the indisputable stars of this tawdry comedy, and for show after show the rest of the cast was subjected to Cyril's excruciatingly unfunny routine of the fairy with the flat feet. After one had sniggered at the hairy legs protruding beneath his tulle costume and the fey waving of his tinsel wand, there was little left to laugh about.

I was told that the corny pantomime was as much an English tradition as tea and cucumber sandwiches, so as a foreigner I was not qualified to criticize, but most of the cast found it difficult to respond to the painfully flat jokes. Worse still, all the dancers were required to remain on stage for most of the show to spur the audience on. I was inclined to think that after a couple of hours of such unadulterated rubbish the audience's main source of pleasure would be a sense of relief that the show was over.

The ballet's choreographer and my performing partner was a demented Scottish soak called John. As a dancer he was inadequate, and as a choreographer he was devoid of creative ideas. I determined to protect my dignity as best I could, and made some suggestions to enhance the mundane choreography. So our *pas de deux* included a few exciting Bolshoi-style lifts and lunges—though I lived to regret having suggested it, as John's doddery condition often made the *pas de deux* a close call with death. Apart from his clumsiness, his chauvinism aggravated me intensely. 'Why won't ye have me then?' he would ask in his thick Scottish brogue, as I was poised in tense full flight towards his limp outstretched arms.

Probably the highlight of the panto season was the reappearance of my menstrual cycle after more than a year's absence. For weeks I listened enviously to my colleagues' complaints, as the curse claimed

The programme for *Sleeping Beauty*: the reality was less romantic.

its victims with clockwork precision. I coveted this most feminine malaise more than anything else, but I had almost abandoned hope. When I began to feel unwell in one particularly cold week in mid-winter, I immediately assumed I was coming down with yet another rotten dose of influenza. But I could now join the others in their plaintive moaning, and how I did sigh and affect boredom at the inconvenience of it all!

I was also aware that my whole way of life was undergoing a major transition. I was now living in a world without any clearly defined moral boundaries. I desired things I did not know. They came from the gut, exciting, stimulating and frighteningly physical. Though I liked to believe that I was tolerant of most of my friends' sexual activities, I had steadfastly protected my own virginity. I would not give myself except to the man I loved, and on the proper crisp clean bridal bed in the nuptial chamber. Though my parents had never overtly stipulated any such rules—they did not talk about such matters much at all—a moral code *was* implied, and underlined by references to other women who were thought to be 'wanton'. Certainly there was a double standard; it was considered natural for the boy in the family to satisfy his sexual desires, but women were still largely bound to premarital celibacy, more out of fear than conviction.

I believed in true love, respect, monogamy and the whole damn thing, but there was no denying my developing sexuality. My over-disciplined ballet life had not only retarded my physical development, but had effectively suppressed my sexuality. While my school friends in Australia had engaged in furtive necking, my eroticism had been satisfied by a leg mount at the classroom barre. A number of men had shown more than a passing interest in me, but until now I had felt little desire to respond to it. Now I too began to explore the world of sexual conquest. I began to accept invitations to parties after the show, where the carousing went on till the wee hours of the morning. Rather than depleting my physical energies, these late nights left me happy and relaxed, and the subsequent performances had more zing. Boring as the panto was, life was generally full of fun.

But I saw in 1963 in a blue funk. It had been a rough week, and I was feeling too exhausted to contemplate going to a New Year's Eve party. I staggered out of the theatre for home and bed, but missed my usual train back to London and ended up stranded in the middle of a blizzard on the Croydon Railway Station. I was not the only performer on that miserable elevated platform in the middle of nowhere. My partner John stood at one end of the platform, swigging down a hip flask of whisky and trying to pretend that he had not seen me. Suddenly, on the stroke of twelve, John began to jump up and down, screaming 'Happy New Year' at the top of his lungs. Abetted by the hip flask of Johnny Walker he had swigged down during our long wait, he suddenly decided that I was the love of his life. I was whisked off my feet and spun around by this tottering lunatic. 'Come to my room, let's make love', he yowled. Fortunately the train arrived, and we both scrambled aboard, where the presence of other people subdued mad John's histrionics.

I felt lonely and homesick during my first Christmas and New Year away from home, and even more so when my nineteenth birthday came around. In our family birthdays were the highlights of the year. A great deal of effort and creative skill always went into making each one memorable, and preparations usually began at least two weeks before the big event. Birthdays were about surprises, presents, treats and lots of visitors, but above all they were about being with one's family.

I felt a dreadful sense of isolation when I awoke on 9 January 1963. There were no presents at the end of the bed, no warm kisses and cuddles from my parents, no Harry bursting into my room without knocking. Presents and cards from home had already arrived two days before, but they were cold comfort. I read all the words on the pages over and over again, but I only became more and more miserable; 'I miss you', they wrote, and it cut me to the quick.

I prepared for yet another working day. To make matters worse I had a heavy cold, and the thought of two performances in this condition was even more harrowing. When I arrived at the theatre there were a few murmurs of 'Happy Birthday', but no one bothered to glance away from their make-up job. This indifference really upset me. It was hard to apply make-up when my face was set halfway between a snarl and a petulant pout, and it was hard to do a warm-up when my thoughts were elsewhere, but I was determined not to show how hurt I was, and snuffled obstinately through my preparations.

In the first performance my head seemed to be in a fog, and my feet and legs might as well not have been attached to me at all. I must have been in the right place at the right time for the appropriate steps and lifts, as I managed to complete the performance and walk off the stage in one piece, which was a remarkable achievement considering how I felt. But there was still another performance to go.

I flopped on to my chair at my dressing-table and noticed that everyone was busily sprucing themselves up and climbing into their street clothes. This was unusual because there was little time between shows, certainly not enough to go outside the theatre. I was ushered into the Green Room where, to my surprise and delight, the whole company was assembled around a table laden with sumptuous goodies. The *pièce de résistance* was undoubtedly the huge birthday cake with nineteen candles. I was also presented with a superb book on Galina Ulanova, endorsed on the inside cover with greetings from every member of the cast. There was a short silence, then everyone flung themselves on me, to smother me with warm kisses and hugs and chide me for my misgivings.

Eventually the season came to an end. At our final performance there seemed to be a great deal of falling about and giggling, unfortunately not on cue, and we all reacted rather too hysterically to Cyril's lines, even when they weren't meant to be funny. Certain members of the cast seemed to have invented some passionate choreography on the spur of the moment. It was a pretty dishevelled performance, and the audience must have been quite confused, but not even the Fletchers seemed to mind the lunacy on this occasion. When the curtain finally came down, we retired to our dressing rooms with quite warm feelings towards each other, and not a little sadness.

I was free to do what I liked. Though I had been longing for this respite for weeks, now that the day had come I felt let down. During the panto season my life had been mapped out for me, but I would now have to cope with a life without schedules or company directors to pull me into line. I still hoped to return to Moscow, but I realized I could be in for a long wait. The best I could do was wait for my visa and hope that my bank balance would allow me to continue classes and pay for my lodgings.

Although the Fealdmans made me feel welcome, I did feel I had overstepped the bounds of their hospitality by staying as long as I had. Luckily Dell Brady, another Australian who had been a member of the panto company, had a place for me in her flat at Geldstanes Road, opposite the Queen's Club tennis courts, as one of the lodgers was currently away on a tour with the Royal Ballet. It was good to move in with people of my own age, and in particular with Dell. As compatriots toughing it out in cruel, cruel London, we made the most of our poverty and creative frustrations. We laughed a lot, and poured out all our agonies and despair over endless cups of black coffee. I think we thrived on each other's misery.

I found it hard to get used to life without any obligatory schedule, and to drive myself out of a warm bed into the bitter cold outside, and

Two girls on the town: Dell Brady and Alida, 1963

then to an unheated ballet studio. Only my habitual guilt and anxiety kept me scuttling off each morning, rain or shine, to allay the fear of losing form and to try to stay ahead of my rivals in that fiercely competitive world. I was thankful for Dell's company in this daily penance. We both complained furiously, but they were specialized complaints about sore toes and lumpy muscles. Our bodies were in constant protest, but neither of us questioned the necessity of our suffering.

We were joined at the studio by yet another Australian dancer, Gerrard Sibbritt, and together we descended upon the conservative British dance establishment like three maniacal musketeers. Gerry was not only a brilliant dancer, but was also blessed with dark, brooding good looks. His whole demeanour oozed an innate nobility and sense of style.

Night after night the three of us would get together to drown our collective sorrows with some affordable, though barely drinkable, Portuguese wine. Secretly we thought ourselves fortunate to be dedicating our lives to the theatre. We were unique, comrades together, poised and straining at the bit. Not one of us doubted for one small moment that we would pass the finishing post and not one of us viewed our present tribulations as anything more than a necessary if inconvenient staging post on the road to greater things.

In Maria Fae I knew I had found a teacher with whom I could communicate. Her vital, sensual personality appealed to me the instant I walked into the classroom, but it was her expansive honesty of movement that won me over. Maria was a former ballerina from the Budapest Opera Ballet, and had made no concessions to English gentility. Although she was now teaching at the Royal Ballet, she refused to modify her Russian schooling. Watching her demonstrate was a treat. Her musicality simply flowed through her *épaulement* and sweeping *portes de bras*. Her leg extensions seemed to defy normal anatomical limits. Her technique was so solid that she did not need to resort to emotive schmaltz. Her classes were quite similar to the Bolshoi classes, so I felt right at home.

One day, halfway through one of Maria's barre exercises, a small, pale man came into the studio. He sat down on a chair next to Maria's and proceeded to watch with an unsmiling expression, his head cocked wryly to one side. From nervous whispers I gathered that this was Walter Gore, who was looking for dancers for his London Ballet company. In no mood for display, as I did not wish to join a company at this stage, I decided to finish the class as inconspicuously as I could, in a remote spot at the back of the room. Some of my friends were elbowing their way to the front line, and desperately trying to outdo one another. I was relieved not to have to be part of this humiliating competition. My pride, however, would not allow me to disgrace myself, and I did work as hard as I could. Several times I noticed Walter Gore pointing me out to Maria, but as I was wearing my pink Bolshoi tunic while everyone else was clad in leotards I assumed that he was asking about my tunic rather than my dancing.

At the end of the class Maria called me over to introduce me. He asked me a few questions and then, in a banal tone of voice, offered me a soloist position for the coming season. I simply couldn't believe my ears. 'Oh, I am sorry', I stuttered, 'I am only a student. I'm waiting for a visa to return to Russia'.

As I continued my babble I couldn't help thinking that everyone would think me a fool to forgo such a wonderful opportunity, but I had to stick to my principles on this issue. Flattering as the offer was, I needed to continue my studies, and Moscow would have to remain my first priority. I told myself over and over again that if I didn't resist the temptation to join as a soloist now, before I was ready, then I would always be a soloist, never a principal.

Surely there would be other opportunities such as this. If I'm noticed now, then they must surely sit up and take notice when I am technically proficient. Then doubts set in, and I wondered if perhaps I had not been over-confident to presume that I would make the big time in my own time. I felt my confidence draining away as I searched for the definitive refusal. Instinctively I realized the dangers of jumping in at the deep end, and I felt utterly unprepared for such a big undertaking. When I finally said 'No, thank you', I was relieved that I had managed to come away with my artistic integrity intact.

The next few days were anticlimactic, to say the least. There was still no word from Moscow, and only the prospect of endless classes. Try as I might, I found it hard to fall back into the old routine, and hankered for a change. I decided to try some classes with the Ballet Rambert at the Mercury Theatre. Although I did not know who would be taking the class, Maria Fae's class was so demanding that I was certain anyone else's would be a breeze by comparison.

Margaret Scott and other ex-Rambert dancers had told me so much about this famous place, and the legendary Rambert herself, that I felt a surge of familiarity as I walked across that well-worn threshold. The studio doubled as an auditorium, and I found it hard to imagine that such people as Sally Gilmour, Markova, Frederick Ashton and Walter Gore had had their first opportunities here, on this impossibly small stage, which was only eighteen feet square.

The Ballet Rambert's influence on twentieth-century ballet was quite out of proportion to its size and modest resources. So many artists, choreographers, dancers, designers and musicians had reason to be grateful for the guidance of Dame Marie Rambert, in spite of the company's ups and downs, successes and failures. The Mercury Theatre, which had been started as a theatre club by 'Mim' and her urbane playwright husband, Ashley Dukes, had witnessed some of the most brilliant innovative theatre and ballet that post-war England had seen.

I felt suitably awestruck, but I was hoping that I would not have to face the great Dame herself. I simply wanted to do an anonymous, solid workout, and did not want to do it in front of someone so much larger than life. I was therefore relieved to see Angela Ellis, Rambert's daughter, walk into the class, and prepared myself to experience yet another new English teacher. But things did not run entirely to plan. Halfway through the class I realized that a grey-haired man was watching me from the doorway, making no effort to disguise the fact that he was scrutinizing me intensely.

I tried to ignore his presence, but it was disconcerting to feel his eyes concentrating on my every move. The class ended up being a dead loss, as I found myself shifting into performance gear. After the class the man introduced himself as David Ellis, the Associate Director of the Ballet Rambert. He told me that he was intrigued by my work. Everything about my dancing was beautiful, he said, except for my insteps, which he felt I could improve. 'We could use you in the company', he added. 'I think great things could be done with you.' More through mischievous curiosity than genuine interest, I enquired what position I might be offered. David Ellis replied that although it wasn't Dame Marie's policy to employ dancers directly as soloists, he believed that I would rapidly rise through the ranks to the top.

In the space of just one week I had been offered jobs in two of London's most prestigious companies. Trying to sound as if these sorts of offers were flung at me every day, and drawing myself up to my full five feet two inches, I repeated the story I had told Walter Gore only two days before.

News of these offers spread through the London ballet world like wildfire. As if the offers were not enough in themselves, the fact that I had knocked these offers back was the biggest *chutzpah* of all.

I was almost bursting with pride, and poured out my joy in voluminous letters home. At last I was able to assure my parents that their faith in me had not been misplaced. My success was their success. But, exultant as I was, so far my success was purely hypothetical. All that had really happened was that I had been noticed, but I remained untried and unproved, and I knew too well that many a dancer who looks bright and promising in the classroom fails to live up to expectations when finally put to the test on the real stage.

A few days later, relaxed to the point of almost being sloppy, I decided it was time to return to work in Maria's punishing classes. I had no sooner stepped into the classroom than Maria hurtled towards me with such an earnest expression that I thought something had happened to one of my classmates. 'Where have you been?' she asked almost accusingly. Apparently she and Walter Gore had been trying to contact me for days. Throwing her arms around me, she shouted in my ear that Walter Gore was so keen to have me in his company that he had suggested I join as Guest Artist. This meant that if my Russian visa came through I could be released from my contract at any time or place on the tour. And that was not all. Walter wanted me to dance the Sugar Plum Fairy in his production of *The Nutcracker*.

It was all too much to digest in one go. The offer was tempting, though not without its pitfalls, and Wally had left me with a deadline. I would have to decide by 10 that evening, so there was little time for vacillation. In pragmatic terms I did need the money. My bank account was down to £20, and it wouldn't be long before things came to a crisis on that front. But I still had reservations about taking on such enormous responsibilities. Reluctant to believe I was ready for the professional stage, I was even more hesitant about being so presumptuous as to start at the top. I would have nowhere to go but down. I was in a quandary, and as logical as a rabid squirrel. My mind flitted this way and that. I was tempted to say 'What the hell' and throw myself in. But then a warning light would flash, urging me to take heed of my technical limitations and think of the damage that too much too soon could cause. Finally I decided to follow my instincts and send myself out on this new adventure.

That night Dell, Gerry and I had planned to go to see the Royal Ballet perform *La Fille Mal Gardée*, so at least I would have something to distract me until that frightening phone call. Although none of us had a company to call our own, we liked to think of the Royal Ballet as the opposition, and we prided ourselves on being far too individualistic to want to become part of such a monochromatic company. Little did we know that we gave our amateur status away by being so hypercritical. Every flaw we found we discussed mercilessly, and in staggering detail. To say that someone was less than physically perfect was to dismiss them altogether. It was all so easy from the stalls.

We had come to see the famous Nadia Nerina. In our eyes, the very fact that she had an established reputation made her fair game. We wrote her off as a technically brilliant cold fish, and the lower ranks did not fare much better. Jubilantly we ripped through the entire cast until almost every member had been deposited on the 'not good enough' heap, apart from a few who we felt had some unique physical trait or individualistic quirkiness of style.

I wasn't at my bitchy best on this occasion. I was even beginning to feel some furtive compassion for the dancers sweating away on stage. I had one eye on the stage and one eye on my watch. As 10 p.m. approached, I waited until the minute hand made its way towards the twelve, then rang Walter Gore.

I trembled so much I could hardly dial the number. Propping the receiver between my ear and shoulder, I fumbled away in my handbag for a cigarette. 'Yes?' clipped Wally's voice at the other end of the line. I took a long draw on my Du Maurier and tried to sound calm and experienced, all the time feeling that this was surely all happening to someone else. 'I would be pleased to accept the offer', I heard myself saying, 'but only on condition that I could be instantly released if my Bolshoi scholarship comes through'. I was even more amazed to hear Wally agree. Now I was as good as under contract, and as a principal artist with a major British company. My exuberance diminished only slightly when he told me that I would only have a week to learn my new role.

It wasn't until I had put down the receiver and lighted yet another cigarette that the penny dropped. One week, for an entirely new role, for this was Walter Gore's version of *Casse-Noisette*, not the Lichine version I already knew. Quite plainly Wally did not intend to make any concessions to my youth and inexperience, but even by the most stringent professional standards four rehearsals was far too little time to study a major role. Wally had also asked me if I knew *Giselle*. When I told him that I had never danced the role he asked me to learn that main role as well, as Paula Hinton, his wife, needed a second cast to dance the matinees for her. I had been flung in at the deep end, and I suspected there would be few hands offering to guide me to safety; but if I succeeded the rewards would be phenomenal.

I returned to my seat in the darkened auditorium a fully fledged professional dancer. The rest of *Fille* passed me by, as just a whirl of colours, bouréeing feet and transient long-lashed, wide-eyed, smiling faces. I sat through the curtain calls staring blankly at the stage. All I could think of was next Monday. What if the audiences didn't care for me? What if I couldn't measure up? My hands felt clammy and my throat tight. I felt as if I was coming down with a high fever. Still, I did not rush back to the telephone to tell Wally I had changed my mind; I was on the theatrical tightrope, and I could not get off.

Maria didn't entirely share my excitement. Although she had encouraged me to accept Wally's offer, she was dismayed to hear that I had been asked to dance *Giselle*. In her opinion I was far too young and inexperienced for such a role. On reflection she may have been right. The Sugar Plum Fairy in *Nutcracker* is a fairly straightforward classical *pas de deux* and variations, requiring only technical proficiency and style.

Giselle, on the other hand, is not only a most demanding role, but one of the most coveted in the classical ballet repertoire. By taking on such a leading role, I could possibly make my career the shortest ever recorded. Perversely I was also rather pleased; the speed of it all seemed to eliminate the need for too much thought.

I felt I should let David Ellis at Ballet Rambert know about these new developments. Though I was inexperienced in ballet politics, I knew it would be folly to be discourteous to any potential employer, let alone to such an influential figure as Madame Rambert. I felt reluctant to do another class at the Mercury, but thought it was more polite to attend a class than just waltz in and out with the news.

When I entered the studio the class had already begun, and it was being taught by Madame Rambert, who was already prodding some hapless student's stomach muscles. I would have made a quick retreat if I could, but David Ellis had already leapt into the studio to point me out. I felt her dark, smouldering eyes run up and down my body. I had already been as good as totally assessed. Rambert placed a great deal of faith in her first impressions. Before the introductory piano chords had struck up, Rambert would have decided whether or not the new girl would be worth watching. The lesson was, to use the tasteless vernacular of the time, spastic-making. Mim was larger than life. Her pint-size old-lady physique filled the studio. It was like being cooped up with a renegade Spitfire.

Some of the students looked absolutely petrified, but everyone knew that those who were most terrified were the fortunate few whom Madame deemed worthy of her precious vitriol. The rest of the class appeared more rejected than put-upon. Clearly they had been considered too boring to have any energy wasted on them.

'You move like a pregnant peasant!' she screeched at a pretty dancer who was too young to have shed her last layers of puppy fat. The abusive verbiage continued throughout the class, and I received more than a fair share of it. By the end of the barre my body was tied up in thousands of knots. I had been poked between the shoulder blades and told to 'crack a nut'. I had been pitched forward like the Leaning Tower of Pisa, standing in a hermetically sealed fifth position, so that if I had moved I would have fallen flat on my nose. When she had finished prodding and plying and twisting my aching body, she peered straight into my face; Attila the Hun, having turned quite fey, said, 'Come on, darling, shut your mouth. Look at me'. Then, with a most artificial politeness, 'You must try and look like a ballerina. You can't be a ballerina with a slack mouth'.

I was dragged to the front of the group and systematically pulled to pieces. Nothing, just nothing was right about my dancing, my body, my attitude or myself. If this was preferential treatment, I didn't care for it. And if she *was* interested in me, why was she trying to cripple me and put me out of action for all time?

The thing that most struck me on that day was Rambert's unmistakable Jewishness. She looked the archetypal cultivated middle-European, middle-class Jewish matron. No matter what label she cared to put upon herself (I learnt later that Mim had long since renounced her Jewishness to become a member of the Russian Orthodox Church), her expression said it all. As far as I was concerned, Mim reminded me of a thousand other Jewish acquaintances of mine: the extroverted expressiveness, the *chutzpah* that goes hand in hand with someone who knows what she wants, is not afraid to pursue what she wants, and is comfortable and secure with her own rightness. She was as Jewish as a *matzoh*.

It was her turn to be taken aback when I again declined to join her company, but she was not nearly as unreasonable as I expected. She told me she would like to train me in the company repertoire at the school, and that if I did join her company she was quite certain that I would have a great future, though she did add that she would expect me to start off in small parts and develop gradually. All this was like music to my ears, though I couldn't help feeling relieved that I was already committed to Wally's London Ballet. I promised to keep in touch with her, and insisted that I was enthusiastic about joining her company in the near future. Events were racing ahead with such speed that I felt it was just as well that I had managed to exclude that bundle of nervous energy from my already confused life.

16

The London Ballet

My first rehearsal day with the London Ballet was not a satisfying or convivial experience. We rehearsed solidly from 10 a.m. until 5.30 p.m. in a cold, bare church hall. Since I had only four rehearsals in which to learn an excruciatingly difficult version of the Sugar Plum Fairy, I knew I would need every minute of each day. I felt very self-conscious entering a company of mature professional dancers right at the top of the hierarchy. Although no one made any bitchy remarks or behaved discourteously towards me, I could sense that there was a fair amount of indignant sizing-up and restrained enmity in the air.

As well as the usual *pas de deux* variations and coda in the third act, I had to learn an additional *pas de deux* and a few more variations. My partner, Alexis Rassine, had spent many years partnering people like Fonteyn, Nerina and Beriosova, but by the time he got to me he was more of a name than a talent. I needed a partner, not a legend. My Albrecht was so preoccupied with his past that I felt I was dancing with a dusty monument rather than a flesh-and-blood human being. Offstage he was twee, with a Dorian Grey face that, despite the good intentions of some skilled and expensive Harley Street surgeons, showed the ravages of his dissipated years. His tastes and hobbies, however, were a model of British respectability. He lived for his cottage and rose garden, and was an absolute stickler for afternoon tea and scones. He often disappeared, compelling us to interrupt rehearsals until we found him, usually tucked away in some cosy little café, daintily scoffing down his repast with the air of one performing a sacred ritual.

I grew fond of this eccentric character, but on stage he made almost every performance a dangerous expedition. He postured rather than danced, with gracefully charming, limp-wristed gestures. He was far too wary of possible injuries to extend a hand for support, and God forbid he should try to lift a ballerina who didn't jump 90 per cent of the way

Another day, another ballerina: Alexis Rassine partners Alida in her London Ballet debut, 1963.

herself. His body, though still lithe, was not for demeaning physical work. Experience had taught him exactly which lights enhanced his complexion. Many a time I emoted to an absent partner, or lunged on to a phantom Albrecht, for he was busy avoiding all those 'lights that give you ageing circles, darling'. Other times I would find him standing in a dark corner adjusting his wig and pulling down his doublet so that his walk to centre stage might be executed with all the style and elegance of the *danseur étoile*. I would be practically partnering myself in the *pas de deux*. I could not expect heroic acts from this genteel partner, especially anything that might make him appear dishevelled or unprincely.

Just when I needed to be in peak condition, just when I was feeling a little too special, Providence quickly reminded me that I was merely another member of the all too human race. A particularly virulent strain of gastric 'flu was sweeping through London. I had managed to resist it for some time, but in the end I went down with the rest of them. With perfect theatrical timing, the virus struck me at Australia House in the Strand on the day that there was to be a press reception in my honour. I vomited all over the steps, only to be rescued by a pukka British gentleman, resplendent in bowler hat, pinstripe suit and red carnation, who escorted me to a cab that took me home. I collapsed on to my bed, ready to die quietly, but knowing that there was no question of cancelling the press reception.

It was my first press reception, and Wally had asked me to look as glamorous as possible, but even in my best clothes I looked more like a candidate for *Danse Macabre* than a budding ballerina. The motion of the taxi was so comforting that I almost dozed off, but all too soon the cab ground to a halt in Regents Park. A butler pulled me out and thrust me into a room full of people who looked as if they had stepped straight off the pages of *Vogue*.

They had all come to satisfy their curiosity about Wally's new find, and I was it. Wally introduced me to a whole host of people, whose names I instantly forgot. On any other evening I would have been in my element, but tonight I couldn't have cared less which profile the cameras captured, and I felt so woozy that it took all the energy I could muster to manage a weak smile, let alone speak a semi-coherent sentence. I resigned myself to the fact that on my first public performance in London I had been labelled a dumb ballerina.

In the following few days my first press releases, write-ups and photographs were splashed across the principal London newspapers. I didn't fare too badly; even in my gaga condition, I must have made a reasonable impression on the journalists. But as my debut loomed closer I began to worry that these premature publicity splurges might be harbingers of my downfall. One week's rehearsal for *Casse-Noisette* and two rehearsals for *Giselle* did not exactly inspire confidence.

My premiere turned out to be too much of what I had expected and too little of what I had hoped for. The Swansea Theatre did not burn down, though judging by its decrepitude it should have. I suspect my performance was interspersed with too many calamities to evoke the sublime theatrical experience that the capacity crowd had hoped for. All my variations were executed in such a strained state that I could hardly expect to impress my audience with my technical brilliance and sparkling personality.

I had so wanted it to be joyous and successful, not only for myself but also for my brother, who was also experiencing a first of his own—his wedding. But I was filled with fear, and not one step would spring to my mind. It was as if I had stepped out on to the last stretch before the executioner's block. The audience waited, hardly breathing, never moving. They were on my side. After all, they wished to be transported into a world of fantasy where I was *their* Sugar Plum Fairy, the charmer with the power to cast a spell that would not be broken until home time. But I felt like the lady with the wrong dress at the wrong party. As far as I was concerned there was no magic, only an introduction, a finale, and unadulterated hell in between. I did not have the advantage of premiering a new ballet, where the audience would have come without preconceived expectations. *Casse-Noisette* is a pop ballet, and for most of the audience I was only a new dancer offering a fresh interpretation of a tried and true favourite.

The music of the grand *pas de deux*, the highlight of the ballet, is surely among the most perfect pieces of music Tchaikovsky composed for ballet. It is exultant, magnificently sweeping, and has several climaxes which are almost always perfectly transcribed into heart-stopping, soaring balletic lifts. Throughout our rendition of this glorious *pas de deux*, however, our audience was repeatedly reminded of our humanness. It is not a pretty sight to see a ballerina's nose scrape the ground, as mine did on several occasions when I attempted to execute spectacular fish dives into my partner's listless arms. I lost count of the number of times my partner dropped me out of a lift on to full *pointes* like a ton of bricks, then calmly disentangled himself from my floundering limbs to stride on into his next elegant pose. He remained unruffled, while I increasingly resembled a crumpled dishcloth.

We approached my favourite moment in the whole *pas de deux*, a moment that might have redeemed our entire performance. Normally you can hear a pin drop in the auditorium as the ballerina prepares for the jump into the arms of her waiting Adonis, and the audience gasps in wonder as this magnificent specimen of manhood holds the ballerina aloft, well over his head, the Olympian winner brandishing his victory trophy. That is what is supposed to happen.

The music rumbled towards its climax, and I prepared for take-off into our grand lift. I took a deep breath, carefully sighted my partner and took three or four grandiose steps before landing smack bang on my face, dragging my unresisting partner down with me. My toe had caught in one of the myriad potholes scattered over the stage. We lay spread-eagled on the floor, in the ultimate posture of disgrace, then scrambled up to finish the performance.

On the final curtain call I was almost happy to call it quits for all time and collapse invisibly in my dressing room, but I was so overcome with nausea and exhaustion that I didn't think I could make it there without the aid of a stretcher. Preoccupied with my own misery, I didn't think to acknowledge the cast members who had gathered around me. Somewhere out in the distance I heard vague voices congratulating me and telling me that I had danced beautifully. If only I could have believed them. I knew that my first performance had been a disappointment, and although some of the compliments may have been sincere, their expectations and mine were undoubtedly different. I still had a long, long way to go. Strangely enough, Wally and Paula seemed genuinely thrilled with my performance. 'Considering the amount of rehearsal time you received', Wally said, 'you did a splendid job. It was a beautiful interpretation'. According to the rest of the company this was extraordinary praise coming from him.

In spite of all my misgivings, the dressing-room atmosphere was imbued with a sense of occasion. Floral bouquets and baskets filled the room, and my make-up mirror was surrounded with scores of telegrams, mascots, goodwill chukka cards and scrawled messages of good luck. Paula and Wally had given me a Welsh doll to mark the occasion, while the Australian boys in the company, and there were quite a few, had sent me an enormous bouquet with the message: 'Go out there and have a dinky-di bash'.

I returned to my hotel room and collapsed on my bed to have a long weep. Alone for the first time that day, I thought of my family, especially my brother. I could only hope that he had felt more prepared for his ceremonial duties than I had for mine.

My second performance progressed more smoothly than the first, and by the third I was conscious through most of the performance. There was life outside those dark convoluted corridors of my mind after all! I registered the other people on the stage, an audience full of desire to be pleased, and a manageable, if not altogether helpful, partner. After several performances I was able at last to throw myself into the music.

Classical ballet is inherently élitist. The ballets of nineteenth-century choreographers such as Petipa and Ivanov reflected their creators' acceptance of a hierarchical social order. They lived and worked in Imperial Russia, and the characters in their ballets covered the spectrum of Russia's feudalistic society. At the bottom of the pecking order there were dances for the happily carousing Cossacks and their beautiful, shy peasant maidens, the rustics at work in the fields or performing ancient primitive rites; then there was the lesser aristocracy, dancing stylized court dances for the benefit of the King or Queen, or bearing gifts of homage to the supreme ruler.

To be given the role of a prima ballerina in a classical ballet is a chance to taste absolute power. There is nothing quite like the thrill that goes with being the central character of one's own little empire, even if it is only a fleeting phantasm. The highlight of a traditional classical ballet is usually the grand *pas de deux* in the final act, after the prince has won his princess. Their soaring movements symbolize the ecstasy of their spiritual consummation (in classical ballet the coupling is always spiritual). Before this magic moment transpires, the *corps de ballet* assembles in neat artistically placed groupings for the *tableau vivant*. Enhanced by this background montage, the two principal dancers make their entrance, followed by a breathtaking moment of motionless silence in which the dancers impress their luminary presence on the awe-struck crowd both on and off the stage. Aware of the reverent hush, the dancers poise themselves until, just beyond the bounds of reasonable suspense, the conductor lowers his baton and the magic unfolds. But there were many occasions when this sense of power completely eluded me. The *courant* style of the Sugar Plum Fairy, for example, was just a lot of hard work with little to show for it. I always felt relieved if I managed to get through the variation without too much huffing and puffing, and still with enough grace and dignity to make my curtain call.

The sobering reality of a ballet dancer's life on tour makes it impossible to take one's public image too seriously. Every few days, or, if one was lucky, at the end of every week, there was a new theatre to acquaint oneself with, a new town with new people to win over, and that infernal search for a bed to lie in at the end of the day. This nomadic life made it all the more necessary to create a little bit of home away from home. Home was wherever one hung one's toe boots. Any space, regardless of its shape, size or form, was soon transformed into one's personal territory. The familiar odours of greasepaint, methylated spirits and drying tights soon pervaded and obliterated the last lingering geists of the room's previous tenants. I don't know why performers seem to be more superstitious than other people, but even the sceptics were wary of breaking theatrical taboos. We all clung to our private little mascots as if our sanity depended on them.

As soon as each dancer had staked out her territory she would set up house with all the dedication of a new bride in her first home. We strung up our chukka cards, break-a-leg and congratulatory telegrams, photographs of our loved ones (these always took pride of place), ribbons and pressed roses preserved from our first-night bouquets and an assortment of mascots, each one of them concealing or denoting a secret message or cherished memory. Our wandering life made this kind of reaffirmation of identity absolutely crucial. How could one put up with the monotony of the constant array of faces, repetitive conversations and petty feuding, if one lost touch with one's true self? Touring certainly can distort one's perspective. It was as if we were constantly cooped up in an orbiting satellite that never touched base. Although we could justly say that we had travelled all over Great Britain, our association with most of the places we visited was purely ephemeral.

The end of the performance was normally followed by a long cold wait at a bus stop along with other plebeians, and on my return to my digs I thought myself lucky to find some stale white sandwiches, for usually supper was a piece of charcoal-black toast, cooked illicitly on a single-bar radiator. Then, having washed my smalls and ballet tights and prepared my *pointe* shoes for tomorrow's trip into fantasy land, it was off to sleep on a strange lumpy bed, feeling alone and decidedly unglamorous.

A ballerina reflects: Alida in her dressing room with mementoes and Bolshoi tunic (hanging behind her)

My position within the company was awkward. I was too young to be befriended by the other principals, who were all seasoned performers at least six years older than I was. I would normally have found much more in common with the younger members in the *corps de ballet*, but my position put me into the untouchable category, so I didn't have much luck among my peers, either. I could understand that young dancers might gaze on the likes of a Fonteyn or Ulanova with misty-eyed awe, but I certainly did not delude myself that I could claim such star status. At only nineteen, clearly immature in many ways, and not predisposed to the posturing of the prima donna, I did not feel at all self-sufficient. I needed a friend to confide in, and I often became acutely homesick. Eventually I became friends with a soloist in the company, Moya Knox, and together we managed to laugh our way through a lot of the rough spots and the monotony of provincial touring.

178   Out of Step

Although Wally said little to encourage or discourage me, a few weeks into the tour he asked me to dance the role of Odette in the second act of *Swan Lake*, and later gave me a new role in his ballet *Light Fantastic*, where I danced the part of a dizzy coquettish character, in marked contrast to the grandiose classical eloquence of the other ballets

Making up for *Swan Lake*, 1963

in my repertoire. This was not a bad thing for someone who was inclined to take herself rather too seriously. Obtaining this role meant that I had finally been accepted as a bona-fide member of the company. Wally's own ballets were the true jewels of his creativity. Although his productions of *Casse*, *Giselle* and *Swan Lake* were excellent, they could only ever be derivative; they were the bread-and-butter ballets.

Most of the leading newspaper dance critics turned up to see the company in Cambridge, and *The Times* and the *Telegraph* hailed me as an exciting new talent of the calibre of a young Beriosova, Fonteyn or Nerina. In Dublin Mícheál Mac Liammóir wrote a glowing review—so glowing that I hardly recognized myself in its flattering description of my dancing.

News of my success also reached the Australian newspapers, but they were less interested in my dancing than in sensationalizing my Russian experience for their own purposes. 'Reds expel Aussie dancer', the headlines shouted, and the accompanying story seemed to suggest that a host of evil Russians had physically hurled me out of their country and banned me from their shores forever. Nothing could have been further from the truth, and the Russian Embassy was quick to respond with a letter to the *Age* denouncing my apparent ingratitude and pointing out that the Soviets had acted extremely generously in allowing me to study at the Bolshoi despite the lack of formal cultural exchange between the two countries.

I was livid when I received word of the newspaper reports. I would never have referred to the Russian people as 'Reds', and I had made it quite clear that it was the Australian Embassy that had suggested that I leave because of the worsening political situation. I had only spoken in the highest terms of the kindness and hospitality of the Russian people I had associated with. But, being thousands of miles away from home, it was difficult for me to refute all this nonsense, so I asked my brother to do so on my behalf. Then, for sticking out his neck in what was perceived to be a left-wing manner, Harry almost lost his chance of taking up a Fulbright Scholarship for postgraduate studies at Chicago University.

Meanwhile, back in England, the press attention I was receiving was creating different problems. A few of the soloists in the company became noticeably cooler towards me, and one or two were downright hostile. From the company's point of view, my Bolshoi student days were excellent publicity. At almost every press reception in every new town I was asked about my experiences with the Bolshoi, so when I was asked to be interviewed on a local television programme in a provincial town I felt relaxed and ready to take on what had now become quite a familiar barrage of questions about Russia, my career and the London Ballet.

I expected the interview to be a light-hearted chat, a genre that I had now learnt to handle quite comfortably. The timing of the interview was tight, so I was whisked to the studio and back in a car, which would leave me just a little time to do a warm-up before the performance. The interview flowed along famously, and I immersed myself in chit-chat about dear old Moscow and the Bolshoi. Asked how I felt Russian and English ballet differed, I replied that I felt Russian ballet was perhaps more emotive than English ballet, and that the Russians tended to use technique to express their emotions or relate a story, rather than as a spectacular visual end in itself. If my memory serves me well, I added that I thought the British were more inhibited by nature, and therefore tended to value clean line and technical precision more than overt displays of emotionalism. The discussion went on in this vein for some time. Then the interviewer suddenly said 'We have a surprise for you', and we were linked up to a London TV studio for a three-way conversation with a young British pianist who had also studied in Moscow. We continued to discuss Russia, and before the interview could get on to other matters we were wound up by the floor manager. I sped out to the waiting taxi and back to the theatre.

As I ran across the empty stage, my mind now firmly fixed on preparing myself for the coming performance, I noticed Ken, our company manager, sitting in prompt corner. 'How did I do?' I called, more by way of a rhetorical question *en passant* than a genuine enquiry. 'You were a disgrace!' replied a shrill female voice from quite another direction. 'You are an evil, evil girl', the disembodied voice persevered. 'How dare you go on television without once mentioning the London Ballet? How dare you say Russian dancers are better than English dancers? You are an evil girl and I never want to speak to you again.'

Paula appeared, aptly bedecked in evil bird make-up for her role as the bird enchantress in Wally's *Eaters of Darkness*, and proceeded to attack me with unbelievable venom. 'What a bloody cheek!' she spat, the blue veins swelling dangerously around her delicate throat. 'You were sent to that interview to publicize our company, not you and your blessed trip to Russia.'

The arrogant bird of prey began to strut back to her dressing room with her feathers flapping defiantly, as if to emphasize the utter contemptibility of it all. It was only then that I found my voice.

'I didn't realize he wasn't going to ask me any further questions', I squealed. 'I had absolutely no idea we were going to do that three-way conversation.' But even if Paula had heard my protestations, they would have fallen on deaf ears. She had decided I was a traitor, and that was that. Not even our diplomatic company manager could appease Paula's anger. Her anger and jealousy had been building up for quite a while. It doesn't do for a press notice to read, 'the highlight of the performance was two young performers, Alida Glasbeek and Jane Roland Evans, both of whom stole the show'. It is a lot to ask that any mature dancer should accept an up-and-coming young minion with magnanimity, especially when the little bitch is up and coming to the detriment of one's own position.

This episode spoilt the rest of the tour for me. Performing was far less pleasurable with Paula glaring at me from the wings, or hovering peevishly behind me at the barre. But I could not bring myself to be obsequious. As far as I was concerned I had done no wrong, and the whole argument seemed ridiculously one-sided and petty.

Wally, on the other hand, did not change his behaviour towards me at all. He remained as remote and correct as ever. His main preoccupation was with his own ballets and, as his wife was the principal inspiration for his work, the rest of the company sometimes seemed almost superfluous. For all that, Wally was inspirational, his choreography brilliant, his method of working unique. In everyday life he appeared an ordinary little man, neither handsome nor striking; no one would have suspected that this vague Scotsman could unleash such passion and inspired sensitivity in his ballets. There was never a moment's hesitation. While the music played, Wally moved and we followed. He spoke through movement with the eloquence of the articulate interlocutor delighting in his native tongue. Dance was so natural to him that he found it difficult to understand other people who did not share this special aptitude.

Most other choreographers in my experience take their dancers through their paces phrase by phrase, but Wally would bolt away, and after fifteen minutes of the chase we ordinary mortals would be no wiser. When we eventually managed to learn, we felt all the more privileged for having been allowed some insight into this remarkable man's poetic world. Then Wally would stop work, the screen would drop down, and in an instant he would disappear into his own private world. It was not unusual to see him wandering down the city streets, eyes aloft, casting handfuls of birdseed out to his feathered friends, too preoccupied in communicating with these little creatures to notice anyone else's existence.

People didn't seem to interest him much at all. He made no effort to engage in small talk at functions or even with his own company members, but he cared passionately for animals, pigeons in particular. It would be no exaggeration to say that he was obsessed with pigeons. 'Birds are taking over Wally's whole being', we would joke, 'and Paula is transforming into a bird in front of our eyes'. Paula had certainly done justice to her role as the bird-woman in *Eaters of Darkness*. She studied the role so intensely that she carried the twitchy, bird-like movements into her other ballets from sheer force of habit.

It was said that Wally and Paula always left their apartment windows open so that the pigeons could fly in and out at will. There was, however, a favourite bird by the name of Eric, to whom they were both so attached that they dedicated a ballet in his honour. Shortly after we went on tour, Wally received a telegram. He blanched and rushed straight into the dressing room to pack his belongings. We were told our director had to return to London on some urgent business. The company was thrown into disarray by the news, as we were in the middle of rehearsals for our next change of programme. When we were told that Wally was rushing back to nurse an injured Eric we could hardly believe our ears. The entire company had been jilted for a pigeon. Two days later Wally returned looking pale and jaded, but he did not tell us that his mercy mission had had an ironic twist. Wally had sat up all night to tend the ailing pigeon, when at dawn who should hop in through the window but a thoroughly fit Eric. Wally had left his entire company in the lurch for an imposter.

Having achieved so much, I should have been happy, but my physical self was in rebellion. Though I was eating less and less, my body continued to blossom. When I least expected or wanted it, I suddenly acquired a substantial bosom. I detested this new body image, and found it difficult to fend off the consequent barrage of sexist remarks with a semblance of humour. I felt so cumbersome with my huge mammary glands that I would gladly have had them surgically removed. But there was little the doctors could do. I could only wait patiently for my body to adjust to my new environment. By ordinary standards I was slim, and most people would have considered my desire to be pencil-thin a little perverse, for I was beginning to look womanly at last. I starved myself and ladled Durolax down my throat, yet my breasts persisted in straining the seams of my 34-inch bra.

One day I noticed that my left breast seemed to be blowing up like a balloon. When this was followed by quite a lot of discomfort, I realized that I needed medical attention. As we were all on tour I had to rely on the theatre doctors in each province. One doctor said my left breast was absorbing too much hormone, and gave me tablets to counteract this problem. The next doctor told me that I had an infection and prescribed an antibiotic. Another told me that I had a particularly virulent cancer, and there was little that could be done to help me. Other doctors also suspected cancer. Some administered pills and potions, others settled back into their black leather upholstery and tried to look pragmatic and professional; it's never pleasant having to break bad news to a patient. I began to believe my days were numbered, and lay awake at night imagining my funeral in Melbourne. I could see my family's tear-streaked faces. Though I was careful not to let on in my letters to my parents, my mother sensed immediately that something was terribly wrong.

Eventually my deformity became so grotesque that I could hardly hook up my costume. I was so lopsided that all the excess flesh was squeezed over the top and out the side of my tutu like an obscene pink blancmange. The other company members could not resist making quips about my malaise. 'We all watch from prompt corner', Mary said. 'That's her sexy side.' And Barry, my lovely Australian partner, would moan and groan as he supported my pirouettes: 'For Gawd's sake, Glad, lean to the right! We're both toppling to the left'.

One night the theatre manager in a dreary northern town told me that the telephone exchange had notified him that my parents had booked a call to me for 7 p.m. International calls were an expensive, complicated matter, and I think this was the first time I had spoken to my parents by phone since I came to Europe. I felt excited and nervous at the idea of hearing my parents' voices once again, but I hoped that I wouldn't become too emotional and spoil the whole thing by crying.

Fortunately I was not dancing that night, because the call did not come through until 11 p.m. I was a bundle of nerves by then, but when the warm voices of my mother and then my father came through (surprisingly clearly), my tension evaporated. This was a thousand times better than letters. I could feel their emotions flowing through the line. If Harry had not taken over, nothing would have stopped my babbling.

'Before you start nattering, shut up and listen to me', came the voice of authority. 'Gideon Goldstein has the name of a specialist at St Mary's Hospital, Paddington, for you to go and see.' Gideon had already briefed the specialist about my problem, and Harry was certain that he would come up with a cure. The official part over, Harry slipped out of his 'I talk, you listen' manner. 'Hi, Puss, how are you, all right?' His inane chatter brought a lump to my throat. Now that the family had taken charge, I had no doubt that my sickness would be cured.

As it turned out, it was not such a rare malaise after all, and there *was* a cure. I had mastitis, a disease that I had always associated with cows, not human beings. After a few weeks of treatment my breasts returned to their normal size, though they did not shrink as much as I had hoped.

As the tour entered its final stages we began to see our colleagues and our gypsy life in a more favourable light. Even the hardships of provincial touring seemed to diminish in importance; we realized that we would wither in a less highly strung environment. The life of a travelling trouper is no bagatelle, but where else can one expect to live in the lap of luxury one minute and in squalor the next? Where else could one be entertained by the Governor of Northern Ireland in the evening, then gag on a breakfast of greasy fried eggs and chips slopped on to the plate by a sluttish waitress?

The last day was predictably tearful. I gave everything I could to the final performance. The music had never sounded so sweet, and my stage relationships were never so emotional. There wasn't a dry eye as the full company took its final curtain call, stepping gingerly over a festoon of bouquets, single flowers and streamers. The curtain fell, and the London Ballet ceased to exist. Suddenly we were all displaced persons, searching for another surrogate family to provide us with the elaborate life-support system essential for us to practise our art.

17

A Chance and No Chance

I was no longer expecting a breakthrough regarding my Russian visa, as there had been no thaw in the international situation, and I felt the bad press in Australia had prejudiced my future at the Bolshoi. But I did not want to go back to the colonial outposts of the Royal Ballet that Miss van Praagh was busy establishing Down Under. I would stand a far better chance of finding a company suitable for my style of dancing here in Europe. But first I needed a little recreational happiness.

I went for a fortnight's holiday in Paris with Moya Knox. We took the £10 shuttle service, and found lodgings in a cheap, tacky hotel on the Boulevard St Michel. It mattered not one bit that we didn't have a basin to wash in and that our mattress was hard and lumpy. The sheer exhilaration of being in Paris compensated for the lack of creature comforts. For me Paris was a banquet of the senses. It was alive, romantic and mystical. If only the Marquis de Cuevas ballet company had still been in existence, or the Paris Opera Ballet had not sunk into mediocrity, I would have gladly hung my *pointe* shoes in that shabby room for a chance to live in this exquisite city.

In the 1960s, however, London was definitely the centre of all that was innovative in the arts, and London artistic life had a brashness and unrestrained anarchy that attracted young people from all over the world. So it was back to London, to a new bedsitter in Earls Court. Searching for low-cost accommodation in London was an arduous experience, but I got lucky, and was able to take over a bedsitter in the Cromwell Road from another dancer who was moving to Paris. For a rent of £3 10s I had a spacious, clean room with a gas ring for cooking and expansive double-glazed windows overlooking the rooftops of Earls Court. The room was in a 'girls only' guest house, which was looked after by a fastidious couple, Mr and Mrs Crystal, and their neurotic poodle, Piccolo. A set of rules was issued with the first receipt, and throughout the house strategically placed, neatly printed notices reminded us of our proprietors' earnest desire for order. There were notices over the loos asking lodgers to refrain from pulling the chain too vigorously: 'Three firm pulls are adequate'. 'Do not drop cigarette butts here' said the note above the wall telephone, with a red arrow pointing to the floor. And in the bathroom there were complicated, long-winded instructions concerning the use of the 'sensitive geyser', which had an insatiable appetite for shilling pieces and an annoying reluctance to keep its end of the bargain. Those shilling pieces were the bane of my bedsitting life, for without them there was no light, warmth or hygiene.

At this stage I was not at all worried by the notice at the entrance stating that all guests had to leave the premises by 11 p.m. and that no further guests were to be received after 10 p.m. Nefarious bedroom activities were not part of my current agenda.

With a roof over my head and a small reserve of money still in the bank at Aldwych, I placed myself back on to a diet of cottage cheese, yoghurt and liverwurst to prepare for an intense bout of training. After the slackness of our training on tour, I began to feel quite excited about getting back into shape and was delighted to be back at the barre of Maria's spacious studio. For the time being there were no pressing problems to solve, no decisions to make. All I could do was work and wait, and I was grateful for the mental respite that such routine classes allowed.

But after only a week of classes I came home to find a letter from Marie Rambert asking me if I still intended to return to Moscow and, if not, whether I could be persuaded to join her company. I was flattered by Madame's interest. I had been hearing stories about Rambert since I was a little girl. Always her name was uttered in hushed tones, like those of other ballet luminaries such as Diaghilev, Pavlova, Nijinsky and so on. I also knew that Rambert's leading ballerina, Lucette Aldous, having found her adult artistic feet, had left the fold, in accordance with a sad but steadfast Rambertian tradition. I discovered that I had friends in high places. Edward Mason, the *Sunday Telegraph* critic who had already helped my career along by writing a glowing review of my London Ballet performances, had decided that Mim needed me almost as much as I needed her. Apparently he had personally prompted Rambert to consider me as the replacement for Lucette.

Rumour had it that Mim preferred to sniff out new talent in interviews disguised as têtes-à-têtes rather than hold regular studio auditions. Rambert seemed interested in me right from the beginning of the interview, and I got the impression that she was so confident of her intuition that she took all our mutual future accomplishments

Marie Rambert

for granted. 'I am certain that with my guidance you will develop into a very fine artist', she said. Was this the direct line to artistic success I had dreamed about? Mim had been responsible for producing so much British dance talent that I would have been a fool not to recognize the possibilities of a future with her company. Furthermore, her company was a company of individuals, a rare thing in the cloned world of ballet.

In the end I clasped my hand over my eyes and jumped into the unknown. 'It is good to have self-doubts', Mim assured me. 'Complacency is the worst enemy of any artist. The more you learn, the more you will discover how little you know. *You*, my dear, are only on the brink of a voyage of wider and wider artistic discovery.' Who was I to question this doyenne of the arts? So I entrusted myself, self-doubts and all, to Rambert's magical powers, and hoped that I might be the next lucky young protégé bound for fame and fortune.

Ballet Rambert had only a fortnight left on tour before its annual four-week vacation, but Mim asked me to come to Canterbury for these last two weeks of the tour. 'You'll be able to watch the company and get a feel of our style and method of working', she told me, 'and I shall have the chance to work on you in class. Every moment is precious. I am going to enjoy working with you, but I want to develop you slowly and carefully'.

If only she had remained true to these wise words! I didn't know Mim well enough to realize that she was too impetuous to exercise caution and restraint. With Mim all tests were instant, spontaneous and resolute, and once her mind was made up it took a lot to dissuade her. 'She won't be able to keep her hands off you, you wait and see', one of the Australian boys had warned me. He was right. It was all a matter of staking a claim. If I *did* prove to be a valuable find, then Mim wished to have exclusive rights. Be damned if she would let her son-in-law have any of the kudos; the Ballet Rambert was her baby.

David Ellis, the Associate Director, was a flat-footed, doughy-faced man, and I deduced from the start that Mim did not have much faith in his judgement. Sharing power did not come easily to Mim. She preferred to be a benevolent ruler of a Utopian dictatorship. The company, however, had grown a great deal since its ballet club days. It received government funding, which implied it had to gain the allegiance of board members and public servants who knew little about the inside world of ballet. Though Mim involved herself in almost every aspect of her company's work, she could no longer expect to be entirely indispensable.

Though I enjoyed looking around historic Canterbury, the theatre where the Ballet Rambert was performing was a great disappointment. As in so many of these provincial towns, the tiny theatre had obviously been built for repertory. If theatre is the art of illusion, then the Ballet Rambert did not have a hope in hell of succeeding in that place. Far from being mesmerized by the beauty of the dance, I am sure the audience must have felt threatened by the proximity of the dancers' thundering feet. Sitting in the stalls, I had to crane backwards to see any action on the raised podium, and if I wished to see the dancers' facial expressions as well, it was like straining to see the topmost branches of a Huon pine forest.

When I did my first class in Canterbury the company was sardine-packed into a tiny church hall a short way from the theatre, for a class and routine adjustment rehearsal. Mim's class was impossible. There seemed to be no connecting thread of thought from beginning to end. We were left to sit out our *pliés*, over-taxing our thigh muscles, while Mim waddled away to poke and chastise the victim of the day. If we dared to stretch our legs to relieve the agony, Madame would berate us like a deranged harridan. We had no staying power. Why couldn't we take a lesson from her hero and paramour Nijinsky? To these ghosts from her past Rambert attributed miraculous feats, which seemed to grow more incredible with each day's embellishment.

'No wonder they're dead', snarled Ken Bannerman under his breath. 'Still, they're lucky not to have survived. They'd only have been expected to take Rambert's ghastly classes, and that would have killed them anyway.'

Throughout it all our pianist, Cyril Preedy, continued to play 'Falling in Love Again', his favourite tune for *pliés*, with a wonderful nonchalance. Rambert's antics left him unmoved; he played on, his repertoire ranging from saloon-style tunes to exquisitely played classics. Cyril had been a superbly talented concert pianist who, having lost his nerve one night on the concert platform, had resorted to drink to bolster his ego. Mim loathed human weakness of any kind, expecting from others the same Spartan discipline she imposed on her own life, so Cyril was often the target of her barbs.

If there was no consistent theme to Mim's classes, her rehearsal seemed even more erratic. As she called the variations and scenes she wished to see, I was told that none of these ballets was in the current repertoire. Apparently she pulled ballets out of the air to satisfy a passing whim, and the ballet of the evening or following season would go under-rehearsed and neglected. Once her mind was made up, however, no amount of protest from the company could deter her.

As the new girl I was the recipient of all the loving abuse the occasion allowed. The rest of the company gazed on with a mixture of respect and sympathy as Mim reprimanded me. While some people undoubtedly envied my good fortune, others were clearly relieved. To be ignored spelt artistic failure; to be deemed worthy of attention meant a life of being cajoled and prodded to such an extent that the strength of one's commitment was severely tested.

'How can you move after Rambert's class?' I asked fellow Australian Johnny O'Brien. 'You can't if you do it all', he replied. 'The trick is to learn how to do her class without doing it.' So began my first lesson in the grand deception that was essential for survival in the Ballet Rambert.

> When she looks into your eyes and says 'Oh, close that mouth and open your eyes', or when she pokes you between the shoulder blades, just smile sweetly, look back into her eyes, and rest your feet and legs. Immobilize any part of your body that is not being scrutinized. Learn to spare your muscles when you can.

I swear the Ballet Rambert's reputation as the intelligent British ballet company was due in part to the fact that a dancer had to be intelligent to survive Rambert's classroom training. She had no peers when it came to her instinctive feel for what was artistically right, but as a teacher of classical technique she left a lot to be desired. The fact that she fervently believed in her own talents as a pedagogue was perhaps the most worrying thing of all. Her teaching methods were often anathema to the laws governing human mobility. It was a case of survival of the most canny, and intelligent dancers soon learnt to distinguish between her good artistic advice and her bad advice in matters of performing technique.

For instance, if your arms are to move freely and with breadth, the shoulder blades should be spaced but flattened in a triangular shape down your back. In scrunching your shoulders back military-style—to 'crack a nut', as Mim put it—you simply lock your back and arms into such a fixed position that arm movement is almost impossible. Another comical obsession of hers was to demand a hermetically sealed fifth position, then suddenly materialize directly behind you to poke you in the back. 'Pitch forward!' she would screech. If you were fool enough to take your hand off the barre, you would land straight on your nose. But if she demanded you take your hand off the barre to test your balance and you *did* land on the floor, Mim would assume that you had deliberately bruised your nose to make a fool of her. Humour was an instrument for her use alone, though sometimes, when it suited her, she could play gentle games of self-derision.

After the Canterbury class Mim invited me to sit with her and watch the matinee. The ballet was *Coppélia*. In spite of the ridiculously small stage, Lucette Aldous was breathtaking in the role of Coppélia. Her technique was flawless, and not one movement was left to chance. I immediately panicked. There was no way that I could compare with such impeccable control. My own performances were still rather too dependent on what I euphemistically called inspiration; and depending on the intangible does not produce artistic consistency.

Mim, impervious to my anxiety, seemed delighted to have a sounding board for her sporadic outbursts; she did not invite any response from me. I felt sorry for the dancers as they went through their paces. Rambert seemed contemptuous of the audience's pleasure—or was it an attempt to win some audience for herself that made her behave so outrageously? Surely she couldn't have believed that no one heard her moan loudly and then berate a male dancer for dancing with 'so much luggage on his back'. The criticism was all the more cruel for being true: the dancer in question had high shoulders. But for Mim even one's genes were no excuse. As far as she was concerned it was all a matter of will, and she had a point. Many dancers have changed the contours of their bodies through scientific training, and many dancers have created a wonderful sense of physical length or breadth by skilful deception. But right now Mim's rhetoric was not exactly reassuring. If she thought of me as a conspirator, the conversation was manifestly one-sided. I tried to keep an open-minded attitude to the performance. After all I couldn't be sure that this scene wouldn't be repeated, with myself in the role of victim.

I couldn't imagine anyone being brave enough to argue a point of view with Mim. Her feelings ran hot or cold, her outbursts swung from gushing enthusiasm to acerbic criticism. No dancer could ever take Mim's feelings for granted. She would be all over you one day, but the next morning, swayed by an adverse newspaper review or an insidious whisper in the ear from some high-born lady with useful contacts, she would turn on you with unwarranted spite.

I was not impressed with the company's performance of *Coppélia*. Many of the solo dancers seemed miscast, and the *corps de ballet* looked like a raggle-taggle of character dancers. Rambert had a glorious heritage of superb masterpieces, not on the grand classical scale, but brilliant, more intimate dance treasures such as Tudor's *Lilac Garden* and *Dark Elegies*. Why, then, was Rambert attempting to stage a ballet better suited to the large showcase companies?

The audience hushed to mark the entrance of a new soloist. Feeling Mim tense, I turned to see her grimace. 'Horrible, horrible', she groaned. Most of the audience turned to watch her. 'That girl is not Dawn', Mim continued. 'You, my dear', she said, gripping me tightly, 'you must dance Dawn tonight'. 'But I don't know it', I stammered. The woman was crazy. Maybe she was joking? I scrutinized her face for some telltale sign of humour. 'I have never learnt that solo', I repeated more loudly. 'Well you must learn it, darling. I'm sure you are a quick learner, you are *so* intelligent.'

It was time to take a stand. 'Madame', I said, as politely as possible, 'you asked me to come to Canterbury to observe the company, and I have come totally unprepared for performing. I have no new *pointe* shoes, no make-up'. 'Don't worry', Mim coaxed, putting her arm over my shoulders, 'this is a most friendly company. Girls will lend you some make-up, and there will most probably be a pair of *pointe* shoes in the wardrobe department to fit you'.

By now I was in a fearful state. The woman had clearly taken leave of her senses. Mim had obviously decided to arrange a quick spontaneous audition for me while the company was out of London. Obviously Canterbury audiences did not rate highly in her opinion. I had three hours to learn an entire solo, and a technically exacting one at that, but I didn't have too much choice. Mim was in the commanding seat, and she could literally make or break me. Her face had set into unmoveable determination. She would see me on the stage that evening, ready or not.

I had heard that Mim was more interested in assessing performing quality than pyrotechnics. She didn't care if I knew all the steps or not. The rest of the performance was blacked out by a cloud of paralysing fear. This, then, was to be the end result of all my sacrifice. I was a dancer with no rights. I was being given a chance and no chance.

The girl whose position I was about to usurp was disconcertingly delighted. She had always hated that solo, for it entailed a lot of hard work for little reward, and now she sincerely wished me all the luck in the world. The solo was a stinker, with no redeeming features. Before I could even begin to think of mastering the technical side of it, I had to try to retain the sequences in my scrambled mind.

The whole company seemed glad of the diversion. Not that the dancers were unsympathetic, but it was a case of rather her than me. So for three hours I repeated the steps over and over again, phrase by phrase, saying the steps out loud as if I were learning my multiplication tables. I didn't dare let go of that all-important visual design—not on the loo or eating a sandwich or through a hurried costume alteration. Even when people spoke to me I could not afford to listen; just one word out of context and the thread of the pattern would be broken. To make it worse, the only shoes that the wardrobe could find to stay on my feet were horrendously misfitting, and despite the hurried tucks here and there the Dawn tutu swamped my body like an overgrown mushroom. I was now legless from the knees up and couldn't even walk in those shoes flat without sharp pains shooting up my legs. *Sur les pointes* was hell.

Apart from the pain, the inflexibility of my shoes posed another problem. I could not control the transition from flat to point and vice versa, which is essential to a sense of fluidity and grace. Yet it seemed ludicrous to worry about the aesthetics of the dance when I was struggling to remember the steps in the first place.

At the five-minute call Mim passed me on the stairwell, still rehearsing my steps out loud, and gave me a cheerful wink and a smile. Her apparent lack of concern was the last straw. Tears welled up in my eyes, and my stomach felt dangerously active. Anyone with more experience would have known better than to attempt such a foolhardy thing. Certainly anyone with an established reputation would never have risked losing it because of one old lady's selfish compulsion. But I was not experienced or established, and was devil-may-care enough to take the gamble. Besides, I still believed in the miracle of inspiration, and my nervousness had not entirely quelled my determination.

Soon the basement dressing room was empty. Dawn does not appear until the third act. I longed to rush up and get the wretched thing out of my system. Overhead I could hear the drumming sound of *pointe* shoes, nervously trying out problematic steps. My boxed-in space hummed with instruments tuning up, accompanied by unhappy tirades about the wretched stage surface, unco-operative shoes and tight costumes. Then there was a sudden quiet. My heart accelerated as the national anthem was played, followed by the overture, and the huge unwieldy curtain was cranked into the rafters. The performance had begun. I repeated the steps over and over again, adjusting my make-up for the eighth time while the sound of carefully synchronized feet and music thronged over the intercom. Suddenly the clamour of hundreds of appreciative hands shocked me back to my reality. There were people out there! Until now I hadn't even considered the audience. 'Full house', one of the girls remarked cheerfully as she puffed back into the dressing room for a dab of tissue on her dripping face.

The moment finally came; time to set my teeth and endure the agony. There was no turning back. 'Come on, Alida. If the steps fail, turn on the schmaltz', I told myself as I resined my feet for the last time. The curtain was still down for the intermission. 'Don't tire yourself', I heard someone say behind me as I threw myself into my last desperate rehearsal. 'You'll be beaut', my new Aussie friend Johnny said, throwing his arm around me. 'Be brilliant just to spite the old harridan.'

'Clear the stage, please', came the crisp order from prompt corner. 'Dim the auditorium lights. Company, take your places.' For the last time that night, the ancient curtain wobbled its way up to the rafters to let in a rush of cold air from the darkened auditorium. I was at my wits' end. 'I'll never do it.' Then I was on.

For the first few moments I was conscious of the scores of eyes peering at me from the wings but then, thank the Lord, my survival instinct took over. Sharp pangs gripped my chest as nerves and physical exertion took their toll. 'Push, push, come on you're nearly there!' was all I could say to myself throughout the three-minute ordeal. 'Come on, legs, don't give up', I pleaded. One more bout and I was off. I collapsed in the wings with a myriad of well-meaning hands and fingers reaching down to me.

'Can you make it for a curtain call?' the stage manager asked. I struggled up, and somehow found the strength to stagger out into the glaring lights to receive the audience's approval. Now there remained only one more lady to please. Her voice reached me well before her physical presence. 'Oh, what exuberance, such artistry!' it gushed. Then she dragged me back on to the stage, where the stage hands were busily dismounting the set. 'You were beautiful. *Now* we will rehearse. There were a few weak spots', Mim continued, 'but we will go through all those parts carefully now'.

Fortunately, or so I thought, there were no more *Coppélias* to be danced for the remainder of the season. The following evening was a triple bill. I don't remember what the first two ballets were, but *Les Sylphides* was the third, and it was to play a significant role in the continuing trial orchestrated by Dame Marie Rambert.

With Dawn over and done with, I believed I had passed muster. I was relieved, but far from content. To say I had *done* Dawn was fair comment, for I could never have said that I had danced the role to the best of my ability. The thing had been punched out without any consideration of light or shade, strength or subtlety. I had been like a wind-up toy, stepping out the programmed dance before my spring wound down. And in my case it did, for I don't think I could have managed one more step.

There was no respite in class the following morning. Mim's sensible walking shoes and ankle-length plastic mac looked strangely incongruous among the leotards and woollies. She looked like a fey little goblin. That evening I was taken by the hand again to watch the performance out front, but first I was paraded in the foyer like a prize Hereford cow. 'Oh, there is Mrs So-and-so', Mim would suddenly announce. 'Darling Mrs So-and-so, do come and meet my talented little ballerina, isn't she beautiful? She's *so* intelligent, but'—turning to me—'we have a lot of hard work to do together, haven't we? Stretch out that neck, dear, we must go'. And Mim dragged me on to meet her next contact.

Though I was the subject of these one-sided conversations, I never got to say more than 'how do you do' and 'pleased to meet you'. June Sandbrook danced a magical Sylphide; she was like thistledown, with an angelic face to match. This time I was impressed. The production was a gem, for Mim had been lucky enough to have Karsavina reproduce the ballet just as Fokine had first devised it. Now here was a ballet I fancied. The wonderful Chopin musical score and the exquisite lightness of the Fokine style appealed to me enormously. Mim could see that I was entranced by this performance. 'Are you prepared to work hard to be as good as that?' she asked, turning to me in the dark. 'I think you'll be just as good as June, who is the perfect Sylph, but I am warning you, I'm a hard taskmaster.' That was the understatement of the decade.

On the surface everyone seemed eager to welcome me. I was taken by the sense of unity that seemed to will everyone into doing their best for the sake of the company and the end performance. It was also refreshing to note that, although there was a hierarchical structure in the company, there was no posturing or rank-pulling on the part of the principal dancers. This may have been due to the fact that Mim cut *everyone* down to size with little regard for rank or status. As queen bee she was as obsessively critical of the leading ballerina as of the spear-bearer in the back row. As far as Mim was concerned, an eye for detail was crucial to the success of any production.

As yet no one had bothered to clarify what position I would hold in the company. All I knew was that I would be earning £15 a week and that I should be prepared for anything. Lying awake in my hotel room at night, I tried to surmise Mim's plans for my career. I guessed she would probably start me off in small roles like Dawn and gradually build me up to bigger and better parts. That would have been the logical course to take, assuming that Mim was a logical lady. I longed for the authoritative protection someone like Mim could offer, and was grateful that I was being tried in relatively undemanding roles where my technique would not be placed under a magnifying glass. In this way I believed I might be able to grow both artistically and technically at a leisurely pace. But I was wrong.

By my third day in Canterbury I was feeling relatively happy and relaxed, despite the physical side-effects of Mim's classes. It was too early for cynicism; I was inclined to disregard all the other dancers' complaints against Mim as normal dancers' gripes, or fanciful anecdotes to add to that ever-growing collection of Rambert legends. After class on the third day, however, I was physically exhausted. Even after the sweat had gone cold and I had flopped into the wings to watch another dancer in the throes of graceful anguish, my muscles continued to shudder. Then it was my turn again.

This time I was not sure that I could manage another step, not even to please Madame. 'You poor darling', Mim said as I limped centre stage. 'Yes, you are right, I have worked you like a slave. Go home and soak in a nice warm bath, and then have a good night's sleep, because I need you well for tomorrow night.' Panic—why tomorrow night? My muscles stopped shuddering as frigidity set in. 'Tomorrow night you will dance the *pas de deux* and Mazurka in *Les Sylphides*. I think *Sylphides* will suit you beautifully, with your classical face and those lovely, lovely lyrical *portes de bras*. Now, darling, do you think you can do it?'

It was not a question. Even if I had followed my first impulse and said 'no', Mim would have taken no notice. If she thought I could do it, it was as good as done, and I was expected to rise to the occasion. Mim had already seen the finished result in her mind's eye. But to me this looked like another deranged scheme. It was absurd to imagine that I could master the intricacies of Fokine's superb *pas de deux* and

Mazurka in one day. Fokine would no doubt have turned over in his grave to learn that someone was so audaciously attempting to dance his magnificent choreography after only a day's rehearsal.

But the adrenalin was already flooding through my body at the thought of this crazy challenge. This time I was not being asked to learn a three-minute solo, but an entire one-act ballet; at least I *had* been promised a day's rehearsal. I did not sleep well that night, although I did have a lukewarm bath. All night I only heard Chopin and saw lines of sylphs floating three inches above the earth. I tried to recall as much of the ballet as I could from having watched Paula Hinton in the wings.

Next morning I arrived on stage in full practice attire, bleary-eyed and neurotic, ready to throw myself into a full day's hard slog. Rambert, however, had other intentions. For no accountable reason, she coolly demanded that we rehearse *Czernyana*, a ballet that had not been in the repertoire for ages. I was left to hover agitatedly in a corner while Mim amused herself with other ballets from other times and places.

Finally, after a ghastly lunch break, she graciously deigned to pay me some attention. I had by now developed a nasty case of diarrhoea to add to my woes. With half a mind on what my belly and bowels might do, I found it hard to cope with the strain of having to absorb so much in such a short space of time. Gone was the sense of challenge, to be replaced by dire confusion and fear. This time I *longed* for an out. I felt defeated, and I hated Mim for being so cruel. Had I been halfway sensible I should have turned my back on it all there and then.

By 4.30 the steps were almost all there, though I wasn't confident that I could put the mechanics out of my mind and concentrate on artistic expression. Then the problems with the costume began. Not one costume fitted me, as my bust was far too large for Lucette's tiny shapeless dress. While one flat-chested dress was brought out after another, Mim contemptuously declared my bust out of bounds. 'Wind bandages around your chest. It must be flattened', she sneered. By stoking my paranoia about my body, Mim only succeeded in flattening my ego.

And, having begun to notice my faults, she didn't stop there. 'By the way', she went on mercilessly, 'the tip of your nose should be shaded with some leichener and, oh yes, I think your cheeks could do with some shading as well. We can't have a bonny little sylph, can we? You must adapt your make-up so you will look willowy. I know all the tricks of the trade to help you create that effect.' That was *all* I needed. An inadequate knowledge of the ballet I was supposed to dance, an inadequate body and a less than pleasing face. Not much to hang a career on.

After I was slapped and shaped into a new improved Alida, I hoped my mirrored image would substantiate Mim's claims. Instead my reflection was forlorn and slightly petulant—not at all the charismatic ballerina to merit our combined labours.

The curtain rose to reveal the beautiful black-and-white tableau that opens Fokine's somnambulistic *Les Sylphides*, with sylphs in calf-length tulle tutus aesthetically grouped around the stage, perfectly offsetting the soloists at centre stage. The poet, the only male in the ballet, stood plumb centre, head inclined in deep contemplation, supporting an ethereal sylph on each arm. I was one of the spiritual threesome, gazing out into some imaginary infinitude, poised to fly out

Alida with Ken Bannerman in the Ballet Rambert's *Giselle*, directed by Joyce Graeme

into Fokine's poetic vision. An eerie enchantment hung over the stage, enveloping spectators and dancers alike. Everything was unreal, a vision. The dancers should move as if in a trance, the long skirts that often conceal the feet creating an impression of weightlessness. Everything should be as in a puff of wind. And everything was, until I began to move. Why was it I felt so inexorably human, a useless mound of trembling flesh, caught up in a nightmare full of floating white geists? Though the poet's arm was meant to be purely decorative, I clung to it for dear life. Ken Bannerman, who was playing the poet, whispered through clenched teeth, 'Come on, girl: eyes, tits and teeth!', while the sylph on the other side did her best to maintain some semblance of serenity.

Ken had to think for two that evening. All through my Mazurka he darted from wing to wing, calling out steps and directions for exits and entrances. I don't know what I should have done without him. Ken was the most reliable partner I ever had. Unlike many other male stars, all his concern was for the well-being of his ballerina. He was always the chivalrous gentleman who remained quietly in the background while the ballerina took most of the credit for his fine helmsmanship. With his help, I managed to make most of the pieces fit. But I was more nervous after the performance than before it. I did not know what Rambert had thought of my performance, and, judging by her mercurial behaviour to date, anything was possible.

I returned to my space in the box-like principal's dressing room. We could all hear Mim coming down the corridor, peppering the rest of the cast with mild admonishments. I tried to pull myself together for the onslaught. 'Don't worry', Lucette Aldous said, 'I'm smothered in wintergreen linament. It's a Rambert repellent—she won't come anywhere near us when she smells it. Let's prop a few chairs up against the door as well, just for good measure'.

Nothing would stop Rambert. Our barricade came tumbling down as the door crashed open, and she didn't notice our attempts at chemical warfare. Mim was exuberant, and in two minutes flat I was dragged back on to the dismantled ruins of the *Sylphides* set. Mim wanted a repeat performance. I floated around with a feigned moodiness, while Mim seemed much more interested in my facial expressions than in anything that happened from below the waist. Just as well, as my bloodstained, stockinged feet, picking their way over tacks and splinters, were not a pretty sight. Two down, I thought. Could there possibly be more?

There could. Lucette was leaving at the end of Canterbury, and Mim wanted an instant replacement. Like Lucette I was small, vivacious and dramatic, and Mim clearly thought me a contender for the position. There was no time for gentle nurturing. Rambert simply assumed my shattered nerves were young enough to regenerate themselves, and I think she genuinely believed that all this nerve-racking business would strengthen my character. The company needed a new star, and Mim intended to find out if I could be the new name the company needed. Where better to risk a little loss of quality than in Canterbury?

The next day Rambert coolly announced that I would dance Giselle on the Saturday matinee. This time I had a day to learn an entirely new production of *Giselle* with a new company. Each of Mim's demands seemed more audacious than the last; in these past few days I had begun to discover that she was not only a hard taskmaster, but also incorrigibly Machiavellian.

My one rehearsal day was a shambles. It took place on the narrow strip of carpet between the front row of the stalls and the orchestra pit. While the rest of the company were rehearsing other sections of *Giselle*, their new leading lady was navigating herself around the kettle drums and the conductor's podium. 'Shut your mouth, drop your shoulders and look coy', Mim said; she seemed to be taking the situation seriously. A rehearsal was a rehearsal, wherever it might take place. Apart from Ken, who I had already been told would dance the role of Albrecht to my Giselle, I had not the foggiest notion who else was in the cast. I presumed that I would recognize Hilarian by his villainous make-up and attire. But how would I recognize the friends with whom Giselle had supposedly grown up? I had never seen the Rambert production, so I had no idea of the sets, the costumes or even all the choreography. This time Mim had gone too far.

When I *ballonéed* out of Giselle's cottage on that Saturday matinee, I felt so disorientated that I might as well have landed on the moon. I tried to familiarize myself with my new terrain, new props and people as quickly as I could. It wouldn't do to look as if I didn't recognize my own front door! Once again I was steered through most of the first act by assorted helping hands, Ken's brilliant partnering and some (at times conflicting) instructions from the wings.

But the mad scene was an opportunity to let rip, and let rip I did. I raged like a mad bull, I was so relieved to release all the emotions that had been festering inside me for the past four days. I had never felt more inclined to become publicly deranged. What did it matter if

I was grieving for unrequited love, a young life already spent, or the knowledge of my own exploitation? What burst forth was a torrent of genuine emotion.

As the company meandered back to their dressing rooms at the end of the first act, there were no theatrical gushings. I felt a real sense of solidarity. There was an occasional reassuring hand gently laid on my shoulder, and a few sincere warm embraces, but the general atmosphere was one of respectful sobriety. And, having purged myself of most of my canker and frustration, I found it relatively easy to drift weightlessly into the second act.

This time I was spared the rehearsal after the event. Mim was rapturous. She confessed that she had been moved to tears by my performance. 'You are a fortunate child', she said. 'You have the precious ability to move people to tears or laughter. You will be a very fine artist.' That was a great day. It was the day Madame decided my future.

Even though I was still not officially with the company, I was scheduled for several performances the following week. On the Monday evening, when the programme changes were announced to the audience over the public-address system, I was appalled to hear the announcement that Alida Beech would dance the Mazurka and *pas de deux* in that evening's performance of *Les Sylphides*. Mim had brazenly decided to change my name for me, without even consulting me. My surname might not roll easily off the tongue, but it was mine, and my father's and grandfather's in turn. I was indignant that Mim had assumed I had so little pride or attachment to my ancestry. I confronted her with my protest after the performance, but she had already decided that I could not possibly be a ballerina with a name like Glasbeek. The name Alida must be followed with a name of one syllable, she insisted. I was determined to hold my ground, but so was she. Over the next few performances I was announced as Alida Birch, Beck and so on, until finally I gave in. Though I couldn't imagine what my name had to do with my dancing ability, I realized that Mim would simply continue to invent names until I caved in. Riled by my defeat, I insisted that I at least choose my own name. I became Alida Belair, but at heart I knew I would always remain Alida Glasbeek.

18

'The Name is Alida'

The holidays finally arrived, and Mim flew off to play grandma to her daughter's children in Trinidad while I returned to some *real* ballet classes in London. I was still no clearer about my status at Ballet Rambert. No one had told me what was happening, and it was left to the press to convey the good news that I was the company's new principal. The London newspapers went on to tell the British public—and myself—that I would soon be seen dancing the leading roles in *Giselle, Coppélia* and *Don Quixote*. It seemed that I was still on a winning streak.

I was eager to establish my own little home away from home, using London as my base. London seemed a great deal less foreboding and lonely now. With a secure position and an ever-growing circle of friends, favourite shopping haunts and eateries, I felt I had a right to call London home.

I had recently acquired a new flatmate in my bedsitter. Anna Roberts, a friend from Australia, had arrived at Cromwell Road carrying all her worldly possessions: two pairs of trousers, a leather jacket and a suitcase filled with records and books. As flatmates we were an odd couple. Anna was in her late twenties, a handsome woman with a keen intellect and a vast knowledge of literature and music. Our bedsitter became our salon, where we spent many a wonderful evening listening to records, chatting or entertaining our migratory friends with some surprisingly sumptuous meals downed with copious amounts of wine and port. Our literary conversations ranged from Koestler to A. A. Milne, our musical interests from Lena Horne to the Mendelssohn violin concerto. There were some complications; Anna's drinking seemed to liven her up as the evening progressed, and as a result I often turned up to morning rehearsal looking ghastly. But I didn't mind too much. Those dark circles under my eyes were all part of my new, independent lifestyle, a sign of maturity.

Nevertheless, by the last days of the holiday and rehearsal period I was dying to get back to work. As soon as I was back on tour, lousy digs and all, I was happy. I disregarded the moans and groans of my more seasoned companions, and hoped that Mim would arrive back soon. And she did, refreshed and ready to eradicate the slightest tinge of slackness that might have crept into the ranks while she had been away.

Now it was known that I was the company's newest ballerina, Mim insisted on displaying me at every given opportunity. Whenever we happened to be together in a public place—a street, a shop, a theatre foyer—I was urged to shut my mouth, drop those shoulders and smile sweetly while she crowed my praises to her rapt entourage. For all they knew, I could have been a deaf mute.

The parameters of my relationship with Mim were defined from the start. Mim would take control of my ballet life and see to it that I received my due rewards, provided that I remained an obedient little hard-working underling. I was happy with this arrangement. Self-abnegation was part of our classroom and rehearsal ethics. We never complained about being called boys and girls rather than men and women. Being still a raw fledgeling, I needed my directress, and entrusted myself entirely to her care.

But Mim had retained some of her summer madness. In York, in the first week of our tour, she decided out of the blue that I should dance the role of Swanilda in *Coppélia* in the Saturday matinee. This decision may not have been as spontaneous as we thought; it transpired that she had important friends in York, and we knew she always liked to impress her friends. Just as in Canterbury, Mim refused to go through conventional rehearsals. For some unfathomable reason I was rehearsed to death in the first and third acts, but the second act, which is by far the most difficult, she simply refused to acknowledge.

Once again Ken came to the rescue. He arranged to meet me at the theatre at 7.30 on the Saturday morning, and fed me the steps like meat into a mincing machine. And, though I still felt ill-prepared as I went into the performance, I was beginning to feel like an old hand. I improvised through my memory lapses, and hammed up the rest for all I was worth. I got through the second act with the usual verbal goading from the wings and a lot of fill-in activity by Dr Coppelius's dolls, but then I barely had enough strength to make it through to the end.

The performance was a huge success. Curtain call followed curtain call amid foot-stomping applause, cheering and encoring. I was flabbergasted, and Mim was beside herself. She rushed backstage with the entire blue-rinse set of York in tow. 'Wasn't she just perfect?' she asked shrilly. 'She was vivacity herself. Do you all realize the poor girl danced the entire second act without any rehearsal?'

I *was* rehearsed in due course, and I was well cast as Swanilda, but I soon began to chafe at the limitations of the role. Though technically demanding, *Coppélia* is pure family entertainment, and I longed for something more emotionally and intellectually demanding. Though Mim tried to persuade me that the role had depths that I hadn't yet managed to explore, I needed a respite from this 'happy land' with its mechanical toys, eccentric toymakers and juvenile delinquents. I was hard put to endure so much gaiety night after night. Fortunately the company had a true spirit of co-operation on stage. Bawdy jokes and rude heckling (all in stage whispers) were a sure remedy for flagging smiles.

Rambert, on the other hand, believed artistry fed off insecurity and competition. She deliberately provoked rivalry among her principal dancers, and she liked dancers to dance in spite of her. It was a dangerous game, for in her prodding and probing she laid bare her artists' rawest emotions. Often the results were superb, but the process of wrenching these emotions out of their safe inner recesses could also break a dancer's spirit. Many talented dancers fell by the wayside, broken in mind and body, but the ballet world did not care to remember these anonymous victims. I am sure Mim would have brushed all this aside as being a matter of the survival of the fittest. She would have said that those who did not make it lacked the mettle that makes great artists, and were never *really* in the running.

Mim could drive the mildest mortals to unprecedented fits of pique. One day she set to work on Ken Bannerman. Ken was a reserved Scotsman, always more concerned with his partner's welfare than his own presentation, and as a result his own performance was often almost too low-key. Mim respected Ken and believed in his talent. She also knew that he was one of her most reliable and faithful dancers. But when a well-known critic reviewed Ken's performance in *Giselle* as being 'inhibited to the point of being wooden', Mim set to work. She was determined to expose the passions that lay under Ken's quiet reserve.

She needled away at Ken in that shrill accent we had all grown to love and fear. For most of the rehearsal Ken kept his temper, and showed a genuine desire to abide and learn. But eventually the slights become too malicious. He began to smoke cigarettes one after another. Smoke signals were a warning of an imminent explosion, but Mim continued to provoke him. Finally Ken went over the top. He pushed aside his friend Johnny, who was trying to restrain him, and strode towards the piano with clenched fists. To everyone's amazement Ken picked up this enormous instrument and carried it at a 45-degree angle into the centre of the room. 'Oh put it down, put it down', Mim flapped. 'It is a delicate instrument, it will be out of tune.' Ken opened his arms and dropped the piano with a crash. The whole company looked on in astonished silence as he calmly marched back to the dressing room. It was Mim who broke the silence. 'Ah, he will dance so well tonight', she said.

Mim did encourage a certain degree of independence in her dancers; she wanted us to be eager to learn, to make new discoveries in art and life. But our independence was conditional. She believed that her company would disintegrate into anarchy unless she was there to wield the whip.

Anna Truscott was set up as my sparring partner. Anna was a superb dancer in her own right, but after playing second fiddle to Lucette Aldous she now had to endure yet another of Mim's little discoveries. Anna and I were totally different, but we were cast in the same roles, and Mim had decided that it would be good for us to feel some honest resentment, jealousy and insecurity towards one another.

Anna was tall, elegant and sensual, with high cheekbones and the longest swanlike neck in the business. She was superb as the gypsy or Kitri in *Don Quixote*, or as the arrogant Russian ballerina in Tudor's *Gala Performance*, but she was no Swanilda. To watch her knocking over toys and running around the stage was like watching a dowager in the throes of senile dementia. Wisely Anna persuaded Rambert that she ought to relinquish Swanilda, which meant that I was lanced with the full workload until our newest ballerina, Cecilia Barrett, was groomed for the role.

Cecilia was also thrown into the fray, and what a merry little triangle we made! Rambert soon announced that I should learn the role of Kitri, and alternate with Anna. Under the circumstances Anna did not feel at all disposed to help me learn the role, and our working relationship was brittle to say the least. To make matters worse, Mim made a big show of changing some of the choreography to show off my 'superior technique', and she made some embarrassing references to my vivacity and ability to spin like a top. Anna had long limbs and high insteps, which made it hard for her to spin or hop *sur les pointes*. With my ironing-board feet I could hop for hours and manage any number of turns. I would have swapped my attributes for Anna's any time, but it was hard to be objective when poison was being ladled down one's throat. It was a while before Anna and I worked out who the mischief-maker was, and realized that we were both being fed similar stories about each other. After that we became firm friends, solidly opposed to Mim's machinations to drive a wedge between us.

When Anna fell in love with one of the musicians in the Rambert orchestra and her personal life assumed greater importance to her than her career, I found myself dancing more and more of her performances. Dancing two performances daily with any number of different partners was no joke, especially when working conditions were often terrible. But the harder I worked the more exhilarated I felt. I loved having my days filled with performance; it gave me a focus for my energy. I never stopped to consider that I was being blatantly exploited.

Mim drove me hard in the *Don Quixote* rehearsals. As always her reputation was on the line, and she was determined that I should outshine Lucette. I was rehearsed at every opportunity. After a full day's work Mim, fresh as a daisy, would set up a private rehearsal for my partner, Alexander Bennett, and myself. We would struggle through all the *pas de deux* over and over again until we could only mark the steps. Mim always seemed oblivious to our fatigue, and continued to exhort us to keep on until *she* felt ready to call it a day. It was hard to remind myself that such exclusive punishment was privilege.

There were still days when I felt homesick and lonely. It was on such a day, my twentieth birthday, that Mim chose to mount a relentless attack on my confidence. My feet were like Kirby grips, I didn't have Anna's elegance, and so it went on. I was made to feel like a lumpy peasant instead of the seductive maiden I was supposed to be portraying, and it went on for hours until I ran into the dressing room in tears.

This time I was past caring. I wanted to go home. Finding myself alone in the dressing room, I let rip. My tears turned to rage. I hurled everything I could find across the room, beginning with my *pointe* shoes.

Mim, astute as ever, and presumably working on her favourite tenet that raging was good for one, left me to rage to my heart's content. And finally, when I had cried myself out, I felt a great deal calmer. I sat down to contemplate the opposite wall, then put my *pointe* shoes back on and returned to rehearsal.

When I walked back into the studio everyone continued as if nothing unusual had happened. Mim held her tongue, and I worked well. At the end of the rehearsal Mim put her arm around me and said,

> You are a brave girl, that is what I like to see—a girl who has the courage to return to work. You think I'm a witch? Perhaps you are right, I am a horrible witch but I only scream at you more than the others because I love you and care for you and I also think you're worthy of more attention than the others. Darling, you are special and it is only for people like you that I still make the effort to come on tour. You make me feel young and give me hope for the future.

This was Mim at her oratorical best. All the blame had been thrown back into my court. There we both stood, locked in a tight embrace, with Mim in the dominant role, consoling her weeping ward.

The Scarborough Theatre, the venue for my opening night of *Don Quixote*, was a hell-hole. The stage was like a minefield, and the roof leaked. Gales howled around the stage, and icicles formed on the dancers' eyelids if they stood still for any length of time. Some of the dancers didn't even make it to the battlefield, but fell victim to the almost perpendicular stairs that led down from the dressing rooms to the stage. Backstage, the four principal females had to share one tiny dressing room. The other three had taken pity on me because it was my first night, so I had a wash basin to sit in. The others had to apply their make-up standing up. We had wound plastic around our bodies in a futile bid to keep warm, and I remember thinking that if the plastic did not stop crackling I would lose my mind.

I must have been getting used to adversity, for the performance went off with a bang. I loved the role of Kitri, with its fiery virtuosity; it gave me a chance to show off all the flashy technical feats I had performed since I was a child. I'm sure I gave Mim many moments of concern during the rehearsals, but by now she had probably realized I was not a classroom dancer. I needed the stage, the lights, the orchestra and the audience to make it all happen.

After a trial run in York, Scarborough and the rest, I was launched into the big time at the Richmond Theatre in London. Mim had already

With Alexander Bennett in *Don Quixote*, 1964

sounded the fanfare. 'You wait until you see my jewel!' she would say, inclining her head in my direction. 'This is one to be treasured.'

If it is possible for a life to change at a given time, if it is possible to feel that all one's work, powers and desire have reached a single moment of reward, then my moment was the final curtain call of that first *Don Quixote* in Richmond. I received a standing ovation. No feeling in the world can compare with such exultation. As the audience chanted 'Alida, Alida', I stood centre stage, covered in flowers, amazed that the tumultuous ovation could be for me. Unashamedly I let the tears erode the face that I had carefully painted to give me courage. There was only one thing missing: my parents.

Rambert was pleased. I know she was pleased, because she created a spectacle at my expense for the benefit of her entourage of backstage visitors. 'You must not hold your flowers like this', she scolded, making me rearrange all the bouquets in my arms. Then she made me take all my curtain calls again.

I knew that audience acknowledgement is no guide to press reactions, so I was apprehensive when the newspapers dropped through the slot in the front door the next morning. Then I saw the headline on page three. 'The name is Alida.' The critic, Clive Barnes, went on to say: 'Britain can add a new name to her list of promising young ballerinas this morning, the name is Alida Belair'. Some of the other papers were even more lavish in their praise. This time I had stepped through the doorway of my life's ambition, and I wanted to go on and on. In any case there could be no turning back. Like it or not, and at the moment I *loved* it, I was now walking the same tightrope as any principal dancer in any other major European ballet company. It was too late to plead youth as protection against unfair criticism. I would just have to accept axes or orchids alike. Yet I still felt that I was a student rather than a fully accomplished ballerina, and was surprised to read some of the extravagant claims made by the London press. One of the papers stated rather too unequivocally that I was the Ballet Rambert's trump card. I was the 'Dancer you will know' of 1964 for the dance magazine *Dance and Dancers*, which predicted a great future for me. All this did me no end of good in Mim's eyes. She chuckled as she told me that one critic had told her he thought me so ravishing that he was almost prepared to turn heterosexual.

My success was proof that Mim had lost none of her talent for discovering talent in others. She seemed ecstatic. As a reward I was offered a new status in our relationship. I became a sort of foster-child as Mim set about shaping me into a well-rounded artist. She gave me a wide range of literature to consume, and she would ring up ordering me to dress up and accompany her for an evening at the theatre, sometimes at less than thirty minutes notice. I was paraded in the foyer as a kind of live promo for Ballet Rambert, then taken backstage to meet Mim's theatrical friends. Rambert was always outrageous, always the leading lady. Wherever she went she found her own opportunity to create theatre. And these performances had their embarrassing moments.

Mim and I went to see a performance by Ram Gopal, who had obviously seen better days. He was overweight, and had unwisely left his torso flab exposed and squeezed his spreading posterior into transparent harem pants. His face was a caricature of an ageing Parisian harlot, heavily rouged, and with lurid vermilion lips. We were seated in a row reserved for critics and other luminaries, and Mim could not resist making some mileage out of this situation. A few minutes into the performance, when Gopal moved towards the wings, Mim yelled 'Oh, thank the Lord he is going!' Then '*Au secours, c'est une faute*, he is coming back!' Feeling confident that she now had all eyes upon her, Mim warmed to the occasion. 'Ah, now I know who it is', she whispered, loudly enough to be heard two blocks away. 'That man on stage is not Gopal, it's Gertrude Lawrence.' For the rest of the performance she wrote notes on scraps of paper, which she passed down the line of chortling critics, all of whom had lost interest in Gopal, and were busily memorizing the quotable quotes of Dame Marie.

It may be almost sacrilegious to admit it, but I found Martha Graham's performance equally repulsive. The woman was seventy-five, and that sort of maturity is no great advantage in the dance world. Every time she plunged down into one of the falls for which she and her dancers were famous, I feared that she would never again make it back to an upright position. In any case, I wasn't taken by all that grovelling and swivelling on the floor. The style was rather too earth-bound for my liking. Though she looked macabre, the choreography was certainly impressive. This was a whole new concept and vocabulary of dance movement. Martha Graham devised a new dance language, which has spawned derivative styles in dance companies throughout the world.

Mim had no reservations at all. For once she did not utter a word through the entire performance. After the performance we went backstage to meet the great lady, who looked even more repulsive without the aid of her lighting technicians. Mim, however, stopped short only of kissing Martha's feet. For at least six weeks the company had to endure Mim's Graham phase, which proved to be a pain in the arse in more ways than one. Without any apparent logic, Mim made us sit legs astraddle (as close to the splits as we could manage without detaching a limb or two) while Mim took her time hitching up her own skirts to her knickers in order to strike a similar pose. 'If Martha can do it, so can I', she declared. Mim often passed through such obsessive phases, but mercifully they were short-lived. It was always a relief when she returned to her dear old French tango.

Mim liked being famous. She liked being the centre of her arty world. She was the *grande dame* of English ballet, the witty raconteur *par excellence*, the European urbane intellectual known to quote Racine in superb French or to run through all Shakespeare's sonnets at the drop of a hat. She was the establishment's pet eccentric. Mim, the Polish renegade, longed to be accepted by the aristocracy in her adopted country, though she loved to joke that the day she was made a Dame had been 'the Daming of the Shrew'.

Another of her little anecdotes is legendary. The story goes that one day Mim was at a Royal Ballet rehearsal at Covent Garden, and found herself being distracted by a young lady seated across the aisle, who insisted on waving to her all through the rehearsal. 'I didn't know who it was', Rambert said, 'but I was sure I recognized her from somewhere. After the rehearsal she rushed over to me and embraced me. Huh, do you know who she was? She was Princess Margaret'.

Mim's personality had been crystallized in the Paris of the early 1900s, in the epicentre of European culture. Paris was also a city where eccentricity and extravagance mixed readily with decrepitude and decadence, and it was in that city, where almost anything goes, that Mim formed her moral attitudes and social mores. She tried to pass on this broadmindedness to her company members. She positively encouraged love affairs, and even managed to derive pleasure from the scandals that ensued from some of her less successful attempts at matchmaking. She abhorred on-stage campery, however, though she closed her eyes when company members had homosexual relationships in their private lives. Her emphasis was on living life fully, and her ultimate aim was to produce artists who were capable of drawing on their own experiences to express the whole gamut of human emotions.

Mim did her best to invest me with some of her enthusiasm for the good things of life, and I was a willing and receptive pupil. She took me to the plays of Brecht, Noël Coward and Shakespeare, to orchestral concerts, museums and poetry recitals. She regaled me with her renditions of bawdy French songs and *risqué* anecdotes about famous people. Though she had a dressing room of her own, she preferred to visit me in my dressing room, and arrived at some inopportune times. Yet I respected Mim's intellect and cultivated taste. I also understood exactly what she meant when she said, 'You are already a ballerina. Now you must work hard to become so, so much more'. How I longed to be so much more!

With a host of new and challenging roles ahead of me, there was no danger of my becoming complacent or bored. About this time Norman Morrice, our resident choreographer, asked Mim if he could use me in one of his modern ballets. Although my heart was still very much in classical ballet, I was eager to extend myself. Mim also appeared very much in favour of the suggestion, but nothing definite was arranged and the idea was shelved.

Although the company had a hierarchical structure, there were ample opportunities for all the dancers in the less structured ballets—*Dark Elegies,* the Norman Morrice ballets and other dance dramas—where it was less a matter of singling out people with the best classical technique than of casting the right people to portray specified characters. In a short time I added several exciting roles to my repertoire. I now danced Swanilda in *Coppélia,* Kitri in *Don Quixote,* the snooty Russian dancer in *Gala Performance, Giselle* and *Les Sylphides.* But I didn't expect to go on receiving such rewarding roles, and, sure enough, I soon landed a solo I loathed. It was an extremely demanding virtuoso piece called '*M'as tu vus*' in Frank Staff's *Czernyana.* I couldn't think of a worse punishment than to be put through that number. From the moment I bounced on to the stage in a *grande assemblée,* it was all *ballon,* right up to the end. Just to add a little sadistic touch, I was expected to maintain a pert little smile throughout this torture session. '*M'as tu vus*' was the only solo I ever tried to relinquish, and I didn't even care to whom I gave it. But no one else *wanted* to even attempt to dance that three-minute killer. Mim insisted that I was brilliant in the role. Edward Mason of the London *Sunday Telegraph* only wrote my epitaph when he confirmed Mim's view by writing that he couldn't recall seeing the role performed better.

With the triumphs and praises came disasters as well, and they occurred precisely when I was seeking to impress. One ghastly incident occurred when Alex Bennett and I were dancing *Coppelia* together. Everything was progressing smoothly until we reached the climactic section of the ballet in the third act *pas de deux.* The entrance of this *pas de deux* can be a beautiful moment. The ballerina bourrées graciously towards her humbled partner, who is waiting in a kneeling position. His right arm is outstretched to receive Swanilda as she gently lowers herself into the crook. Having secured her there, he rises to his feet, with Swanilda appearing to hover in space, in a graceful swallow position. It is a theatrical piece of choreography; when executed perfectly, it is quite breathtaking. On this occasion, however, I lowered myself on to the wrong section of Alex's arm; then, instead of moving his arm to readjust the balance, he said, in his very refined voice, 'My God, I think we are falling. Oh yes, we are falling', and I felt our pose slowly disintegrate like a melting candle, until we were lying side by side on the floor. For a moment I was blinded by the chiffon frills that had flopped over my face, then I jumped up to try and salvage what was left of our performance, but Alex had other intentions. 'For goodness' sake don't hurry', he mumbled as I bourréed self-consciously on the spot, waiting for my errant partner to return to me. 'Don't rush, you'll get an injury.' The music flowed on while Alex languidly rose to his feet. 'Must get yourself together *first*, darling', he continued laconically. Then, when he felt composed, he joined me as if nothing untoward had occurred. For me it was a devastating experience, but Alex never spoke about it again.

Other touring mishaps were quite outside our control. When we arrived to perform in Torquay we discovered that British Railways had managed to rail our costumes somewhere to the north of the country, but Mim insisted the show must go on, without sets, costumes, shoes or make-up. So we danced *Coppélia* in our practice clothes, and in stockinged or bare feet. Then there was the unforgettable time that I danced *Les Sylphides* topless. Right in the middle of the ethereal solo in the prelude, both my shoulder elastics snapped simultaneously. I hastily

Rehearsing for *Coppélia* in leg-warmers

bourréed off, trying not to notice the leering gazes of a couple of horny men in the front row.

These were the spectacular disasters, but it was the trivial discomforts of touring that wore our spirits down. Most of the time it was cold, so very, very cold, and through it all we had to endure subhuman living conditions and ridiculous travel arrangements, which had us zigzagging all over the English countryside just to travel fifty miles from London. Add to that undanceable stages, unappreciative audiences, claustrophobic relationships within the company, and you are bound to have some pretty grizzly dancers.

The long tours made one feel rather like an assembly worker; one town began to look much the same as the next, and the ballets were churned out repetitively, night after night. Our only relief was to be cast in a new ballet. The cloistered quality of touring life also presented a problem for me. While I was immersed in learning new ballets or correcting faults, I didn't give a damn where I was, but from time to time I became desperate to return to London just to re-establish my own identity. A few other members of the company felt the same way, and we would madly dash back to London whenever we were within striking distance. Sometimes I would not arrive until 3 or 4 a.m. on Sunday, but it was worth it just to get a few hours' sleep in my own bed and spend a glorious day pottering around the flat and walking around London. Then on Monday it was back to the provinces, just in time for morning class and 'shop' as usual. It was amazing how those short spells away from the company helped raise my tolerance level for the rest of the week.

One night I arrived back at Cromwell Road at about 2 a.m. to find Anna up and obviously intent on keeping *me* up. She was wearing her sensible Bonds knickers and singlet, and pressed me to have a glass of Scotch; I think she had consumed a vast quantity already. Reluctantly I settled for a quick nightcap, but when Anna went to balance herself on the arm of one of our fauteuils, the chair overbalanced and came crashing on to the floor with a loud bang. Almost immediately the door flew open and an irate Mr Crystal barged straight in to confront Anna in her undies. 'Where is he? where is he?' he demanded, searching around the room. 'I know you have a man in here, Miss Roberts, we're quite aware of what you're up to. You've given poor Mrs Crystal a headache and the poodle is a nervous wreck.'

Drink seemed to loosen Anna's tongue and release her mind. Even I knew never to cross her when she was in such a state. Obviously Mr Crystal did not know what he was in for.

'How dare you burst in here and invade my privacy?' Anna began, slowly and clearly. 'Have you never heard of knocking?' Then there followed a diatribe so vicious that I could only stand there speechless, completely overawed.

The next time I arrived back in London, Anna was waiting for me at the door. 'Alidushka, I am sorry, but I have bad news. That pathetic Mrs Crystal has evicted me, although she emphasized that you, my sweet little dancer, are most welcome to stay.' Naturally I said I would go with her, and I went downstairs to the Crystals' flat to give notice immediately.

19

A Classical Cul-de-Sac

Our next flat was a much grander affair. It was in Bedford Park, and had a huge bed-sitting room with French windows opening on to a lovely garden, plus a second bedroom, bathroom and small kitchen. After Cromwell Road it seemed positively rural, and we were both delighted to have some greenery around us again.

Mim continued to drive me pitilessly, and persisted with her campaign of introducing me to the world of London theatre and high society. I was invited to Lady Bonham-Carter's functions, drank cocktails with Princess Margaret after a gala performance, opened the newly restored Georgian Theatre in Richmond, and became close friends with the Pilkington family, who had been Rambert supporters right from the earliest Mercury days. In class-ridden Britain, to be called an artist was to be given a free pass that transcended all barriers.

Around this time I acquired a new friend. The friendship had not been the result of an instant mutual attraction; on the contrary, Wendy had been foisted upon me by Mim, and if we did become an almost inseparable couple it was no thanks to her. As soon as Wendy walked into the rehearsal room I knew she was an Australian. She bounced in, bronzed and energetic, brimming with determination. By now I had been well and truly toned down in complexion and manner, and I found her conscientiousness and sincerity quite sickening. 'How obnoxious!' we all groaned when Wendy jumped in to do all the exercises, with every group, boys or girls. She practised like a little dervish in the tea break, and smiled obsequiously when Mim corrected her.

Mim's favourable response to this tarted-up mallee bird made the rest of us bare our teeth and wince.

At the end of our rehearsal Mim called me over to introduce Wendy formally. 'I have a fellow countrywoman here', Mim said, implying that I should jump up and down with joy. 'I know', I snarled. But Mim persisted: 'Wendy is joining the company, and as she doesn't know anyone I thought maybe she could share digs with you. You know how it feels to be so far away from home and alone'. 'OK', I grunted, and strode away without looking back. But to my surprise I grew to like Wendy, with her single-minded resolve to make it to the top. She had a strength and self-confidence that I came to envy.

Wendy was a devout Roman Catholic, and never missed going to church. No matter how early the train call, or how high or impassable the snow drift, even after a night of carousing at a club or disco, Wendy would rise at 6 a.m. for church on Sunday, and return with a glowing face and shining eyes. I respected her religious convictions, even though I did not share them. We simply made a tacit agreement never to discuss the subject. And otherwise we were just two libidinous Aussie maidens determined to enjoy life while remaining paragons of virtue. I think we made a rather formidable twosome.

Like two escapees from Dartmoor, Wendy and I lived it up in the little spare time we had. We discoed in the famous Cavern in Liverpool, home of the Beatles and Cilla Black; we ventured into casinos in the smoggy towns of the industrial North, and we drank many an Irish coffee in the taverns of Dublin, especially the theatre pub, where we were enchanted by the vibrant loquacity of the regulars. Dublin was a great place for me in more ways than one, for we performed to packed houses, and I received yet another glowing notice from the respected local critic, Míchéal Mac Liammóir.

Oxford and Cambridge were two of our favourite spots. Apart from their scenic appeal, I was drawn to these beautiful historic places of learning by a baser attraction. I was most definitely into intellectual men, and there was no scarcity of that particular species in Oxford and Cambridge. In our spare time Wendy and I sat in the busy student cafés and observed the parade of male talent. Rambert had friends in Cambridge and Oxford, and was in her element there. Mim adored excellence in any endeavour, as well as social status; I am sure she would have preferred to sit down to a bad meal with a member of the intelligentsia or aristocracy than a good meal with someone she considered uncultured. So in mid-tour she would often make us switch from our scheduled repertoire to the more highbrow ballets. It was important to her that Ballet Rambert should continue to be considered the thinking person's company.

Wendy and I were always delighted to meet people outside the ballet world. We became acquainted with the cast of the Royal Shakespeare Company's production of *Marat/Sade*. Their world had a carefree abandon that we as dancers could never dare to experience fully. Though the actors were all dedicated, and worked hard, they could punish their bodies in the name of pure pleasure and still go on to perform. On nights when we were not performing we would meet our friends at the Opera Tavern to chat and drink until their half-hour call. Then our friends would saunter off to put on their make-up and walk on to the stage, stone cold. After curtain down it was back to the Tavern for some more drink and discourse until well after closing time, which was just a matter of closing the curtains and locking the doors. Indeed it was not unusual for the bobby on that particular beat to come in and join the rest of us for a few pints.

I was attracted to these suave, articulate men, and the fact that actors had a reputation for being 'fast' only made them more appealing. Every time we came to the Tavern, we were greeted extravagantly, and we were introduced as 'our *beautiful* ballerina friends'. But my friendship with this group of actors—Patrick McGee, Robert Lloyd, Freddie Jones, Anthony Hopkins, David Warner and others—stimulated far more than my adolescent sense of sexual daring. By contrast with *Marat/Sade* and Peter Brook's wonderful production of *A Midsummer Night's Dream*, my own art form began to seem facile. I began to feel that Ballet Rambert was arrested in limbo. It was neither a great classical company nor a hotbed of innovation. The members of the RSC were witty, physically confident and politically and socially active. They were not submerging themselves in a demure fantasy world.

In spite of my burgeoning disillusionment, I was still riding high. I continued to receive glowing notices in the London press, and there was nothing like the London seasons and the possibility of critical acclaim to spur me on to greater feats than I ever imagined possible. The climax of every year was our short but important season at the Sadler's Wells Theatre in Islington. Suddenly all the wounded and ill dancers in our ranks would make miraculous recoveries to join in the wrangle for first nights and prominent billings. The London seasons provided us all with the glamour and credibility we needed to survive the provincial tours.

For our next season at the Wells I had been chosen to dance the technically difficult polka in a revival of Frederick Ashton's *Façade*. My predecessors in the polka were formidable—Markova, Fonteyn and Sibley, to name but three—and Mim was determined that I should uphold the high standards these famous dancers had established. She set out a harrowing training programme, and even wrote me a letter of instruction for when she was not on tour to supervise my rehearsals in person. 'Learn the polka phrase by phrase and then the whole', she wrote,

> and do it right through twice every day at least. You may not find it as difficult as Lucette and Maggie found it, but to do it on the first night in London, it must be perfect. When Ashton was teaching it to Margot, he made her do it twice through so as not to get puffed. The turns must be done with absolute certainty, so practise a dozen running in a circle.

She added in a postscript: 'Sibley does it all to perfection and you must beat it, my love to you, M.R.' I did not let down the side. I received great notices, the company's honour remained intact, and my relationship with Rambert continued to ebb and flow as usual.

When the ballet season finished, Wendy and I booked for the Costa Brava. For months I had been longing to escape the English winter. We had a thoroughly enjoyable vacation, surrounded by a large circle of suitors with whom we flirted and danced the balmy nights away.

Renée (Wendy) and Alida in Spain, 1964

Thoroughly intoxicated by so much Latin charm, we decided to adopt a more exotic identity for the duration of our holiday. Instead of admitting to our boring colonial background, we rolled our r's and became Renée and Alida, the French girls. Wendy, now Renée, immersed herself in this gallicization. She dressed herself as a Parisian coquette, with a beret cocked cheekily on her chignon, and uttered numerous little *bon mots* in her Aussiefied French. From that time on she insisted that the name Wendy, as applied to her, no longer existed. I could not take this impromptu switch quite so seriously, and by way of a friendly compromise, I called her Bon Bon instead. The name stuck, and was adopted by our colleagues in the Ballet Rambert, but the name Renée had been approved and accepted by Mim. Soon it was official; Wendy exited from the company, and Renée Valent discreetly slipped in to take her place.

The Tudor ballets *Lilac Garden* and *Elegies*, and Walter Gore's *Sweet Dancer*, were the gems of the Ballet Rambert repertoire, and reserved for the most mature artists. Mim felt that I was still not ready to dance roles that demanded such a depth of emotionalism. Rightly or wrongly, company circumstances demanded that I be moulded into a classical ballerina because of my superficially strong technique. I yearned to dance demi-character parts that had more humanness about them, but to my chagrin I was left to re-create roles that had already been danced by a continuous line of dancers before me. Though it was an honour to be part of that immortal line-up, at the age of twenty I was still intent on self-discovery. I turned these recycled ballets sideways, upside down and inside out—I did everything in my power to claim these roles as my own.

Most of my life I had been driven to dance, but now that pillar of certainty seemed less than sound. My cerebral needs were far from being satisfied, and my artistic needs were being ignored. I began to ask myself if all the effort had been worth while. My work was so all-encompassing that I was certain my perspective of life beyond the resin box had become distorted. Maybe it had been a case of too much too soon, but I felt I had outgrown my world of bird-women, enchanted maidens and virtuous demented peasants.

Night after night I stood in the wings watching the more mature artists perform those Tudor masterpieces with tears streaming down my face, responding to the sublime beauty of these works of genius, and anguished at being denied a chance to dance them. I found it hard to enjoy dancing at the cost of so much emotional suppression. Worse still, I realized that, although Rambert presumed to know me, she saw only the person she wanted to see. My performances were still being acclaimed, and to Rambert that was all that mattered. I began to push for some more fulfilling roles, but was told to be patient and bide my time. As far as Mim was concerned, my progress was up to her; my duty was to work and have faith.

Rambert also had problems of her own. More than at any other time in the Ballet Rambert's existence, Mim's unique talents were being inhibited by the need to secure government funding. When the Ballet Club was formed it had provided a nurturing ground for the talents of people like Ashton, Tudor, Gore and Staff. The club's development reflected the taste of its owner, and because the property was a freehold the theatre was in a position of modest independence. Now it was a different ball game. The Ballet Rambert had entered the ballet establishment, and it had to conform to the requirements of the theatre boards and arts councils. The company's creativity plateaued while it struggled with its identity crisis. Ballet Rambert was dependent on the public purse, and the public was notoriously intolerant of artistic experimentation. Furthermore, the company was expected to tour extensively, and provincial audiences mainly attended performances of well-known ballets. So Rambert the innovator found herself having to perform the classics that should have been left to the Royal in order to fulfil her obligations to the tax-paying public.

Everyone in the company realized that the Ballet Rambert was running out of puff. In her efforts to please all her clients, Mim was in danger of pleasing no one, least of all herself. We did not have the technical or financial resources to make a success of the ambitious classical productions. As a product of *La Belle Epoque* in Europe, Mim seemed at odds with the changing cultural mood of the 1960s. Her creations had arisen out of an intimate, clubbish atmosphere where risks could be taken. I believe that Rambert was also out of kilter with the contemporary ballets that her resident choreographers were creating, though instinctively she knew that she would have to move with the times or face oblivion. After the première of one of Norman Morrice's ballets she came hurtling backstage, gushing, 'Wasn't it marvellous! I didn't understand it at all, but I know that it was wonderful!'

While I was in the company it was divided into two schools of thought. There were those who believed that Ballet Rambert should continue to exhibit its real artistic gems along with some carefully selected classical ballets suitable for a small company, while others felt the company could only survive if it swung full circle and again became a small experimental company, as it could not compete with the larger companies in the production of full-scale classics. The latter was the only real alternative but my die had already been cast. To the public and to most of the other company directors who mattered, I was Alida the classical ballerina.

I think my style was more middle-of-the-road, neither extremely classical nor obviously modern. I definitely was not a Norman Morrice dancer, however. When I was eventually cast in his ill-fated *Cul de Sac*, I could not endure having to count the music rather than just feel it. This mechanical way of executing the steps made me feel alienated

Vamping it up with John Chesworth in Norman Morrice's *Cul de Sac*, 1964

from the spirit of the dance. Mim maintained, mischievously perhaps, that my role as the tart in *Cul de Sac* was one of my best, but I felt no inclination to pursue this style of dancing.

It was becoming clear to me that Mim was at a loss as to what to do with her new protégé. We both knew that before long we would have to take different paths. Mim needed her company to survive, and I had just happened to wander in at the wrong time. While Mim was treading water, people who were abreast with the political and bureaucratic wranglings were already devising plans for the Ballet Rambert. I was not inclined to involve myself in such matters. I didn't realize then that the freedom to create ultimately rests with the freedom to control one's own artistic destiny, or to be in a position to control the destiny of others. At that stage I still believed I needed the structure provided by a benevolent dictatorship to help me develop as an artist.

My life outside the ballet company was developing most agreeably. London had closed in around me with the soothing intimacy of a well-used leather armchair. I knew where the action was, and where to find privacy and seclusion when I needed it. Above all, I felt a growing sense of confidence about living independently. Anna Roberts and I had parted on amicable terms after I came home from another tour to find that Anna had again been given the boot by the landlady. 'She may own the flat but she doesn't own me', Anna said by way of apology. The flighty ballerina and the avowed polemicist went their different ways.

With the help of Rambert's estate agent I found a super flat in Linden Gardens, Notting Hill Gate, a stone's throw from the Mercury Theatre. Even on a principal's income I could not contemplate taking a flat on my own, especially when I only used it as a home base and had to pay living costs while on tour out of an inadequate tour allowance. Renée and I, now close friends, set up our own little *pied-à-terre* with another Australian girl. Though our fourth-floor flat was far from grand, we transformed it into a home with a great deal of character.

We covered our tattered Victorian chairs and fauteuils with brightly coloured hessian, and decorated the walls with unframed posters and prints. We had none of the more conventional bourgeois collectors' items, but for us the empty Chianti bottles, first-night mementos, pressed roses and photos and postcards from loved ones had far more meaning. Whenever Bon Bon and I had the opportunity, we hared back from the provinces to spend some time at home. Here in Linden

Gardens we had no bothersome landladies, and we felt free to entertain and party to our heart's content. With hindsight I marvel that the tenants below us did not weary of hearing us stomp out the rhythms of 'I can't get no satisfaction', and seek to obtain *their* satisfaction by having us evicted. Even when we found ourselves counting the days until the next pay packet, we pooled our resources, or begged and borrowed so that there would always be coffee and toast for our steady stream of visitors.

Sometimes the private performances held in Linden Gardens surpassed the best on stage. Where else could one find a Beethoven Concerto being conducted so magnificently as by Freddie Jones? Dawn would still find Freddie, surrounded by empty wine bottles, expounding the intricacies of Ludwig's inner being. We would often philosophize the night away by the dim light of candles stuck in Chianti bottles and the warm glow of our coin-operated gas fire.

The pressures that Mim had exerted on me while I had been settling in to the repertoire were beginning to ease off. Now I was thankful for Rambert's goading when I could get it. Most of the company preferred it when the laconic David Ellis took over the helm, but I loved the instant shot of adrenalin Mim's presence gave me. Eventually, however, self-doubt began to undermine my confidence once again. I did not share Mim's confidence in my ability. I still believed that my fundamental technique was unreliable and insubstantial. Superficially I had it all, and that was part of the trouble. I had so much to lose if I did the righteous thing and declared my fraudulence. How could I turn back without losing face?

I had been offered a chance to return to Moscow shortly after I joined the Ballet Rambert, but I was reluctant to lose the opportunity to work with one of the greatest names in the ballet world, so I had decided to stay with Rambert, reasoning that I could always go back to my studies at some later date. There was no one to advise me, no one who cared enough about me as a person to think what might be best for my artistic and emotional development.

Often when I reflected on the chain of events that had landed me in this coveted position, it struck me just how little control or positive involvement I had had in my career so far. All I seemed to have done was to respond while others had called the tune. I had not spent a lifetime in the *corps de ballet* waiting for a lucky break, or developing a clever plan for self-promotion. My career seemed to have taken on a life of its own, and I realized that it was now desperately out of control. The nature of my vocation meant that others determined what I should dance, when and how I danced it, and even whether I would dance at all. All that I had dreamed and hoped for, all those principles that I held to be true, now appeared far less defined. Once I had mastered the classic roles, a disturbing emptiness soon replaced my sense of achievement. On stage I still enjoyed the exhilaration of the dance, but the warm glow that comes from creative fulfilment was missing.

If a dancer is fortunate enough to share a common language with a choreographer, the result can be pure magic. In responding to the choreographer's thought-processes, the dancer brings his or her own innermost feelings to light. Such conceptual marriages have not only produced superlative ballets, but also allowed such dancers as Nijinsky, Karsavina, Pavlova and Fonteyn to flourish. Perhaps the natural evolution for dancers who need to experience the joy of being creators in their own right is to become choreographers or directors themselves. But I was certainly not ready to take that step. What my career needed was the intervention of a Kenneth MacMillan, Anthony Tudor or Frederick Ashton. I longed to be more than a cliché ballerina.

Often it seemed as if I was the centre of an industry that had grown up around me. Too many people were dependent on my ability to succeed. I felt more and more isolated, floating around in this peripatetic life, a member of a family in which I was the black sheep. The anonymity of the people who adored from a distance troubled me, and I was weighed down by the responsibility of having to try to remain the quintessential idea of beauty in order to retain their loyalty and affection.

My best and most satisfying performances were those in which I could focus on a particular person in the audience. The critical appraisal of a friend or relative whose opinion I respected and who loved me warts and all was much more valuable than any number of press accolades. My diminishing dedication caused me grave concern, for I knew I was moving further and further away from the single-minded sense of purpose necessary for the demanding art of ballet. While other dancers stayed behind for further punishing hours of practice after class, I preferred to go home to a good book or a stimulating conversation. Above all I desired the warmth and companionship of a one-to-one relationship with a man who respected and stimulated my mind.

For some time I had begun to find it increasingly difficult to cling to my old moral tenets with any conviction. I was in love with love, and now imagined that I just might forsake my virginity, if I could expect the same commitment from my partner as from myself. But when it came the event could hardly have been further from my expectations. I fell for an actor named Sylvester, an irresistibly attractive rogue. I was still hesitant about sex, but eventually I presented myself at his flat, feeling like a sacrificial maiden. I am sure he simply decided I had come to have a screw, and complied with my wishes as efficiently and courteously as possible. There were no fireworks, and the earth did not move for either of us. I was left with the pain of realizing that my lover loved me no more for my magnanimous sacrifice. Desperate for solace, I found myself standing with bowed head beside Wendy at Mass, a repentant Jewess seeking forgiveness in the religious mystery of the Eternal Being. My true solace, however, came from mortal parts. In my agony I had written to Harry and, though the letter stopped short of confessing, he read between the lines. His answer soon came back: 'It has happened to you later than it usually happens to other girls. I am delighted, you are now a woman'. At last I could purge myself of remorse.

My twenty-first birthday party was held at a friend's flat in Putney. The place was packed with people I had never seen in my life before. A man approached me, rather too ceremoniously, to announce that we shared the same birthday. 'That deserves a special kiss', he said with a grin. I was too preoccupied to feel elated, though I did think he was nice. Having humoured Mr Nice Guy, I quickly made my exit to return to my rightful position at centre stage. I was dressed in a turquoise sari, which I later found was gloriously unsuited to disco dancing, as it unravelled in a most beguiling manner.

The party was a huge success. By daybreak the flat resembled a battlefield, with bodies strewn all over the place. Judging by the number of couples huddled together in beds, on divans and on the floor, the party had brought people together in more ways than one. I endured an excruciating few hours of sleeplessness, lying on the floor trussed up in my semi-unravelled sari like a bedraggled chook, while beside me my current heart-throb had passed into a blissful inebriated sleep.

The next morning, clasping a mug of Nescafé, I watched the wretched warriors file out, looking very much the worse for wear. It was time to plant a lukewarm kiss on my partner's cheek and board the train for the peace of Linden Gardens. I felt rather down when I got home. Tired and melancholy, I decided to ensconce myself in my bedroom for the rest of the day. And then Mr Nice Guy turned up. 'I didn't have a chance to chat with you at your party', he said, 'so here

I am. I thought I'd drop in to see you without your entourage'. I was surprised how happy I was that he had come. This fellow Capricornian and I had an unusual rapport.

Tall, fair and blue-eyed, Simon was handsome without being seductive, for his face was too finite to lead people astray. Most importantly for me, his face was a strong, constant reality in my life, by contrast with the many masks of the actors I associated with. I felt at ease in Simon's company. He alternately lulled me into a state of comfort from which all triumph was extinguished, and unleashed my mind from its captivity for the first time since I had left my family. It was great to feel my mind flying free without having to worry about the effect my presence was having on my listener. I just talked and talked, as if I had known him all my life.

I found myself confiding my secret fears and insecurities to him. As our relationship developed, we teased each other with the easy intimacy of people who feel secure and happy. Long after the rest of Linden Gardens was asleep, we would lounge around the gas heater reading, discussing books, listening to music, or rolling about with laughter as we parodied the clichéd lines from some movie we had travelled across town to see. In a life that had already had more than its fair share of anxiety, I had always clung to my one source of real strength, the uncritical love that my family had for me. Now, all these miles from home, I had found a friend, lover, poetic mentor and surrogate blood relation.

Simon Sempill, 1967

Yet Simon and I both realized that sooner or later I would have to try to come to terms with that worm of ambition still gnawing away deep within me. I felt caught between two tenses—the immediate calm and happiness that Simon brought me now, and the world of emotion and unreason that I knew I would have to move into. Happy though I was, I could not live on this pink cloud of happiness forever. I needed the daily intensity, surprise and drama that are part of a dancer's life.

I threw myself into an extreme programme of hard slog, hoping to diminish my creative frustrations. Each day I pounded and tormented myself on a dimly lit stage. Wrapped in plastic from neck to ankles, stretching, kicking and flexing, I implored my body to elongate, limber and reconstruct itself. I think most other dancers and ballet critics saw my obsession with my technique as a rather strange quirk. I was, after all, the technician of the Ballet Rambert. But my insecurity was based on self-knowledge. So once again it was back to the drawing-board.

It took a great deal of stoicism and courage to put up with the awkwardness of relearning. Once again I had to resign myself to frustrating periods of ineptitude while I stripped myself of all my former fluidity and naïve aplomb. I felt like an infant struggling to take her first steps. My talent seemed to evaporate into thin air. Gone were all those technical feats that I had hitherto executed with an almost unconscious arrogance. Gone was that large vocabulary of dance phraseology that I had always been able to articulate so freely. Steps and movements that had been second nature now began to expose enormous problems. Once I had analysed, dissected and absorbed each step, the total sum of the components didn't seem to resemble what I had once put out so naturally. Gone were the pirouettes that had earned me the nickname of the 'Aussie spinning top'. Gone was the natural spring that was driven by my need to move with the music.

I felt like a constipated slug. Dancing had been a way of life for me, as spontaneous as my desire for verbal communication. Now that I was forcing myself to pre-empt each step and phrase, now that I tried to approach each performance with premeditated, methodical calculation, for the first time I began to fear having mental blackouts. I had the frightening experience of being frozen mid-dance, gripped by paralytic anxiety. My pursuit of technical honesty became a neurotic obsession, which other people attributed to my inability to feel satisfied with any level of personal achievement. They were probably right, and it was all connected with my chronic anorexia, which was still a factor in my London life.

My stringent exercise programme was not enough to satisfy my zeal for improvement. My weight worried me even more than my technique. So, in spite of the taxing demands I was making on my body, I continued to sap myself of strength by shovelling those handfuls of Duralax down my gullet, with less and less effect. My greatest wish was to be a fawn-like, leggy will-o'-the-wisp, but I wasn't. As one critic put it, Miss Belair was 'delightfully amply upholstered'. He swore he meant it as a compliment, but I felt like kicking him in the crutch. On the one hand I resented my 32-inch bust, but on the other I wasn't against flaunting my cleavage whenever I had the opportunity to do so in mixed company. I wanted to remain the ballerina, but I also didn't want to miss out on being the young attractive gal about town.

We Australian dancers had kept abreast with the news of our burgeoning national ballet company, and when we heard that the company was visiting London to dance at Covent Garden some of us thought seriously about exploring the option of going home. The English audiences were eager to see this new group from Down Under, having already experienced the individual dancers who had made such successful inroads into ballet companies throughout Britain and Europe. Peggy van Praagh's English peers were also curious to see the results of her work in the colonies.

For their part the Australian Ballet, still basking in the pink of their newness, wanted to show the creaking British ballet establishment a thing or two. They bounced into London with all their youthful athleticism. Though many of the girls were the predictable Royal Ballet clones, male dancers such as Karl Welander and Garth Welch were refreshingly virile, handsome and technically strong. There was a lot of advance publicity, most of it focusing on the guest stars, Fonteyn and Nureyev, whose services had apparently been necessary to assure British bums on seats. Indeed the Australian Ballet was introduced more as an adjunct to these two famous artists than as an entity on its own. Artists like Kathleen Gorham were relegated to supporting roles.

My own disillusionment made me look to the Australian Ballet as a way out of my predicament with Rambert. Although Peggy van Praagh and I did not see eye to eye, I now began to view this company as a possible future employer. Returning to Australia was inevitable, as I never doubted for one moment that I would eventually return to my family. My attendances at the Australian Ballet classes were not quite as casual as I made out.

When I first met the company management, there seemed to be a mutual sussing out, veiled by an air of nonchalance. On the whole I wasn't much impressed with this revamped version of the Aussie Ballet. Each performance was a showcase for the two stars, and the rest of the company, when they were not being appealingly youthful, seemed rather rough and ill-disciplined. The press reports were a mixed bag, with the predictable accolades for the superstars and a variety of opinions about their Australian entourage. I was surprised to hear that the Australian news reports seemed to be saying that the London season had been a huge triumph.

Whenever I spoke with Peggy van Praagh she seemed delighted with my success in London. At the reception we had a friendly tête-à-tête, in the course of which she intimated that I was the first contender for Kathleen Gorham's position when Kathleen retired. But Mim made it obvious that, as far as she was concerned, her gain was Peggy's loss. Holding me in her arms, she gloatingly announced that I was a superb artist and technician, and that under her guidance I was destined for greatness. Caught between the two of them, I felt like the meat in the sandwich.

I became rather more apprehensive about switching companies as I renewed my acquaintance with old friends in the Australian Ballet, and got to know new members of the company. By living and working in England I had obviously distanced myself from Australia in more ways than one. When I invited a group of Australian ballet friends to Linden Gardens we all found it hard to find any common ground for discussion beyond ballet. I kept wondering if I could bear to leave the ballet mainstream, while they were wondering just how I could stay in London and live in such cramped, decrepit conditions. Word got back to my parents that their daughter was living a poverty-stricken, Bohemian life, and it took me several lengthy letters to dispel their fears. But I suppose the Linden Gardens lifestyle *was* rather unconventional.

There were now four of us in the flat. One of my brother's closest friends, Frank Vajda, a neurologist, had come to live with us. Frank had adapted quite well to our unconventional circle of friends. He wasn't the least put out by our lovesick transvestite friend Bill, nor was he disconcerted by the scantily clad dancers who lounged so provocatively around our flat, intent on relaxation as only dancers and athletes can be. There was one thing he didn't accept, however, and that was that we were on 'dropping in' terms with Lord Wakehurst, the Governor of

Northern Ireland. Frank thought Bon Bon and I were pulling his leg when we asked him to take the message if Lord Wakehurst called. 'You mean I'm to take a message from the Lord Wakehurst himself, himself personally?' he laughed. So Frank took to answering *all* our phone calls with a pompous 'Lord Wakehurst here'. The inevitable happened. His greeting was met with a stony silence, then a well-modulated voice at the other end said: 'It is Lord Wakehurst *here*'.

The combination of physical exhaustion, smoking, a rotten diet and those long dank English winters soon began to play havoc with my health. At first I tried to ignore the racking cough that kept me awake at night on tour, but after a while I could no longer get through the performances. I had sharp chest pains and restricted breathing, and could not muster the energy to suppress my rasping cough while I was on stage. One evening Mim came across me coughing and spluttering in the wings, and immediately rang a doctor, who informed me that I had a lung infection that required a long rest from dancing. Mim was flapping around me like a worried mother hen, revealing a glimpse of her character that was usually hidden by her on-the-job authoritarianism. She insisted that there was no question of my continuing the tour, and arranged for me to take a rest in Northumberland with her close friends the Pilkingtons. 'The fresh air and rest will be just what you need', she said tenderly, and then with just an edge of the taskmaster, she added, 'I have left instructions with Mrs Pilkington that there is to be *no* smoking'. Dutifully I took the train up to Northumberland, where I was met by Mrs Pilkington and driven out to stately Lea Grange.

I could not have wished for kinder and more companionable hosts. The Pilkingtons went out of their way to make me feel one of the family. Although I did not kick my smoking habit, I did return to London with colour in my cheeks and more flesh on my bones. Things were looking up. I had returned to the company to begin a period of rehearsal for a brand new production of *Giselle*, to be directed by Joyce Graeme with sets and costumes by Peter Farmer. Bon Bon was cast as the Queen of the Wilis, a role she imbued with a sinister, spine-chilling coldness that won her accolades from peers and press alike.

I was to be the first-cast Giselle and, although the traditional choreography remained basically unchanged, Joyce added a new dimension to all the characters in the ballet, making them into plausible human beings with whom the audience could identify. It was an exciting experience to work with this highly intelligent woman who had been a brilliant dance artist herself. She lifted the production from the realms of melodrama to create a moving piece of theatre. All my energy was directed towards developing my role to the utmost of my ability. Once again I was totally happy.

Our opening night at Sadler's Wells coincided with the London visit of the Bolshoi Ballet, and, as luck would have it, the Bolshoi had also programmed *Giselle*, starring the young and brilliant Maximova. We felt rather like David pitched to do battle against Goliath, but without his sling. Before long, however, we were too absorbed in the usual pre-performance panic to think about the Bolshoi. Unfinished costumes piled on the machinists' tables, dance excerpts that still looked rough and ready, and hot and cold running company relationships all kept us entrenched in our own little universe.

Renée and I became happily absorbed. *Giselle* and our roles were all that mattered. We decided to make a determined effort to streamline our bodies. Along the ballet grapevine we heard that a Harley Street specialist was doing wonders with other weight desperadoes, including some of the top ballerinas in the business. In only a matter of weeks the dancers acquired that wonderful, wonderful gauntness that is a dancer's bliss. Bon Bon and I took out an advance on our salaries, and fronted up to the fat, affluent-looking specialist. We returned home with our bottles of miracle pills plus a formidable list of eating instructions.

Doctor G. made it clear that we had to go strictly by the book. We were limited to four cups of liquid per day—and this in mid-summer, when we were sweating profusely in rehearsals! Renée and I took to sucking lemons as a substitute for the usual cup of coffee. This regime also took the gloss off our social activities. It wasn't the same sucking a lemon while our friends were sipping glasses of wine or mugs of coffee. But the diet and the pills performed the miracle. In three or four weeks Bon Bon and I were mere shadows of our former selves. Though we weren't told what the pills were, I think they were probably diuretics. I doubt that many other medicos would have approved of our dramatic weight loss, but we were only too happy to risk the long-term consequences for such glorious short-term results.

Our *Giselle* was a tremendous success. The London critics unanimously described our production as superior to the Bolshoi's at Covent Garden. With Joyce Graeme's tasteful production, Peter Farmer's exquisite autumnal sets and costumes, and Graeme's inspired direction, our small-scale effort compared favourably with the Russian *Giselle*, with its cast of hundreds. On a personal level the critics were more than

In Joyce Graeme's *Giselle*, second act

generous. 'The Ballet Rambert trump card is Alida Belair, a dark, vivacious girl whose Giselle makes the whole evening light up', said one. Another stated that I was 'part of the music, part of the notes as they emerged. She was as serious, gay, and sensitive as they were, but never weak. Her enviable youthful vitality also had a magnetic influence over the entire cast'. This triumph put to shame all my doubts and quibbles. I felt gloriously fulfilled. A dancing life *was* quite enough.

Full of optimism for the future, Bon Bon and I joined Jeffrey, our ballet master, for a trip down the Loire Valley from Paris to Cannes. It was magical. We were relaxed and happy, and the French countryside with its enchanting villages filled us with wonder and delight. The Mediterranean climate was conducive to a simple existence. We bought fresh fruit each day at the local market and ate it on the beach, braved the cold public showers to perform our ablutions and, when we weren't being wined and dined, we would turn the bed into a picnic table for a meal of bread and cheese, or treat ourselves to a slap-up meal at a chic waterfront restaurant. We were not beyond playing 'spot the celebrity'. I was thrilled to find myself in the deck chair beside Pablo Picasso's, and I took vicarious pleasure from spotting Bardot, Nureyev and Bruhn as they promenaded along La Croissette. For four weeks we gave our bodies a rest, apart from exposure to the sun and some uncontrolled gyrating in the ubiquitous discos. Though we had started out with every intention of attending regular classes at Rosella Hightower's magnificent studio, we only managed two classes in the last few days in Cannes. After the second class I was offered a position as a principal dancer at the Zurich Opera Ballet, which was most flattering. I returned to the rehearsal period at Ballet Rambert buoyant and full of optimism.

The feedback from *Giselle* also bolstered my self-esteem. A principal dancer from another company had remarked that I reminded him of Spessivtseva, one of the greatest exponents of the role. Even Mim had said that I was the 'perfect Giselle'. And John Field, the director of the Royal Ballet Touring Company, had expressed the hope that he might have a chance to work with me in the future.

But there was bad news as well. All our anticipated trips abroad had fallen through, so once again we had to prepare for those irksome tours around the British Isles: performances in Eastbourne in the off season, or in another pavilion at the end of a jetty in some gloomy seaside retirement resort. Dancers, directors and choreographers settled into their respective niches. And it was still dancers who spanned the classical and contemporary fields who had most to gain from Rambert's latest mixed-bag repertoire.

Maggie Lorraine was the next in line to receive Mim's undivided attention. Maggie, Mim decided, had unusual dramatic abilities, which Mim could manipulate and direct to everyone's advantage. Mim's switch to a new creative plaything left me feeling that I had misplaced my trust in her. Her sole rationale in life seemed to be to preordain and control someone else's destiny, then claim credit for the resulting work of art. The writing had been on the wall for some time. Mim was becoming bored with the predictability of our current repertoire. She needed to work with someone new, and in a more dramatic arena.

20

Bon Voyage

The time had come to cast around to find a new company that would offer me the challenge I needed. I was even prepared to accept a lesser position in a company of high repute. Rambert and David Ellis knew that I was no longer happy in the company, but there had also been developments behind the scenes. A plan for a new company was already in train, though the dancers would be the last to hear about it.

One day Mim came into my dressing room and cried on my shoulder about the demise of her company. 'I don't know what is going to happen', she wept, 'but the Arts Council is no longer prepared to fund the company. What will happen to dancers like you? You know how much I care for you, how hard I have worked on you. I can't imagine the company not existing any more'. I was touched by her sadness and her concern for my well-being. The tears welled up in my eyes and we both wept, clasped together in an embrace of absolute solidarity.

But several weeks later the full company was assembled on the stage to hear a different version of the story. Norman Morrice stood with his arm around Mim, who seemed to have made a remarkable recovery. We were told that Norman Morrice had had the idea of re-forming the company by dismissing the *corps de ballet* and keeping only the soloists. Mim delivered an enthusiastic speech describing this plan as intelligent, practical and completely in accordance with the Ballet Rambert's artistic philosophy. As the news was unfolded, it became clear that these plans had been developing for quite some time, and I was not surprised that Norman Morrice would be the Associate Director, with Rambert as the titular artistic director, although I knew that she would remain in the background in an advisory and critical capacity.

The new manifesto proclaimed that all the company's dancers would be accorded the same status, and that the old hierarchical order would be abolished. I understood at once that I was part of the dead wood that would have to be lopped off in order to create this new egalitarian company. What did surprise me, however, was Mim's change of heart. She had obviously managed to resolve all those worries about her principal dancers' future welfare. With all her old revolutionary fire, she declared that in this company there would be no place for airs and graces, and announced that it had been decided that, as the principal ballerinas might have some problems adjusting to the workings of such a democratic setup, it would be wiser and more considerate to let them go and work in other companies that still had the star system.

Not all the dancers who had been invited to join the new company accepted, as some were not prepared to accept such a narrow area of specialization. For my part, even if I had been offered a position (and I was not), I still felt I needed a balance of classics and contemporary ballets. Although I felt sad to leave the company in which I had spent the formative years of my adult life, I was relieved that the inevitable parting of ways was over. I felt both scared and exhilarated at the prospect of a new challenge at last.

Instead of trying to inject some life into the umpteenth performance of Saint Leon's hateful *Coppélia*, I was out walking the tightrope once again, and the prospect sent the adrenalin rushing through my body. Perhaps I was about to face my first real test against the dancers with whom my reputation had been linked in the press.

On hearing of the Ballet Rambert's change of format, several European directors offered me positions, but of all the offers I received the one that interested me most was John Field's tentative offer of a principal position in the touring Royal Ballet Company. The smaller branch of the Royal Ballet was the more interesting of the two. The larger resident company at Covent Garden had the prestige, but it served mainly as a national museum of dance, a showcase for presenting the full-scale classics and spectaculars, vehicles for the likes of Fonteyn and Nureyev in a grandiose setting. John Field's company, on the other hand, was able to be more innovative. It was a training ground for rising dancers and choreographers, and it could also offer a more varied repertoire than its tradition-bound mother company. After the low-key intimacy of the Ballet Rambert, I felt that it would be a good experience to work in a larger institution and to be just one principal among many.

John Field, however, could not offer me a position without the approval of the board of directors, and I had to resign myself to a long process of bureaucratic wrangling. Still, I took heart from Field's enthusiasm, and did not pursue my other options. One of my offers was from John Cranko in Stuttgart, another from Todd Bolender in Cologne. Germany was never on my list of proposed countries to visit (for obvious reasons), so I wrote to both Cranko and Bolender and told them that I had something else in the pipeline.

Madame Rambert, in a bid to help those of her dancers who now faced unemployment, had talked Sir Frederick Ashton into auditioning her dancers for the Royal Ballet. Usually the Royal did not employ dancers unless they had been trained at Whitelodge, but in this case Sir Frederick and the Board were willing to make an exception, more as a friendly gesture to Dame Marie, I suspect, than for the sake of the dancers, whose style they would almost certainly disapprove of. For Anna Truscott, Cecilia Barrett and myself, clearly not *corps de ballet* aspirants, our chances were slim from the start, but Mim insisted that we go and take the class, just for the experience.

Mim did not know about my negotiations with John Field, and I felt I should keep this little snippet to myself. Though I knew that I was not shown to best advantage in the classroom, I still decided to venture along; after all, I had been 'discovered' in the classroom at least twice before. I did not count on the humiliating experience that lay before me.

We were invited to join in a normal Royal Ballet Company class but we were issued with large numbers in poster colours to wear pinned to the front of our leotards, so that each one of the Rambert dancers could be distinguished not only from each other but also from the resident dancers, who seemed only to have been issued with supercilious expressions. There was no way we could escape the conspicuous scrutiny of the Royal Ballet Constabulary who had come to judge us, or ignore the sideways glances of the company members. Never too confident in the execution of the *adage* section of the class at the best of times, I now found myself gripping the floor, two feet hermetically sealed in fifth position, unable to release a foot to begin the slow tortuous sequence of *développés* and *penché arabesques* that had been set to display our technical control. Sweat ran in rivulets from my wet scalp to eat away my carefully applied wide-eyed look. I knew now that the Muse was not around to help me here. The judges were looking to find raw material with potential. Any outward signs of artistic maturation would be a sure manifestation of talent already spoilt. It was an open cattle market. I had been given a number, then expected to shut up and show off my wares. I could not, and *would* not, bring myself to pass muster. I switched off to the rest of the class and left.

The next few weeks were traumatic. I had foolishly closed off most of my options. By now most companies in England and on the Continent had signed on their full complement of dancers for the coming season. I had also committed myself to my first trip home since I had left in 1962. Harry was concerned that our father in particular was beginning to find my absence hard to handle. As a trip to London for my parents was out of the question, Harry had volunteered to pay for half my return fare to Australia. As the weeks progressed and my Royal Ballet appointment was more off than on, I postponed my departure date further and further, much to my family's consternation. Finally the answer came from the Board. The ruling body, true to tradition, had decided that I could not be brought in as a soloist or principal over the heads of all those dancers who had patiently worked their way up the hierarchy.

John Field obviously felt he bore some responsibility for my predicament, and recommended me to Frederic Franklin, Artistic Director of the National Ballet in Washington DC. I had not looked to the USA as a possibility before. All the American companies I had seen seemed to emphasize an athletic and technical excessiveness that would preclude dramatic dancers of my ilk. And Washington DC was not New York. Nevertheless, reassured that I had some prospect of employment, I began to plan a short holiday with Simon in Greece *en route* to Australia.

Although I left all my belongings in the flat at Linden Gardens, I had no idea whether I would ever dance in England again. Now that I faced the prospect of having to start somewhere new, I realized that I would be desperately sad to leave London, and in spite of everything I also knew I would miss the Ballet Rambert. It would be hard to re-establish myself in a country where I was unknown.

I arrived in Athens a couple of days before Simon. At the suggestion of George Angel, a London TV producer, I stayed at the Ambassador Hotel. George was Greek, and had obviously tipped off the head porter, who was a friend of his, for when I arrived I was welcomed like a visiting Hollywood star. My huge bedroom was full of flowers, and at the press of a buzzer a smiling bellboy would appear at lightning speed to meet my every wish. Two days later the phone rang in my room. It was the receptionist, who asked me if I knew a Simon Sempill. 'This man says you are expecting him', he added in a tone of contemptuous disbelief. Simon had entered the opulent foyer barefoot, in scruffy jeans, with a week's growth of beard. After travelling in a filthy train compartment jam-packed with peasants, students and animals, he was more interested in seeing my big, beautiful bath than in holding me in his arms. After he had washed and shaved, I reintroduced him to the staff, who quite forgave him.

We went on to the island of Paros, where we swam in crystalline waters and strolled hand-in-hand through narrow alleys hewn out of the rock. It was too good to last; though I found the prospect almost unbearable, the end of my relationship with Simon seemed inevitable. There was still too much unexplored territory out there; I couldn't curtail my growth now and settle down to live on my past experiences. None of it was enough, not by a long way.

When I arrived at the airport in Sydney I was met by a flurry of reporters and photographers. The Kinmonts had alerted the press to my arrival. The reporters seemed more interested in my experiences behind the Iron Curtain than in any dance talent I might have had. It was like stepping into a time warp, and the final press releases were every bit as parochial as I feared they might be. 'Aussie dancer prefers Russian men', one headline shouted, after I had mentioned that I had gone out with some Russian dancers and that they were much the same as young men anywhere else.

The Australian Ballet was on tour, so I did not have an opportunity to do classes with the company. Instead I ambled off to Kathleen Gorham's classes in the city. It was a great effort, because my parents now lived in Burwood, quite some distance from the centre of the city. I had forgotten how tedious travel by public transport could be in suburban Melbourne. It was wonderful being with my parents again, but I had little in common with most of the friends I had left behind in 1962. In many ways my homecoming was a disquieting experience. Throughout all those years away from home I had thought of Melbourne as a homely paradise on earth. Instead I found a stultifying parochial town.

I had been shocked by the first sight of my ageing parents as I ran across the tarmac to meet them, but gradually that first impression softened and merged with the picture of my parents that I had carried around with me in my mind's eye. All of us now carried with us

A Ma and Pa Kettle existence: Mr and Mrs Glasbeek outside their new home, 1966

experiences and memories that we would only be able to share on a second-hand basis. I think my parents realized almost immediately that I would not be putting my suitcase in storage. The suitcases remained half-unpacked in the bedroom that could only ever be symbolically mine. With Harry doing postgraduate study in Chicago, my mother and father now referred jokingly to their Ma and Pa Kettle existence. They continued to live on for their children, weathering our physical absence by soaking up every word in our letters from abroad.

After the prerequisite exchange of telegrams between Melbourne and Washington DC, I prepared myself for my new challenge, but with far less zest and confidence than in 1962. It was almost more than I could stand to wrench myself away from my parents, but I boarded the Qantas plane ready to re-establish contact with the person I had become.

The Hotel Du Pont was one of the most expensive hotels in Washington, but after flying straight from Melbourne to the USA I was too jet-lagged to worry about such trivia. Frederic Franklin, my career and my dwindling finances would just have to wait until I could sort out night from day again. I was jolted back to reality soon enough. When I woke from my long sleep and looked in the mirror, what I saw was too depressing for words. Could it be a fattening mirror? I dashed into the bathroom to check. But there was no escaping it, that gross image *was* me, with pounds and pounds of unworked flesh.

Dressed in the most slimming outfit I could find, I made my way to the National Ballet Studios on Connecticut Avenue. I edged my way through the crowded foyer, trying desperately to avoid the eyes of the sylphs who I was sure were sizing me up already. One of the men gave me a look that was openly suggestive. With my red frilly outfit and black Spanish hat, I wondered if I looked more like a voluptuous Spanish peasant than a prima ballerina.

A well-preserved figure eventually bounced out to welcome me. 'Darling!' Frederic Franklin said, kissing me on both cheeks. 'How lovely to meet you! I have heard so much about you.' We began to play the old theatre game, falling into the traditional roles of director and employee. Frederic immediately established his credentials as the experienced director, former *premier danseur* and understanding paternal overlord; for my part I poured out my career credits with accelerating hype, and tried to pretend I didn't care in the least whether I worked with him or not. Never once looking me in the face, he gushed on in a breathless, carefully modulated voice, producing such a stream of compliments that, had I not been a cynic, I might have believed that meeting me was the most important event in his life. I could see no sign of vulnerability in him, nothing that would give me an inkling of the personality behind this glossy, contrived persona.

I was ushered into a classroom of slim, proficient-looking dancers, feeling mortified. From my vantage point at the back of the class, I saw immediately that these Americans meant business. Fed on a diet of steak, orange juice and flapjacks, these kids propelled into action like dynamos. These were no anaemic Britishers standing back to let the Aussies bash past. I heard one Texan ballerina drawl: 'I don't see why we have to import dancers any more, when our schools in Texas are brimming with superb dancers'.

The company had quite a few foreign dancers among its principals, including a fellow Australian, Marilyn Burr, who had made her reputation in London's Festival Ballet. She was an archetypal product of this urbane, showy company, a principal ballerina to the hilt. She knew her rights, had put herself into the hands of a leading English agent and demanded the treatment she felt was due to her. She didn't look in the least perturbed at exhibiting herself in a classroom of strangers, and I wished for just a little of her confidence. After the class she left the studios adorned like a Hollywood screen goddess.

I don't know whether Franklin could see the sprite within the slob, or whether he had decided to take a gamble because of my previous successes, but he engaged me as a principal dancer. I was delighted and relieved, not least because the hotel had already exhausted my financial reserves and I had nowhere else to go. I moved out to an apartment in Connecticut Avenue, opposite the studios and next door to Marilyn Burr. I couldn't believe that for $200, just one week's salary, I could furnish and stock the apartment, right down to potholders and tin openers, from one of the mighty American dime stores. All those expensive labour-saving devices, cheap furnishings and my comfortable spacious apartment gave me a temporary faith in the American way of life—until I saw how people lived in the slum areas that house the black majority.

Our apartments had a black janitor who spoke an almost incomprehensible Southern dialect. One day I ventured down into the basement. I saw a space surrounded with wire netting, like some kind of storeroom, and realized to my horror that a black woman was lying on a bed that almost filled the area. She was perspiring profusely, as the temperature must have been well over a hundred degrees. This was where the janitor and his wife lived.

I soon found that such observations were best kept to myself. Once again the only issues that seemed to count in the minds of most of my new colleagues were the line of their *penché arabesques* and the necessity of resting up between workouts. The average age of most of the company members was about eighteen, and I reckon most of them must have come in fresh from the Midwestern bible belt. The girls were pink-faced, strong-limbed and virtuous, while the boys had the square-jawed, bright-eyed look of the wholesome all-American college kid.

This company made the Ballet Rambert look like a bunch of libertines, though some of the imported principal dancers liked to enjoy themselves after rehearsals and performances. Most of the principals were much older and more experienced than I. They had worked with the ballet legends like Markova and Dolin and had travelled the Continent in a rather grander style than Rambert's provincial touring. My stories of tacky theatres in the English provinces compared poorly with their tales of nights spent dancing in royal palaces and villas on the Riviera. This time the title 'prima ballerina' seemed much more apt than in the London and Rambert companies.

At first Freddie's bonhomie quite pleased me. Here was a company where I was going to be treated like an adult, and accorded some respect as a professional. After the initial convivial junket, I began to look forward to some hard work. But I quickly realized that I would be left to my own devices, my talent taken for granted, though I still longed for some real structural guidance. I also hoped to be cast into a repertoire very different from what I had just escaped. However, this was a commercial company, funded largely by a private benefactor, Mrs Riddell, and she expected the company to function well commercially. So the repertoire was a safe and sure one. There they were, back to haunt me again: *Coppélia*, *Nutcracker* and *Les Sylphides*, and a few ordinary fairy-floss concoctions that could have been part of any one of the older ballets, so derivative were the choreography and music.

Franklin's insecurities also became apparent. Indeed his attempts to be always the affable host, loyal friend and self-effacing artistic mentor were lost in his need to be constantly reassured of his own worth as a person. The remoteness of being an authoritarian figure did not appeal to him, and I suspect his attitude to his directorship was rather ambivalent. By all accounts he had been a beautiful dancer, with a handsome figure complemented by a strong technique and comely stage presence. But his identity and enthusiasm lay with the past. He had the inexorable sense of loss that comes with the demise of every

From left, Ivan Nagy, Alida and Frederic Franklin at the National Ballet Company, Washington, DC, 1966

performer's performing life. To be acknowledged for his input behind the scenes was no consolation to him.

There could be no disguising the fact that he was the loneliest of men, having now to pay the price for all those years spent basking in the adoration of people who knew only the dancer as a transitory work of art and had little interest in Freddie the person. In any case his inability to separate his private life from his official role as company director led to our becoming entangled in a most unpleasant emotional triangle.

Franklin shared his house with Stevan Grebel, the handsome Yugoslav who had ogled me with such arrogant enthusiasm on my first day with the company. Then I had been far too preoccupied with practical matters for playful banter, but after I had settled in I was more than happy to reciprocate. In between *enchaînements* we would attend to each other in a ritualistic silence that left no doubt that our attraction was entirely sexual. The fact that Stevan already had a girlfriend only made me more determined. I decided that I would approach this new relationship with resolute emancipation.

Stevan, however, was still entrenched in the old romantic world of double standards. He regarded it as the male prerogative to initiate the courtship, and saw the act of consummation as a masculine victory; and, as I was to find out later, he held women he had conquered in some contempt.

Stevan and his girlfriend Maxine were lovers, but she did not live with him. Instead Stevan continued to share Freddie's house, with Freddie playing the role of the magnanimous father figure to both. Whenever Maxine and Stevan had had a tiff she would run to tell all to dear old Freddie, who I suspect managed to manipulate this relationship quite effectively. Freddie's affection for Stevan was obvious. Although Stevan maintained that his own friendship with Freddie was platonic, I am sure he did not seriously set out to discourage Freddie's unrequited passion. But then I arrived to disrupt this cosy setup, and poor Freddie had to come to terms with a new rival.

Stevan began to court me in a suave, romantic way. His black MG would materialize out of nowhere, and he always just happened to be going in the same direction as I was. One day while I was out on a shopping spree, I was surprised to find Stevan languidly arranged among the suitcases in the baggage department of the store. Just how he had worked out that I intended to buy a suitcase I don't know. Suddenly he thrust into my hand an expensive red leather suitcase, which he must have seen me trying to ignore. 'For you, *petite*', he said. 'Please let me buy this for you to welcome you to our company.' My stomach tightened into a knot. I was smitten and triumphant. To think that I could attract such a man of the world, ten years my senior, a heart-throb who could pick any female companion he desired!

Though I felt a little guilty when I saw Stevan and Maxine together, I was sure that I was not organizing this *coup d'état* on my own, for Stevan was not exactly acting like a reluctant participant. So I waltzed straight up to him in the classroom and asked him to accompany me to see Odetta performing at a nightclub. I had been asked to join one of Harry's friends and his wife for a foursome. I hoped the presence of two chaperones would dilute the brazenness of my proposal, for I could tell at once that Stevan was surprised by my boldness.

Stevan charmed all of us with his witty anecdotes, smattered with just the right amount of name-dropping. As we pressed together on the packed dance floor, every nuance in Odetta's sensual singing seemed to be loaded with significance for us alone. Stevan teased and tantalized me, and I was intoxicated by the grace of his physical presence and the strength of his desire.

We embarked on a whirlwind courtship. I was wined and dined in hushed élite restaurants, and there was scarcely a day when my gallant paramour failed to bring me some expensive gift of clothing, perfume or jewellery. For a while I devoted myself almost entirely to being the mistress *par excellence*. It was a welcome distraction, at least; Stevan's rapturous love compensated for the excitement the ballet company lacked.

Still, I planned to whittle my body back into nymph-like condition, for my goals still lay far beyond Washington DC. All that wining and dining was bad for my figure, but I hoped that if I did not have to spend so much time despising myself in the classroom, then perhaps all that weight would just drop off as a result of some hard and patient work. Stevan assured me that love-making was the most efficient weight reducer, and said that he would have me as slim as a reed in no time.

Stevan's balletic ambitions had well and truly petered out by this stage. Defecting to the West from Yugoslavia had given him an opportunity to enjoy the good life. He had had his good times in Paris, and had done quite a long stint in Las Vegas, working in a musical; the hedonistic lifestyle of that casino town epitomized to him the good life, American style. Now, in his mid-thirties, he dreamed of finding an easier and more financially secure way of making a living, and of retiring to

Bon Voyage 247

Stevan Grebel

California, where he intended to start a family. This was the Stevan who slowly revealed himself as his love for me grew from being just a lustful fancy to a kindly love with serious and honourable intentions.

Stevan no longer viewed his art with idealism. It was just a job that paid him a reasonable wage to support his fun-loving way of life. He laughed openly when I sought to display a more complicated Alida, and mocked me affectionately when I begged him to accommodate my need for intellectual stimulation. If I suggested an interest in social issues he would nip this train of thought in the bud. 'Ah, *ma petite*, she is a revolutionary. You will see in time that having money and enjoying life is not such a bad thing.' My life's complications were, as he saw it, entirely of my own making. I was his bubble of fun, his lovable little '*petite*', and any ventures into the world of ideas were silly little quirks, to be tolerated only because he loved me.

This facile approach to life soon began to aggravate me. 'Stevan', I screamed reproachfully when he denounced a friend of mine for his dowdy academic appearance, 'he has a wonderful mind and he is a warm, affectionate and caring person'. 'Yes, but his wife just wants a good fuck', Stevan answered, and to prove his point he waltzed my friend's wife on to the dance floor and swept her off her feet.

I began to feel that Stevan's facile behaviour reduced me to the level of an empty-headed concubine. Perhaps originally I did want to experience the mythical perfect fuck, but now, with that little obsession out of the way, I began to realize that I wanted more than Stevan and his mighty member could ever offer me. Yet the more he took from me the more I looked for compensation in him; I felt increasingly trapped by my inability to express my own personality.

Franklin was not a passive bystander in this little love affair. It was clear that he was jealous and resentful of my intrusion. Whenever he had the opportunity he would recount anecdotes involving his friendship with Stevan, presumably to imply that their long relationship transcended such passing infatuations as this current episode. The more Franklin attempted to discourage Stevan's relationship with me, the more determined I became to keep it up. My resolve hardened while we were on tour. The whole company was staying in the same motel, and Franklin had seen that Stevan intended to spend the evening with me. At about three o'clock in the morning Franklin rang my room to ask if Stevan was with me. He was not, but that was beside the point. I was furious. Ballet director or not, I told him in no uncertain terms that he had no business interfering with my private life. This episode sounded the death knell for my career in the National Ballet.

It was impossible to regain my former dancing condition, particularly as Franklin gave me less and less to perform. I became acutely depressed. In the rehearsal room I had nothing to rehearse and so had to put up with working solitarily in front of the mirror in a quiet corner of the room. After the rehearsals I strolled around the lonely precincts of Connecticut Avenue with nothing to look at but apartment blocks and cars, and then, feeling suicidal, I plied my poor body with all the junk food I could lay my hands on. Finally feeling utterly self-disgusted, I wandered in to sit in prompt corner to watch the evening's performance unfold.

Socially, Franklin's behaviour towards me remained cordial and correct. He knew that by denying me the opportunity to perform he was driving me away from the company and, no doubt, from Stevan as well. Through all this Stevan remained infuriatingly noncommittal. At one time he and Franklin were not on speaking terms, but Stevan did not move out of Franklin's house. He insisted on staying put, arguing that he was saving money for our future together.

When Stevan spoke of my giving up dancing, or working on an adagio act to perform in the wealthy clubs of the Catskill Mountains, I became incensed at his trivialization of my desire for artistic gratification. It soon dawned on me that in order to fulfil his aspirations I would have to remain a lame duck, for Stevan was conscious that if I found creative fulfilment then a new, more self-assured Alida would emerge. In my incompleteness I was Stevan's total woman. My incompetence in the kitchen and in other domestic chores only enhanced his notions of masculine dominance. In time, no doubt, Stevan planned to domesticate his pampered little concubine, but for the present he suffered my disorganized housekeeping, while I endured numerous training sessions in which he displayed his exemplary culinary skills.

Ironically my search for a love imbued with risk and recklessness had landed me with a middle-aged Don Juan who was beginning to temper his way of life in preparation for matrimonial domesticity. After we had made love he now talked of the son we were going to have, the boy child with whom he would spend hours fishing, and who would no doubt help carry Stevan's unique brand of manliness through the succeeding generations.

Things continued to fare badly for me in the company. A new tour was in the offing, and to my dismay I found I had not been cast in a single ballet. Stevan did his best to persuade me to swallow my pride and go on the tour. 'Just take the salary and ignore the rest', he argued. 'We will be together, *petite*, and I will make you happy.' But I could not bring myself to suffer such a humiliation.

I went to see the company manager, who listened to my complaints with sympathy. Clearly he knew that Franklin and I had arrived at an intolerable impasse. Fred had stated point blank that he had no use for me in this particular repertoire, and as Artistic Director it was his indisputable right to cast the ballets as he pleased. When I explained that I would prefer to go to New York City, where I could use my time attending classes, rather than to accompany the ballet company as a bored and dissatisfied observer, he agreed to continue to send my salary every week for the rest of my contract, and we parted quite cordially.

I don't know whether Stevan was genuinely sad that I would not be with him on tour, or jealous at the thought of his *petite* in New York City, alone among so many rapacious wolves. I did my best to hold back the tears as I walked across the road from my apartment to the studio, where I bade the company and Stevan *bon voyage*.

I thought how strange it was, how the seductive camaraderie of the theatre always hits you most when you stand at the point of turning your back on it, or when you are trying to convince yourself that you *can* live alone without it. Suddenly everyone loved me; now that I was leaving, I was everybody's friend. All the dancers in turn threw their arms around me, until my reticent tears flowed all over my puffy, appreciative face. The more they kissed me the more sentimental I became, but as they hurried away to attend to their luggage I knew that all traces of my tears had by now dried up on their coat lapels. As they drove away, only Stevan's face remained glued to the window right until the bus turned the corner out of my view.

21

A State of Anonymity

New York City was an unknown quantity. I had only visited the city once, when Stevan and I took the shuttle service from Washington, and though I had fun there, I was overwhelmed by the city's cold grey canyons and sleazy streets. Obviously NYC could not be termed a caring place. I felt that if I tripped on those escalators going down into the subway the people would swarm over me and trample me to death. Dwelling on the periphery of such a teeming multitude was the loneliest existence imaginable.

My hotel on West 78th had obviously seen better days, but I would have to economize if I was to attend ballet classes in New York. A black chambermaid took me up the staircase and down a long corridor to my room. It reminded me of one of those B-grade detective movies where the cop always lies on the bed fully clothed under the glare of a bare light-bulb. When I saw the condition of the bedding and the myriad cockroaches, I realized why those cops never undressed. In any case, it was cleaner on top of the bed than between the sheets. 'Don't forget to put on all the night locks, especially the police bar', the maid warned.

I spent my first night in misery; only the bravest cockroaches ventured out during the day, but at night they were joined by thousands of their brethren. I sat on the bed clasping my knees under my chin, rigid with fear, too terrified to cry. The wailing of police sirens, fire engines and screeching brakes only added to the nightmare. In desperation I decided to seek out some fellow dancers in the American Ballet Theatre Studios.

But even at the studios there was no hint of a smile. The journey from the dressing room to the barre was as suspenseful as Gary Cooper's epic confrontation in *High Noon*. I was immediately hated, for I was a rival in a camp that was already rife with jealousy. And I could see just by the way they stretched their tights and woollies over their long, long legs that these girls were going to be depressingly good.

At precisely 10 a.m. the studio door opened and a tall, elegant lady strode in. Like Madame Boro, she bore the mark of imperial Russia (she even had a fur coat draped over her shoulders). To my surprise she did not stop centre stage, but walked across the now silent classroom to the piano. Then, as if on cue, a small, rotund lady strode in. She looked more like a Russian tractor-driver than a dancer. She wore a plain red cardigan and a pair of black trousers that revealed the tiniest feet I had ever seen. 'Morneeng class', she said, striding in. 'Class commence, pleez close windows, close doors. Vun, tew.' The outside world was closed off, and the first rolls introduced the *plié* music. I glanced nervously at the sealed exit, but the minute I began to follow the familiar routine I felt better.

There were no newfangled methods in Madame Pereyaslavec's class. 'Don't fold your arms across your chest and slouch like that!' she bellowed at some poor dancer who had mistakenly assumed that the rest periods were for resting. 'You stand straight in my class or leave.' Ten minutes into the lesson a sheepish face peered around the door. 'Out!' screamed Madame Pereyaslavec. 'You are late for my class—now you miss it!' The face meekly disappeared. To my astonishment I realized it was Nureyev.

For me the tension of Madame Perey's classes worked wonders. While I was balancing on *demi-point* in an arabesque, Pereyaslavec would put her barrel-like frame under my armpit, and her guttural voice would defy me to come down from my pose. I did not come down. Those controlled *adages* that had always been my undoing simply started to happen. I was executing complicated technical *enchaînements* beyond my wildest expectations.

At first Pereyaslavec hardly seemed to notice me. In accordance with protocol, I kept a polite distance from such celebrities as Fonteyn, Bruhn, Fracci, Maria Tallchief and Nureyev, who were placed in the front line. Pereyaslavec positioned the dancers around the room in order of rank, seniority and talent. I was overjoyed when she began to hold up the class to make me repeat a step on my own. There I would be, in the centre of the room, with stars lined up at the sides waiting patiently for Alida Belair to get the hang of one of Madame's murderously difficult *adages*!

At the end of the sixteen *grands battements* at the barre, the music would stop and Madame would stride out of the room, shouting 'Give me air!', while the dancers opened the windows and took a breather. A few minutes later the tyrannical tub marched back in. 'Windows closed, please learn this *adage*', and the second part of the class began, with all the dancers looking like wet rats.

I thrived in my new state of anonymity. Without any expectations to live up to, I was being given a new chance to rediscover the talent I had *almost* given up on. But I could not expect this luxury to last. When my contract with the National Ballet ended I had two serious problems to face. I could only work in the USA if a company petitioned my services, stating that there were no Americans who could fill my position; and if I did not find some work I would not be able to stay on in any case.

The dance world in New York City was bursting with enthusiasm, vigour and promise. On any one day I could choose to see three or four top-rate ballets. As well as the famous establishment companies there were many smaller outfits appearing and disappearing at an amazing rate. It was not a place for the faint-hearted. Even in large companies, there was no such thing as job security, and dancers had to live with their own dispensability. The working climate was tense and tough.

The greatest exponent of American dance was George Balanchine of the New York City Ballet, who stressed choreographic movement as an end in itself, and trained dancers to enjoy movement, regardless of whether or not there was a story or message to convey. But I was far more impressed by the American Ballet Theatre. I was transfixed by the technical proficiency of the leading dancers, and moved by their vivid dramatic performances. This was a company that managed to blend the new and the old. Its repertoire was a superbly balanced mixed bag, catering for a wide range of audience tastes while providing plenty of challenge to the versatile group of dancers. Only the principals and soloists were permanently employed. The *corps de ballet* members were contracted for each season, depending on the current repertoire's requirements. The Americans had learnt their lessons from the Russians well. They had benefited from the unsurpassed thoroughness of the Vaganova method, and had copied and perfected the Russians' virtuoso tricks, but then had delighted in using all this wholesome knowledge to explore areas that Russian Communism had declared out of bounds.

At the end of class I watched all those sweaty bodies put on their street clothes and become people again, individuals with somewhere to go and something to do. Jealously I imagined them meeting friends to talk about how their class went and share a cup of coffee. Outside the classroom I spent my time in a state of catalepsy. Apart from the corrective verbal projectiles that Madame Pereyaslavec and my other instructors hurled at me, I spoke to almost no one for days on end. The nights were spent in misery as I sat waiting for the day to break and the cockroaches to depart.

And then the hex was broken. A voice penetrated the soundproof wall of glass that seemed to have incarcerated me for so long. 'Why are you crying?' the voice asked. 'I have watched you in class for quite a while now, and I think you are a lovely dancer.' The voice belonged to Andrei, a young university student, who invited me to meet his Ukrainian parents in their two-roomed apartment in one of New York's tough ethnic areas. Over an abundant continental meal they issued an open-ended invitation to me to share the unconfused chaos of their loving home as often as I wanted. Andrei and his family provided a warm human sanctuary in a world that was at last becoming less hostile.

Abruptly, my final cheque from Washington signalled the end of my contract with the National Ballet. I should have begged and scrounged for my fare home, but I could not bring myself to return home as a loser. Besides, my progress in the classroom was consistent. I was now familiar with all of the 'in' ballet teachers, and sometimes took three or four classes at different studios each day. Poverty had taken care of my dietary problems, and I was re-emerging from that hateful, blubbery cocoon with a thin, energetic and reliable body for which I didn't have to make excuses. Though I missed the gentler world of London, the harshness of New York City was beginning to soften. Even a city of this size had its intimate qualities, and I no longer felt as if it was part of a great conspiracy to make me feel non-existent.

For all my gestures of defiance, I found it hard to imagine staying in the US without seeing Stevan. When he reappeared I even allowed myself to take the dubious step of becoming his kept mistress. He rented an apartment for me on the fourth floor of a slummy West Side tenement building. Its charm-proof poverty ruled out any pretensions to romanticism about artists starving in garrets. The place was unbearably hot in summer, and we soon joined the blacks and Puerto Ricans who sat on the steps and watched the children turning on the water hydrants and providing the watchers with some spontaneous street theatre.

Stevan travelled up to New York when he could, while the intensity of our relationship waxed and waned with my fluctuating self-esteem. I spent a lot of time alone in our apartment. In that tenement building I saw the demoralizing effects of urban poverty at first hand. I wanted to cry out that I understood my fellow tenants' predicament, but they knew I was not one of them. This was not my reality, but just a passing inconvenient phase in a life that already had all the hallmarks of that most important privilege, the privilege of choice. Every night when I ran up those rickety stairs I ran a gauntlet of hatred. I constantly expected an outburst of violence. With all the locks securely fastened, the apartment was more like a prison than a home. I became so paranoid that just waking up alive and intact seemed cause for celebration.

It was when I was alone in such a cheerless atmosphere that I became convinced that I was miserable and lost without Stevan, and there was great excitement whenever he called to say he was coming to visit. On the day before he arrived I would primp and preen myself. But five minutes through the door the reality was all too often far different from the fantasy. I longed for some real communication, an honest, heart-felt conversation, a chance to discover the more complex person behind the carnal passions. But the opportunity never arose.

For Stevan the sexual act expressed everything. It was loving, caring, fecundity and friendship. He would have found it impossible to believe that many a time I would gladly have forgone his faultless display of sexual prowess for a companionable talk. I felt that my only hope of regaining my independence was to find my strength again as a dancer. Without my talent to support me, I was paralysed. Sometimes I believed that I did love him, that I could do without this crazy desire for success, but it only took one important person to enquire about me in class, one performance that made me feel the electricity crackling through the air, or a breakthrough in my battle to master my body, to make me resent Stevan's simple-hearted love. At the slightest hint that I could still be extraordinary I became so hostile that I wondered why he didn't dump me then and there. But Stevan just believed these unrealistic fantasies would pass, and he seemed quite prepared to wait.

I felt my horizons narrowing. Confused and lonely, I sought to draw closer to Simon. In spite of all my capricious attempts to prove otherwise, Simon was still my truest friend. I wrote him long, confessional letters. Simon had always understood that I needed a fundamental emotional stability before I could even begin to pursue more creative ideals. But my relationship with Stevan only undermined my confidence. I began to see London as the cure for all my problems, a miraculous escape valve.

Mim and I had kept up a sporadic correspondence. Mim replied to my long letters with whimsical and eminently memorable one-liners scrawled on the back of photographs of herself or other Ballet Rambert members. 'Tear this up when you are sick of it', she wrote with mock modesty, on the back of a photograph of herself curtsying to what was obviously an adulatory audience. And, on the back of a portrait of Gilmour in *Giselle*, 'Oh, if only Sally had remembered to shut that mouth'.

In my mind I had filed away only the most endearing Rambert memories. I had also found that, in every country with some ballet tradition, Rambert stories were always a reliable drawcard. The real multifaceted Mim was gradually replaced by a one-dimensional paragon of wit, artistic virtue and loyalty. I began to believe that Mim would naturally go out of her way to help me, as we had had a special and close relationship.

My return ticket from London to Australia was still valid for a trip to London, and I argued that I needed to return to tie up various loose ends. Stevan, however, was quite aware that the trip was no such casual matter. He realized that I could never commit myself to New York City or our relationship without first laying to rest the ghosts of my past.

The weeks preceding my departure were nerve-racking. With the prospect of my reunion with Simon looming large in his mind, Stevan became more and more jealous. To him Simon was symbolic of the irksome side of my nature that preferred couch confessions to couch caperings. One day in a fit of rage he tore up a bundle of Simon's poetry that I had left in a suitcase. My heart wrenched with every rip. He tore each page into smithereens, then threw them in my face.

Although it was summer, I arrived at Heathrow to be greeted by a genuine English fog. After putting up with a plane-load of loud American tourists it was wonderful to hear Simon's beautiful voice break softly through the strident twangs. 'Welcome back to an English summer's day', he said. We kissed, but I was surprised at my own reluctance, and knew at once that he could not mistake the lack of sexual tension and confidence in my embrace. It had been a long time and I had not exactly concealed the fact that I had been living with someone else. If I thought he had been hurt by my infidelity, I never doubted that he was my anchor, my best friend. As we drove through those joyless, sunless streets, I wondered if London and Simon and the more friendly English ballet could once again be my life.

I don't know what I expected, but nothing came together. Though we didn't talk about it, Simon and I felt the wall of incomprehension that my American experience had placed between us. I wanted so much from him. I longed for him to fill the empty spaces of my frustration and loneliness. I wanted to love him as if he was the last man on earth. But as we lay side by side, separated by an incomprehensible hiatus, it seemed that we had been more intimate in our letters than in our loving.

London seemed torpid against the youthful vigour of New York City. My entourage of ballet groupies had turned their attention to ballerinas of the here and now. Though some of the old faithfuls still traipsed up our formidable staircase, Linden Gardens had been invaded by a delegation of square-jawed, beer-drinking Aussies. Despite her former willingess to diffuse her distinctive Australian characteristics in favour of *La Culture d'Europe*, la Bon Bon had found the temptation of those magnificent brawny Australians with their fast cars and easy intellects too much to resist.

My feelings of isolation were exacerbated by the lukewarm reception I received from Rambert. I had gone to the performance dressed like a star returning to her home town, believing that Mim would be delighted to see me, and would jump at the opportunity to have me back in the company. But on the contrary Mim was determined to emphasize how much she *didn't* need me. What I saw as her disloyalty was probably no more than a manifestation of her need to justify her actions in changing the company into an entirely new format. 'See how *wonderfully* they work together!' she said, then added almost accusingly, 'No one cares about status and position in the company, *everyone* just works for the common good of the final production', and, for her final thrust, 'Your friend Renée is a jewel, she is such a hard worker. That beautiful face, so seductive. She has improved beyond all recognition'. Seething inside, I could only manage a weak, submissive nod, but her indifference made up my mind. I would return to New York City and make it entirely on my own merits.

22

An Errant Swan

I returned to New York fired with determination. Now that I was clearer about my short-term goals I began to regain control of myself. After the first few stubborn pounds had been shed, the rest of my excess weight peeled off, layer after layer. Soon I began to feel as willowy as a five-foot-two Caucasian could feel.

I didn't mind that an element of performance had crept back into my classroom work. This time I was proud to display the technique I had, rather than having to hide the technique I *didn't* have. I was creating quite a stir around the Manhattan studios. My new invincibility seemed to draw people to me. Once again I was pointed out when some ballet VIP strode into the classroom being conspicuously inconspicuous. Then the job offers began to flow in fast and furiously, though I was eager to study for as long as I could, and to re-enter the professional world only when I felt secure about my technical capabilities.

This time I tried to listen to the voice of pragmatism rather than be swayed by the temptation of instant fame. Though I had been offered several positions as prima ballerina, I accepted the unlikely job of understudy to the lead dancer at New York's Radio City Music Hall. I didn't even have to audition: the director accepted me on face value and my new Saks 5th Avenue dress. This was the kind of job all students dream of; all I was required to do was learn a spectacular and difficult *pas de deux*, then call in before the half-hour call to leave a telephone number where I could be reached in the unlikely event that anything went wrong with Christine, who was as strong as an ox and as resolute as a mule. There were some dodgy moments towards the end of the season when Christine was showing signs of wear and tear, and I was worried that I might have to work for my money. But if I was earning $100 a week for doing next to nothing, Christine was earning a fortune, and she was determined to last the distance even if it killed her. I suspect it very nearly did.

I was engrossed in classroom work, deriving *absolute* satisfaction in work for its own sake. I also felt at one with my body. It was sheer joy to look in the studio mirror and see an image that even *I* could feel satisfied with. My legs were more pulled up and lithe than ever before. Every muscle in my body was alive, taut and expectant, and my new Jeanmaire urchin haircut suited the line of my appearance perfectly. I was also relieved to be self-sufficient again. Alone in my tiny new bed-sitter on East 54th Street, I submerged myself in a gloriously self-centred routine. When I had no more classes to attend, I filled in my spare hours browsing around art galleries, gaping at boutiques and department stores, or strolling around Greenwich Village.

I attended as many theatre and ballet performances as possible, both in the prestigious establishment venues such as the Lincoln Centre, and in fringe theatres, with which New York was almost over-endowed. The New York season of the Bolshoi Company showed me just how far my technique had progressed. After an emotional reunion with my old friends, I was invited to join their classes in the Lincoln Centre studios. Although there could be no doubt as to the solidity and thoroughness of the Russian technique, it was pleasing to see that my American schooling, which was after all mostly derivative, compared favourably. Indeed the Bolshoi's performances were a big disappointment. Artistically the company had remained static, and much of their performance seemed *passé*, almost naïve.

One of the highlights of 1968 was the Netherlands Dance Theatre's New York season. The Netherlands company showed that the classically trained body could best convey expression through movement, and that dance could express contemporary life as aptly as it had captured the romanticism of the previous century. I was invited to do classes by the company director, Benjamin Harkavy. All these dancers had trained their bodies to the highest degree of technical proficiency. There was no *corps de ballet*; each person was an accomplished artist in his or her own right. It was a stimulating atmosphere, but in the final analysis I decided I would not be compatible with this new-wave company. What I needed was a company with a diverse repertoire to allow me to indulge in the more egalitarian contemporary ballets from time to time, without

A new haircut, a new image: Alida rehearses at the American Ballet Theatre, 1968.

having to forgo that incomparable experience of being the pivotal character. American Ballet Theatre was such a company. I was setting my sights for the top.

The competition for places in the American Ballet Theatre was fierce, but some friends who were former members of the company seemed to think that Lucia Chase would like my style of dancing, and the critic Clive Barnes, now at the *New York Times*, offered to put in a good word on my behalf. Then there was Job Sanders, choreographer for the Netherlands Dance Theatre and other international companies, who was determined to bring me to Miss Chase's notice.

I heard that Ivan Nagy, a young Hungarian dancer whom Frederic Franklin had brought out to dance with the National Ballet, was also trying to join the ABT. Ivan had a great deal of talent and an abundance of charm. I can't help admitting I was flattered when he rang to ask me if I would teach him the Springwaters *pas de deux*, which I had learnt at the Bolshoi. Very few people in the West knew the choreography of this spectacular *pas de deux*, but I had the piano score, complete with markings and instructions for the whole piece. Perhaps if I taught Ivan and rehearsed this *pas de deux*, we could show it to Lucia Chase.

I set to organizing a rehearsal venue at the American Ballet Theatre Studio, and talked a friend of mine, James Clouser, a notable choreographer and composer, into playing the piano for me. Jimmy was apprehensive when I mentioned Ivan, but he consented to play for me as a personal favour. Jim and I were already in the studio when Ivan sauntered in. 'Nocoddly', he gushed, 'how sleem you are'. Then Eleanor D'Antuono strolled in, a huge ballet bag slung over her shoulder. 'Where do I get changed?' she called cheerfully in my direction. Mouth agape, I turned to Ivan for explanation. 'Nocoddly', he simpered, 'I hope you don't mind. Eleanor and I thought this would make a superb audition piece for Lucia Chase to see'. I caught Jimmy Clouser's meaningful glance, and conveniently lost my memory. Not even bothering to conceal my disdain, I showed them some smatterings of the whole and flounced out, muttering obscenities about Hungarian opportunists.

Job Sanders soon managed to get me invited to an American Ballet Theatre Company class where he sat next to Lucia Chase, lest she should forget who this little Alida Belair was. For once I tried to do the class as purely as possible. I strove for neatness rather than attempting a brilliant display of pyrotechnics, and hoped that some inner quality might manage to shine through despite this modest, artless statement. Even my attire was aimed at conspicuous tastefulness, rather than my usual sloppy layer-upon-layer workout gear. I wore a pastel pink silk crossover tunic over matching leotards, and with my pink tights and pink shoes I looked like a benign kewpie doll. At the end of class Lucia Chase walked up to me and said how much she had enjoyed my dancing, and asked me to see her in the office when I was dressed.

Seated across the desk from this powerful ballet magnate I couldn't help thinking that she reminded me of so many other dynamic American women who ran their organizations with a no-nonsense attitude, and a little help from the family coffers. After she had managed to extract my *curriculum vitae*, she said she would love to have me in the company, but as a soloist first and not a principal. 'No one is ever taken into the company as a principal straight away, unless they are guest artists', she said, 'but after a few months we can re-negotiate the contract and if we are both satisfied you could be promoted there and then'. I was thrilled to gain a foothold. 'I cannot offer you a definite contract yet', Miss Chase added. 'I have a board to look to, but if you let me know where we can contact you, we shall do so as soon as possible'. End of interview.

Then, typically, other excellent offers came along to confuse me. Although the other companies offered me principal positions, I hoped for the position in the American Ballet Theatre. I heard on the grapevine that Ivan Nagy had been made a similar offer. To keep the wolves at bay in the interim I accepted a short contract with members of the New York City Ballet to perform at Saratoga Springs. This was hard work; as well as performing for adults, we were required to tour the colleges in and around Saratoga and Detroit. We often had to have our make-up and hair done at 6 a.m. ready for the bus call. Luckily there were some live wires who helped to divert us from our constant exhaustion and fraying tempers. Jon Benoit was one of the naughty boys of the troupe, a former New York street kid with a reputation for taking drugs, and it was with Jon and his friend that I smoked my first joint.

I think the illicitness of the situation was far more exciting than the drug. It was all very *risqué*, sitting on Jon's bed with the door locked, engaged in our antisocial behaviour. Very soon we were falling about, laughing hysterically. But then a voice drifted up the stairs, and I realized that my name was being called. Someone wanted me on the phone. The thought of speaking into a phone had me in more fits, but after moon-walking over Jon's bed, which seemed as big as the Atlantic Ocean, I managed to float over to the phone. When the voice announced that it was the Manager of American Ballet Theatre, it seemed like an eternity before I could muster a reply. The Manager was saying that I had been offered a contract, but I could only blurp out a thank you between suppressed giggles.

Buoyant in the hope that at long last I had found a company where I would have an opportunity to develop into an artist, I drove myself mercilessly. In my triumph, I was determined to keep my body in a state of subdued starvation. In the weeks before my first rehearsal I could think of nothing else but the dance, myself and the dance. I arrived at the American Ballet Theatre studios blinkered, whittled and uncharacteristically confident, because my new-found strength of technique gave me a sense of liberation. Now I would be able to express and communicate without reservation the world of images and symbols that lay deep within my consciousness.

But as I walked into the gloomy American Ballet Theatre rehearsal studio I could feel the air vibrating with disharmony and collective insecurity. These paradigms of order and discipline remained islands unto themselves. There was not a flicker of emotion to flaw their perfection, not an inkling of a smile, let alone a gentle nudge or pat on the shoulder to reassure the newcomer that she was among friends. Here in the big time every dancer was set to go in his or her own lane, determined to get to the finishing line first. Ivan looked at home, hobnobbing with the top dancers; he did his best not to be too friendly to me. No one liked me, no one disliked me and, worst of all, no one cared.

Right from the beginning it seemed to me that to survive this war of nerves a thick skin would be more valuable than any amount of talent. There was no gentle nurturing of the creative spirit, no careful fortification of fragile psyches, and little attempt to bring to light any submerged talents. American Ballet Theatre had an impressive line-up of stars. No one could resent the eminence of such people as Tony Lander, Bruce Marks, the superb dramatist Sally Wilson, Gayle Young, Cynthia Gregory, Ted Kivitt and Royes Fernandez, the dark, handsome prince who had transported me on his shoulder from the kingdom of snow to the land of the sweets in the Borovansky production of *Nutcracker*. Now I was dancing alongside Royes as an adult and he looked as if he had just stepped from those years of my childhood into the present.

This was finally the big time. I could already see my parents' proud faces as they saw my name at the head of the bill for the American Ballet Theatre, on tour Down Under. Ensconced in Clive Barnes' huge luxury apartment while he was abroad, I entertained all my friends in the Manhattan style, and splurged on a wardrobe suitable for my new 'rising star' status. All at once the inaccessible became accessible. Hard-to-get tickets were thrown at my feet. My list of acquaintances began to resemble a *Who's Who* of the international art world, and, much to my amusement, my name was also added to the invitation lists for high-society dinner parties and soirées.

Yet I soon began to suspect that American Ballet Theatre might not prove to be the uplifting experience I had hoped for. The company was like a factory, and the dancers sensed their own alienation and dispensability. My loneliness made me more determined to step up control over my body to make sure I could determine the way I would present myself to survive the ABT initiation trials.

The company was presenting a new lavish production of *Swan Lake*. As well as having to learn the *pas de trois*, with Ivan as the cavalier, I was one of the six leading black swans and—horrors!—one of those four revolting little swans who are required to beat out a monstrous little rhythm in unison. The only other ballet I was cast in was Balanchine's *Theme and Variations*, with music by Tchaikovsky. It was all threatening to be a major anticlimax. I was to be buried away in a flock of swans, where I was constantly getting my wings tangled in someone else's, or falling over their *courant* feet, which these malicious birds used like machetes. I could never find my place, constantly forgot my number in the pecking order, and couldn't tell the difference between the others. Seen one swan, seen them all, perhaps, but all I seemed to be doing was flapping on and off the stage, madly counting the music and searching for my place in that over-populated mess.

I derived no pleasure from perching on one leg with my neck twisted under a contorted arm, waiting for the Swan Queen to finish her majestic solo. When I began to experiment with my make-up Lucia angrily snapped me back to order: 'You must look the same as the other swans'. As part of this militaristic line-up I was a dismal failure. I was sure I would initiate some monstrous traffic jam, and all those hybrid swan girls would come tumbling down on top of me. Smothered among those perfumed armpits and deodorized crutches, I felt no empathy for the music, the dance or the audience.

My disorganized ways were attracting a considerable amount of flak from the other more efficient swan ladies. They had no time for bumbling individualists; I was spoiling their parade.

I was feeling apprehensive and despondent when we set off on tour to Japan. Stevan was on the West Coast, and met me at the airport in San Francisco, where we had a few hours stopover. At the sight of a friendly face I broke down and wept. Only then did I realize the strain I had been under. But I said goodbye and pulled myself together, determined to reinforce the barricade around myself.

In many ways ABT presented the most difficult challenge I had faced. Alone and without encouragement, I had to rely on my own resources for the strength and self-discipline to keep up my solitary work. Once again I overstepped the mark in my quest for thinness. Lucia, intent on achieving uniformity among her swans, felt compelled to reprimand the scrawny runt of the flock. Her advice that I should put on weight filled me with joy and guilt.

Once again my life became a complicated round of subterfuge and defiance as avoiding food became my major preoccupation. It was almost impossible to get salad or lean steak in the restaurants, and I had been conditioned to believe that every grain of rice was a poisonous fat globule. If I couldn't get the protein value in foods I was used to, better not to eat at all. To stave off my hunger I chewed dried salted fish, seaweed and rice savouries. I resorted to my old trick of pretending to take food, mulling it around without swallowing it, and then pretending to blow my nose.

I was convinced that I was going insane. As my body faded away, my brain raced off on some hyperbolic charge of its own. I couldn't sleep, so I chain-smoked until breakfast, where I turned up partly for the sake of having something to do, and partly out of an ambivalent desire to be close to food. I would be the first seated in the vast dining room, where I would down as much coffee as I could and take as much toast as I could chew, without actually having to swallow it. I was often joined by another early bird, Lucia Chase, who was up and about for different reasons. We had some pleasant conversations; had she not been the boss, we might well have got along well together.

Shortly I would have to perform my audition piece, the *pas de trois*, and there was no pretence that this would be the beginning of a gentle period of artistic development. There were to be no laurels for trying one's best; at that level there was no encouragement for a show of promise. In a sense they were calling my bluff. I had said I was good enough, and now it was up to me to deliver the goods.

Even in rehearsals the tension was all-pervasive. My every move was scrutinized. It was difficult to feel free and expansive when all those eyes were pushing me into a corner. For the second time in my life I fell prey to blackouts. Instead of being able to leave the mechanics of the dance to second nature, each step jerked out like the pellets of a constipated rabbit. I was tormented by the fear that I would freeze up and forget the steps of the solo. I felt intimidated, and as a result I smothered every ounce of natural dance instinct, every vestige of pleasure, in a conceptualized straitjacket. Control, control, control; in my supposed hour of triumph, I felt controlled to death.

Now more than ever I dreamt of Australia, where I could be the child sitting on my father's knee, in his comfortable armchair, and feel the reassurance of my mother's arms. There was still that 'real' world out there, beyond this stage of impossible perfection.

After some rushed and inadequate rehearsals, my big day was upon me. Finally I was going to be allowed on in the *pas de trois*. The big bosses congregated po-faced in prompt corner, where they could oversee their little performing minions and decide their futures. Beyond the proscenium arch the anonymous audience waited benignly. Although I never felt more like running away, I stayed in my corner in a blue funk. The idea of dancing just to please the piranhas in prompt corner seemed preposterous, but I didn't have the moral courage to say 'Up yours!' and flounce on and dance for myself, the music and the joy of it.

The *pas de trois* was exhausting, and a few minutes into the dance, gasping for air like a constricted mullet, I knew I would be hard pressed to get through to the end. The first *pas de trois* came to an end and I was left to recuperate in the wings while the other girl danced her solo. She had never danced better, this superb little dynamo with her huge radiant eyes, and the audience loved her. As I stood waiting for the hushed silence to drown that obscene round of applause, I wanted to sink into oblivion. The chords resounded and I was on. No matter what I felt, no matter how I ached, I clung to my mechanical smile, which I prayed would disguise all my fear and pain. Even if I had been well on top of my emotions, which I was not, the disdainful stares of the other dancers would have been enough to stop me. I managed to push out all the dance steps in the correct sequence and finish in time with the final note of the music.

By now I was past caring what anybody thought of me. I wanted out of this hell-hole. The final coda resounded and the last bars came crashing to the climax. The three of us stood side by side as the curtain came down to a thunderstorm of applause. Dazed, I took my three steps forward to curtsy, clinging to Ivan's hand for a supportive warmth that was not forthcoming, and after we had repeated our three steps forward, three steps back four or five times I wandered off-stage, still in a daze, to await the verdict of my trial.

Some of the dancers rallied around to offer me their congratulations. So unexpected was their sudden burst of enthusiasm that I deluded myself into thinking that maybe I had crossed the barrier and become an accepted member of their clan. Lucia seemed delighted, and I *should* have been, but I wasn't.

By now I was reaching the danger zone of advanced anorexia. I was becoming lightheaded, and my spirit was beginning to take leave of a world that was bounded on all sides by rehearsals, classes, footlights and discipline. In my need to restore contact with my being, I began to distance myself from that suffocating world in which I could find no comfort.

When I wasn't on call I left the hotel at the crack of dawn to explore Tokyo, and, in search of a distraction from my depressed state, I followed up an American colleague's suggestion to contact a Japanese friend of hers, a Mr Yagisawa.

Mr Yagisawa was well worth meeting. He was a frail, aesthetic man in his mid-seventies, yet he was also a wealthy industrialist. Though he was married, with several children and many grandchildren, the only other member of his family I met was his eldest son. I saw a photograph of his wife, but I was never invited to his home.

Mr Yagisawa and I spent many hours discussing literature and philosophy. Always punctual, he would be waiting in the hotel lobby at the appointed time, carrying with him some snippet about a book we had discussed the day before. He would take me walking through one of Tokyo's formal gardens, or to lunch at an elegant restaurant, and gradually, as we talked, I felt I came within reach of this fascinating old man.

His generosity was overwhelming. If I expressed the slightest wish to go somewhere or see something, a chauffeur-driven car would roll up for me to use for as long as I wanted. I only had to show interest in any item and it was mine—delivered by the hotel porter to my door in a mountain of boxes. When I protested, Mr Yagisawa replied that he earned more in one day than I would see in a year. 'Please', he said 'just think of yourself as one of my grandchildren while you are in Japan. It gives me enormous pleasure to give'. My surrogate grandfather provided me with comfort and love at a time when I felt close to total collapse.

Mr Yagisawa seemed to understand my torment. Perhaps this old man and I, who were born in two different worlds, were in essence not so very different. He knew nothing about my past and cared little about my balletic aspirations, but he allowed me to be. He wasn't there to judge my talent, my intellect or my sexuality. I talked about the pain of being separated from my family. I talked about my parents' pride in my success, and about how important it was to me to repay their love. I talked myself around in circles, saying nothing and everything. Soon Mr Yagisawa was referring to my family by name, as if he had known them for years.

'You need to go home to your family', Mr Yagisawa said simply one day, for he was as economical with his words as he was Spartan in his lifestyle. 'That is what your mind needs. I think that maybe you need to find a balance between your clever mind and that very talented too thin body of yours.'

The next day Mr Yagisawa picked me up for our daily walk. He seemed far more outgoing than usual. 'I start my day at 4 a.m.' he said.

Mr Yagisawa and his grandson in a characteristically simple setting, Tokyo, 1968

I read business journals, gazettes and newspapers. Then for my pleasure I read one or two chapters of a few books, all in their original language. I eat one meal a day, usually a bowl of soup and some rice. In the evening, after returning home from work, before I devote myself to my family, I meditate in my own room.

I marvelled at the iron discipline of this old man who was both gentle and hard, a cultural traditionalist and a progressive, successful businessman.

Stopping outside a drab grey office block, Mr Yagisawa said, 'And now I would like you to see where I work'.

As we stepped into his neat office the telephone rang. 'That will be for you, Alida', Mr Yagisawa said. 'Please answer it.' Too befuddled to question the absurdity of receiving a phone call in an office I had never been in before, in a country where I was unknown, I strode over to the phone and picked up the receiver.

'Darling!' said my mother's voice.

'Where are you?' I asked, almost speechless. For one moment it crossed my mind that somehow she had materialized in Tokyo; or maybe Mr Yagisawa, the maker of miracles, the bearer of incredible gifts, had somehow brought the disembodied spirit of my mother into this room.

'Wasn't it kind of Mr Yagisawa to arrange this phone call?' she went on, and then the flood of tears came, and I knew that more than anything else in the world I wanted to go home. My family didn't care if I fell on my nose in the middle of that precious *pas de trois*. I couldn't cope with the pressures any more, and didn't want to. I felt sick and tired, fed up with playing the star. I just wanted to roll up into a tight little ball and become ever so little.

'I'm coming home', I announced. 'We have four weeks' holiday, and I'm going to spend it with you.' Worn out but becalmed, I put down the receiver and smiled at a beaming Mr Yagisawa. 'Thank you for knowing me so well', I said. 'Thank you for giving me the opportunity to find myself again.'

I knew the admission that I needed to go home was a sign that my resolve to 'make it' had weakened, maybe beyond redemption. I had begun to think the unthinkable. I had begun to see those four weeks as extending into months, years, maybe even forever. It was not that I was homesick for a country or base to call my own. I was responding to a need to rediscover the sensibilities that had been lost to me in the urge to be *more* than myself.

For the first time in my life it was easy to say goodbye to the company. I had no feelings of sadness, no optimistic expectations; it was just a sheer relief to let that super-talented squad take their super-trim little bodies back to the Big Apple. Who cared if I was flying off in the wrong direction? They certainly didn't. I was turning my back on the big time to fly home to the backwater of suburban Melbourne, where

I was going to let myself degenerate into an undisciplined, complacent blob, basking in a great big pool of non-judgemental love.

High up in the sky, I felt betwixt and between and nowhere in particular. My horizons had widened dramatically since I had first left the new world for the tainted old one. I had come within an inch of achieving everything a dancer could hope for. I had wanted it all so, so much. But—and wasn't that just the problem, there was always that 'but'—none of it had given me the inspiration or answer I had hoped for. Whichever way I seemed to jeté, pirouette or bourée, whichever companies and dancers I worked with, it had become apparent to me that *I* was the one who was always out of step.

Index

Aborigines, 101–3, 109
Adelaide, 36, 41–6
Age (Melbourne), 179
Ailey, Alvin, 86
Aldous, Lucette, 186–7, 191, 197, 199, 200, 205, 219
America, 239, 241–56, 258–65
American Ballet Theatre, 251, 253, 260–8
Amsterdam, 8, 20, 22, 128, 156
Angel, George, 239
anorexia nervosa: beginnings, 50–5; acute, 64–81, 106; in London, 130–1, 182–3, 206, 228–9, 232; in Russia, 143, 151–2; in Washington, 241, 246, 249; in New York, 258; in Japan, 265, 267
Antwerp, 1, 7–10, 20, 22; Opera (House), 10, 20
Arts Council (New South Wales), 93–4
Arts Council tour, 93–103
Ashcroft Theatre (Croydon, UK), 128, 157
Ashton, Frederick, 164, 219, 221, 225, 238
Astell, Betty, 128
Auschwitz, 10, 129
Australia, 1–113 *passim*, 240–1
Australian Ballet, 109, 229–30, 240
Australian Embassy, 141, 154, 179
Australian Women's Weekly, 34

Balanchine, George, 136, 253, 264
Ballet Russe de Monte Carlo, 28, 85, 126
Bannerman, Ken, 189, 198–200, 203–5
Barnes, Clive, 209, 261, 263
Barons Court, 122, 125, 136
Barrett, Cecilia, 205, 238
Barrett, Daphne, 73, 92
Belgium, 7, 9
Bennett, Alexander, 206, 208, 212–13
Benoit, Jon, 262
Benson, Alice, 20, 58
Ben-Uri Gallery, 127
Blankenberg, 9–10, 21
Bogomolova, Ludmila, 88, 151
Bolender, Todd, 238
Bonham-Carter, Lady, 216
Bolshoi Ballet Company, 83, 86–9, 108, 118, 123, 125, 127, 131, 133, 140–51, 179–80, 232, 259, 261
Bolshoi Theatre, 139, 142, 148
Borovansky, Edouard, 14, 25, 28–34, 38–9, 47, 68, 80–1, 84–7, 90, 110
Borovansky, Xenia, 4, 5, 13–14, 16, 26–7, 31, 33, 40, 47, 52–6, 58–60, 64–6, 74, 79–80, 82–4, 89–91, 93, 105, 109, 110
Borovansky Ballet Academy, 5, 13–14, 16, 24–7, 33, 40, 53–4, 59, 62, 67–8, 74, 79, 82–4, 90, 105
Borovansky Ballet Company, 14, 27, 84, 86, 95, 124, 263

271

Bourmeister, Vladimir, 151
Brady, Dell, 161–2, 166
Brisbane, 46–9
British railways, 213–14
Bruhn, Erik, 234, 252
Burke, Walter, 109
Burr, Marilyn, 242–3

Canterbury (UK), 188–9, 191–2, 196, 200
Card Game, 25
Casse Noisette, 167, 173, 179
Chase, Lucia, 261–2, 264–5, 267
Chesworth, John, 222
Clara (*Nutcracker*), 27–8, 30, 34, 41–2, 46, 48–9, 93, 96
Conservatorium of Drama (Antwerp), 20
Cooma (NSW), 102
Coppélia, 191–2, 194–6, 202–4, 212–13, 237, 244
Corrida, 33, 96
Costa Brava (Spain), 219
Covent Garden, 98, 121, 211, 229, 232, 237
Cranko, John, 238
Crystal, Mr and Mrs, 186, 214–15
Cuban missile crisis, 154
Cul de Sac, 222–3
Czernyana, 197, 212

Dance and Dancers, 209
D'Antuono, Eleanor, 261
Davidson, Jeffrey, 234
de Basil, Colonel Wassily, 28
Diaghilev, Sergei, 126, 186
Dolin, Sir Anton, 243
Doof, Gerrie (cousin), 1, 9, 23
Doof, Maria (aunt), 3, 9, 11–12, 17, 22, 34, 36–7, 76
Doof, Nico (uncle), 3, 9, 11–12, 17, 22, 23, 34, 36–7, 76
Don Quixote, 151, 202, 205–8, 212
Dublin, 217
Dukes, Ashley, 164

Earls Court, 121, 185–6
Eaters of Darkness, 180, 182
Ellis, Angela, 164
Ellis, David, 165, 168, 188, 224, 236
Elizabethan Theatre Trust, 95

Empire Theatre (Sydney), 32
Esmeralda, 150
Estonia (ship), 132
Eureka Youth League, 113
Evans, Jane Roland, 181

Facade, 219
Fae, Maria, 163–4, 165
Farmer, Peter, 231–2
Fealdman, Mr S., 127, 157, 161
Fernandez, Royes, 35, 263
Festival Ballet, 122, 127, 242
Field, John, 234, 237–9
Fletcher, Cyril, 128, 156–7, 161
Fokine, Michel, 136, 195–9
Fonteyn, Dame Margot, 86, 177, 179, 219, 225, 229, 237, 252
France, 5, 7, 8, 10, 126, 185, 234, 246
Franklin, Frederic, 239, 241–2, 244–5, 248–50, 261
Fraser, Anna, 41–2, 44, 47–8, 56, 61

Gala Performance, 205, 212
Gaskell, Sonia, 157
Gerdt, Elizaveta, 147, 149, 151, 155–6
Germans, 7, 63, 86, 135
Gilmour, Sally, 164, 256
Giselle, 33, 86, 167, 173, 179, 198, 200, 202, 204, 212, 231–4, 256
Glasbeek, Celien (mother), 1, 2, 5–14, 19, 20, 22, 26–8, 33, 37, 42–4, 46–8, 54–5, 57–65, 67, 69–70, 72, 74, 76, 79–80, 109, 111–12, 153, 183, 240–1, 269
Glasbeek, Harry (brother), 6–7, 11–12, 14, 18–20, 23, 46, 54–5, 57, 59–61, 70, 79, 86, 88, 93, 103–4, 107, 112, 146, 173, 175, 179, 183–4, 226, 239, 241
Glasbeek, Simon (father), 1, 5–14, 19, 21–3, 27, 32, 37, 46, 54–5, 57, 60, 63–5, 69–70, 79, 90, 91, 111–12, 130, 153, 183, 240–1
Goldstein, Gideon, 184
Gopal, Ram, 209–10
Gore, Walter, 163–7, 172, 174, 178, 181–2, 220–1
Gorham, Kathleen, 16, 33, 93, 229–30, 240
Gosler, Alida (cousin), 2, 3, 5, 8, 12, 14, 18, 20, 57, 59
Gosler, Maurice (uncle), 8–10, 17–20, 22, 57, 83, 89–90

Gosler, Rosa (aunt), 8, 10, 18–20, 22, 57, 89
Government House (Adelaide), 43–5
Graeme, Joyce, 188, 198, 231–3
Graham, Martha, 210
Grant Street (Malvern), 17–18, 22, 50, 56, 89
Gray, Beth, 39, 42–3, 48
Grebel, Stevan, 245–51, 254–6, 264
Greece, 239–40
Gregory, Cynthia, 263
Grinwis, Paul, 37, 93–7, 100
Gusev, Piotr, 88–9

Hammond, Paul, 93, 106
Harkavy, Benjamin, 259
Harley Street, 170, 232
Haskell, Arnold, 123, 127, 130, 132, 156
Helsinki, 107–8, 111, 117–19
Helsinki Youth and Students for Peace and Friendship, 109, 113
Hennessy, Christine, 258–9
Her Majesty's Theatre (Melbourne), 45, 86
Hightower, Rosella, 234
Hinton, Paula, 167, 174, 180–2, 197
Hippodrome Theatre (Eastbourne), 128
Hitler, Adolf, 7–11
Holocaust, 63–4

Indonesia, 113–15
Intourist, 132, 141
Ivanov, Lev, 136, 175

Japan, 264–9
Jedda, 109, 118
Jews, 5–9, 18, 31, 36, 65, 68, 108–9, 116, 129–30, 146, 155, 169
Jones, Freddie, 218, 224

Kalinin (ship), 119
Karelskaya, Rimma, 88, 145
Karsavina, Tamara, 136, 195, 225
Kellaway, Leon, 33, 84
Khessinskaya, Mathilde, 136
Kings Cross, 34, 36
Kingston, Claude, 42
Kinmont family, 41, 77, 81–2, 119, 121–3, 127, 240
Kirov Ballet School, 125, 136–7

Kivett, Ted, 263
Knox, Moya, 177, 185
Koval, Jeffrey, 94–5
Kulyk, Andrei, 254

La Fille Mal Gardée, 166–7
Lediakh, Gennady, 87, 145, 151
Lely, 113
Lenin, Vladimir Ilyich, 139
Leningrad, 134–7
Lepeshinskaya, Olga, 144–6, 151, 155–6
Les Sylphides, 195–6, 198–9, 201, 212–13, 244
Lichine, David, 27–9, 41, 96
Liddell, Jeanette, 109
Light Fantastic, 178
Lilac Garden, 192, 194, 220
Linden Gardens (London), 223–4, 226, 230, 239, 257
Lisner, Charles, 94
Lloyd Street Primary School, 26
Lodders, Corrie, 13
London, 85, 118–20, 122, 124–8, 136, 141, 155–7, 161, 165, 170–2, 180, 184–6, 214–16, 218, 223–4, 226, 228–30, 232, 239, 243, 254, 256–7
London Ballet, 163, 169, 180, 184, 186
Lorraine, Maggie, 235

Mac', John, 157, 159–60
Mac Liammóir, Micháel, 179, 217
MacMillan, Kenneth, 225
MacRobertson Girls High School (Melbourne), 50–1, 67, 89, 92, 104
Magner, Helen, 109
Malvern Town Hall, 109
Margaret, Princess, 211, 216
Marken (Jewish district, Amsterdam), 20–1, 36, 80, 129–30
Markova, Dame Alicia, 164, 219, 243
Marks, Bruce, 263
Marquis de Cuevas (ballet company), 185
Maslova, Nellie, 147, 149
Mason, Edward, 186, 212
M'as-tu-vus (solo, *Czernyana*), 197, 212
Matchgirl, 24
Mercury Theatre (London), 164, 216, 223
Melbourne, 1–5, 12–30, 40, 45–6, 50–94, 104–13, 240–1

Index

Mollard, Mr and Mrs, 76
Morand, Sylvester, 226
Moree (NSW), 102
Morrice, Norman, 211–12, 221–2, 236
Morton, Ursula, 125, 127
Moscow, 137–57
Mount Isa, 95, 100–1, 103

Nagy, Ivan, 244, 261–2, 264, 266
Namatjira, Albert, 100
Naples, 11
National Ballet Company (Amsterdam), 157
National Ballet Company (Washington, DC), 239, 244, 249, 253–4, 261
Nazis, 6, 8, 10, 63
Nerina, Nadia, 166
Netherlands Dance Theatre, 259, 261
New York City, 125, 239, 250–1, 253–9, 262, 269
New York City Ballet, 262
New York Times, 261
Nightingale and the Rose, 25
Nijinsky, Vaslav, 186, 189, 225
Nolan, Carmel, 48
Northcote, Anna, 124
Nova, Estella, 94–5
Nureyev, Rudolf, 125, 229, 234, 237, 252
Nutcracker, 27, 32–5, 40, 50, 58, 93, 151, 166–8, 244, 263

O'Brien, Johnny, 190, 194, 205
Ocean and Pearls, 87
Ogden, Karl, 109
Opera Tavern, 218
Overland (train), 42

Palais Theatre (Melbourne), 88
Paris, 185
Paris Opera Ballet, 185
Paul, Ron, 109
Pavlova, Anna, 33–4, 39, 54, 56, 85, 186, 225
Pereyaslavec, Madame Valentina, 252–4
Persephone, 74–6
Petipa, Marius, 175
Pilkington family, 231
Pineapple Poll, 33
Poland, 10
Port Melbourne, 12
Prague, 115

Preedy, Cyril, 189

Queensland, 46–9, 93–102

Radio City Music Hall (New York), 258
Rambert, Dame Marie, 164, 168–9, 186–91, 193–7, 199–207, 209–12, 216–17, 219–21, 223, 230–1, 234–9, 256–7
Rambert Ballet Company, 164–5, 168, 189–90, 198, 202, 218, 220–1, 223–4, 228, 234, 237–8, 243
Rassine, Alexis, 170–2
Reece, Maxine, 245–6
Reid, Rex, 93, 106
Richmond Theatre, 207–8, 216
Riddell, Jean, 244
Riga, 134–5, 138
Roberts, Anna, 202, 214–15, 223
Romeo and Juliet, 86
Royal Ballet Company, 82, 85, 108, 122, 125–6, 161, 163, 166, 211, 234, 237–8
Royal Ballet School, 123, 127, 130, 140–1
Royal Shakespeare Company, 218
Rubinstein, Martin, 84
Ruby, Aunt, 44, 48
Russia, 132–57
Ryabinkina, Yelena, 145, 151
Rye, 76

Sager, Peggy, 16
Sadler's Wells (theatre), 218–19, 232
Sandbrook, June, 195
Sanders, Job, 261
Sascha, Captain, 134
Scarborough Theatre (UK), 207
Scott, Margaret, 93, 106, 109, 164, 219
Segal, Sol, 109
Sempill, Simon-Charles, 226–8, 239–40, 255–7
Sibbritt, Gerard, 162, 166
Sibley, Antoinette, 219
Simpson, Dudley, 124
Skripov, Ivan, 155
Sleeping Beauty, 24, 158
Soekarno, President, 113–14
Souquet, Madame and Monsieur, 6–8
Soviet–Australian Friendship Society, 140–1, 147
Spitalni family, 140, 143–5, 147–8, 151, 155, 156

Springwaters, 261
Staff, Frank, 212
Stalin, Joseph, 135, 139
Stock, Gail, 109
Struchkova, Raissa, 88, 145, 151
Sunday Telegraph (London), 179, 186, 212
Swan Lake, 178–9
Swansea Theatre, 173
Sweet Dancer, 220
Swinard, Valerie, 123
Sydney, 30–9, 41, 82, 95

Tallchief, Maria, 252
Theme and Variations, 264
Tichonov, Vladimir, 145, 150
Times, The (London), 121, 179
Titlow family, 99–100
Topham, Jan, 94–5, 99
Toscano (migrant ship), 11, 109
Tournon (France), 6
Truscott, Anna, 205–6, 238
Tudor, Anthony, 192, 205, 220–1, 225
Tyrrell, Mrs, 28

Ulanova, Galina, 83, 86, 136, 177
United States of America, *see* America
USSR, *see* Russia

Vaganova, Agrippina, 253
Vajda, Dr Frank, 230–1
Valent, Wendy (Renée), 216–17, 219–20, 223, 226, 231–2, 234, 257
Valse Tendre, 118
van Praagh, Dame Peggy, 82, 85–6, 93, 95, 123, 125, 128, 229–30
Villeneuve-sur-Lot (France) 5
Vishnevskaya, Galina, 83
Voice of America, 149

Wakehurst, Lord, 184, 230–1
Warsaw (ghetto), 116, 135
Washington, DC, 239, 241–6, 254
Welander, Karl, 229
Welch, Garth, 229
Wilkinson, Miss D., 123, 125
Williamson's, J. C., 42, 48
Wilson, Sally, 263
Witt, Lynne, 41, 50–1, 56, 58, 67, 72, 93
Women's Weekly, *see* *Australian Women's Weekly*
Wright, Mr, 26–8

Yagisawa, Mr, 267–9

Zak family, 129, 156
Zurich Opera Ballet, 234